India and the End of Empire

Selected Writings of Daniel O'Connor

— EDITED BY —

ANN LOADES & DAVID JASPER

Sacristy Press

Sacristy Press
PO Box 612, Durham, DH1 9HT

www.sacristy.co.uk

First published in 2023 by Sacristy Press, Durham

Copyright © Sacristy Press 2023
The moral rights of the author have been asserted.

All rights reserved, no part of this publication may be reproduced or transmitted in any form or by any means, electronic, mechanical photocopying, documentary, film or in any other format without prior written permission of the publisher.

Scripture quotations, unless otherwise stated, are from the New Revised Standard Version Bible: Anglicized Edition, copyright © 1989, 1995 National Council of the Churches of Christ in the United States of America. Used by permission. All rights reserved worldwide.

Every reasonable effort has been made to trace the copyright holders of material reproduced in this book, but if any have been inadvertently overlooked the publisher would be glad to hear from them.

Sacristy Limited, registered in England & Wales, number 7565667

British Library Cataloguing-in-Publication Data
A catalogue record for the book is available from the British Library

ISBN 978-1-78959-322-8

"Lord, said my mother, God God, said my father—but here's a short one—Farewell, dear rea...."

Irwin Allan Sealy

Contents

Preface v
Introduction: The Life of Daniel O'Connor 1

The Writings 26
Chapter 1. John Cosin: A Collection of Private Devotions, 1627 27
Chapter 2. The Study of Religion and Social Reality 39
Chapter 3. Dialogue as Communion: C. F. Andrews and
  Munshi Ram 47
Chapter 4. Solidarity 61
Chapter 5. Some Distinctive Features of Andrews' Thought 83
Chapter 6. Karanjia 113
Chapter 7. Spring Thunder 129
Chapter 8. "Perpetual Succession": USPG and the
  Changing Face of Mission 149
Chapter 9. The Geography of Anglicanism 161

Appendix: Writings by Juliet O'Connor 182
Afterword by Harish Trivedi 187
The writings of Dr Daniel O'Connor: A select bibliography 198

Preface

Dan O'Connor and David Jasper

The idea for this book began with the vision of our dear friend and colleague Ann Loades, and she was hard at work on it at the time of her unexpected death in December 2022. It was decided with David Brown, Ann's executor, that we should continue the work that she had started, though the form of the book as it developed was not entirely what she had in mind and any shortcomings should be attributed to us. We thank Ann for her vision and her characteristic enthusiasm and hope that what has been done would have met with her approval.

Thanks are due to the Drummond Trust of 3 Pitt Terrace, Stirling for their generous grant towards the costs of this book.

David Jasper

Playing a part in this book has been a double honour for me. Ann was my mentor, and being asked to complete work that she had initiated is something I could never have imagined. At the same time, Dan O'Connor has been part of my life for more than 50 years. We met in Delhi in 1972, when Dan was teaching in St Stephen's College and I was a volunteer teacher in a school in Bihar. On his return to Scotland, Dan's friendship with my father, Dean Ronald Jasper, maintained the family connection. Now we find ourselves living not far apart in Scotland and have been brought back together by our common friendship with Ann.

The Introduction is in the form of a brief biography of Dan and his wife Juliet, focusing particularly on their decade in India in the 1960s and 1970s. India, both before and after independence in 1947, lies at the heart of Dan's life and work, though the first extract from his writings, drawing upon his early interest in the devotional writings of the seventeenth-century Bishop John Cosin, sets the tone for the whole book: Dan's deeply sacramental Anglicanism which took root in his training for the ordained ministry in Cuddesdon in the 1950s. It found its spiritual roots in the pre-Oxford Movement High Church Anglicanism that can be traced back to the Caroline Divines, to Archbishop Laud and above all Bishop Cosin. More recently, as we shall see, Dan became more conscious of the more questionable aspects of the cultural context of such spiritual writings, but the luminosity of their spirituality remains, as does the literary beauty of their language.

Featuring largely in Dan's thinking since his days in Delhi in the 1960s are two remarkable Englishmen from the early and mid twentieth century, who devoted their lives to India, Charles Freer ("Charley") Andrews and Verrier Elwin. Both of them were ordained Anglican priests who moved away from their priesthood, if not their faith, to espouse the life and culture of India and the cause of Indian nationalism in the face of late British imperial rule. Andrews, the friend of Rabindranath Tagore and Mahatma Gandhi,[1] was finally to return to his priestly vocation and though, like Elwin, he was never attracted to the conventional notion of missionary work, and although he certainly knew and visited British figures in India as senior as the Viceroy, he is something of a model for later missionaries whom Dan was to describe in 2001 as "some of the most committed and effective anti-colonialists that the modern missionary movement has seen. They are our heroes today."[2] We may even catch an early glimpse of missionaries of their kind, not portrayed with much sympathy and on the edges of British society in India in E. M. Forster's *A Passage to India* (1924), and they are certainly present in the less well-known fiction of Edward Thompson and novels such as *Farewell to India* (1931).

---

[1] The rather tepid character who is Charlie Andrews in Richard Attenborough's film *Gandhi* (1982) does very little justice to his robust and independent intellect and spirit.

[2] Daniel O'Connor, "'Perpetual Succession': USPG and the Changing Face of Mission", The Inaugural Lecture of USPG "LINKS". USPG, 2001, and see below, pp. 150–60.

Dan's work on Andrews and Elwin remains of central importance to the understanding of India before and after independence in the first half of the twentieth century. In some ways, Dan's own time in Delhi is a continuance of their spirit, a period of his life that is glimpsed in the eighth essay printed here, concerning his links with the radical intellectual students of the Naxalite movement in St Stephen's College.

On his return to the United Kingdom in 1972, Dan became, after a time as chaplain in St Andrews University, during which he was awarded a doctorate for his work on C. F. Andrews, the Principal of one of the Selly Oak Colleges near Birmingham. Here was begun his seminal work on the history of the United Society for the Propagation of the Gospel (USPG) and of British missions overseas. This is represented here by his remarkable essay "The Geography of Anglicanism" from 2015. The final brief essay is not by Dan himself, but by his wife Juliet from her book on prayer and spirituality, *Beyond Words* (1987) which she published under the name "Beth Collier".[3] It seems appropriate to end with a writing about the spiritual life that expresses so much about Dan himself, just as we begin with the devotions of another great Anglican, Bishop Cosin.

At a time when the idea of the worldwide "Anglican Communion" is frequently debated and often divided by cultural and theological differences, it is highly appropriate to listen to the voice of Daniel O'Connor as one grounded in humility, in the Book of Common Prayer and its spirituality, a tradition with roots also in the Oxford Movement and the great Bishop Brooke Foss Westcott, and yet always critical of injustice and power, not least imperial power, wielded inappropriately. The pieces reprinted here extend back some 50 years in Dan's long career as a priest and teacher. References, terms and even spellings have changed during that time. Generally we have decided to leave them as they were first written, making occasional comments in the footnotes. We understand that a term like 'Third World' was perfectly acceptable in the past though now very much frowned upon. We hope that our readers will understand this decision.

Dan O'Connor is a man with an enormous capacity for making and keeping friends. Friendships made in India some 50 years ago remain

---

[3] See below, pp. 182–6.

strong and lively, while the beginnings and makings of this book are found in friendship. For this gift I am profoundly grateful.

Daniel O'Connor

Behind this book stand devout but unfussy parents, lovers of the countryside on our doorstep. My father was conscious of his Irish origins and my mother was an enthusiastic writer. Her novella *A Far off Bell* was published by the Hutton Press in 1987. After my ordination in the Church of England, there was, for me, a marriage of 53 years to Juliet, who bore our two sons and was a source of endless love, faith and fun, capping my naivety and frailty.

India and our ministry there were supremely important to both of us, and Juliet had quite as significant a role as I at St Stephen's College, Delhi, hosting our many later Indian guests. But she, eminently practical, got over the experience better than I have or have even wanted to. By the time we reached our later short decade at the College of the Ascension, Selly Oak, Juliet's arthritis was becoming serious, all the more so to an art and crafts practitioner. But our time there was important to me, for it allowed me to place my Indian experience in a broader framework, thereby enabling me, for example, to write the last essay in this book.

As for my writing, almost all of it happened because I was asked to do it, and thankfully I have always found it to be one of the most enjoyable aspects of my life. I was thankful when, after I retired and was feeling guilty that I was not getting very involved in leading worship in local churches, Juliet insisted that writing was my ministry. This was affirmed a few years later when I met Ann Loades at a seminar in the University of St Andrews. In her inimitable and forthright way, she announced that she was going to write a book about me and my work. I was, of course, flattered and glad to co-operate when she set about this task, but even more stricken when she so suddenly passed away in December 2022. Her friendship and, with David Brown, her hospitality in their nearby village in north-east Fife, was a lovely thing in my widower-hood.

David Jasper's taking up "Ann's project" has been remarkable, and for his care and perception and friendship I am deeply grateful.

INTRODUCTION

The Life of Daniel O'Connor[1]

David Jasper and Ann Loades

Early life and education

Daniel O'Connor was born on 9 January 1933 at 7, Boyes Hill Grove, Darlington, the home of his parents Daniel George and Gladys O'Connor. For most of his working life, his father, Daniel George O'Connor, was employed by the London and North Eastern Railway, eventually taking charge of the accountancy team at the railway's Shildon Works. His mother Gladys was a schoolteacher and prolific writer of children's books. Dan had a happy childhood in the countryside just beyond their home, and although it was overshadowed by the Second World War which brought rationing, gas masks and blackouts, there was no great interruption of the "green beginning" to his life. Life in the countryside eventually led him to a recurring subject in his later reading which included *The Creator Spirit* (1927) by the Anglican priest and theologian Charles Raven; his writings have been described as early examples of ecotheology.[2] Through Raven, and later John Habgood, Dan's reading came to echo an Anglican claim

---
[1] Spellings of the names of cities such as Calcutta and Bombay have been retained in accordance with the use of the time and as found in publications by O'Connor here used.
[2] Charles Raven (1885–1964) was Regius Professor of Divinity and Master of Christ's College at the University of Cambridge. *The Creator Spirit*, based on the Hulsean Lectures in Cambridge (1926–7) and the Noble Lectures in Harvard (1927) traces the work of the Holy Spirit in "the creative as well as the inspirational energies of the Godhead" (Preface).

that the study of the works of creation was the proper occupation of the Sabbath day. John Habgood, later Archbishop of York, was a member of the Association of Ordained Scientists, as was Dan's close friend David Gosling,[3] who later became a colleague in India. Gosling's book *Science and the Indian Tradition: When Einstein Met Tagore* (2007) is among his most important works.

The town of Darlington, with its tall-spired twelfth-century St Cuthbert's Church, provided the focus for Dan's earliest, and diverse, experience of institutional religion. A prosperous Quaker town it never, however, displaced the green world of nature that was gifted to Dan and his sister Kath in their early childhood. Theirs was a stable and secure family home, enjoying some prosperity and close links with the parish church of Holy Trinity, Darlington. Dan attended the local Queen Elizabeth Grammar School, where he developed his lifelong love of literature, though largely through the influence of his mother rather than through his formal education. In due course, he moved on to study at University College ("the Castle") in Durham University during the years 1951–4. Dan's school days were not especially memorable and certainly engendered no aspirations to the Christian priesthood.

But Durham, with its university and cathedral, was different. A mere 18 miles north of Darlington it opened up a new world for the young Dan O'Connor. In his first year, as a student of University College, he lived in the keep of Durham Castle close to Bishop Cosin's Library with the great mass of Durham Cathedral just across Palace Green. He read English Literature in a then small department. There were a mere 18 honours students in the first year, working under the careful gaze of Professor Claud C. Abbott, who was best known for his edited volumes of the correspondence of Gerard Manley Hopkins. Also on the staff, teaching Jacobean and Elizabethan drama, were Clifford Leech, and Bertram Colgrave, a scholar of Anglo-Saxon and Middle English, who introduced Dan to the early Christian sites of Monkwearmouth and

---

[3] David Gosling trained in nuclear physics and was Principal of Edwardes College, Peshawar University, Pakistan, and now teaches ecology at the University of Cambridge. He has also taught, like Dan, at St Stephen's College, Delhi.

Jarrow, and the lives of the great northern saints—Cuthbert, Bede, Aidan and Wilfred. Among Dan's fellow students was Hamish Swanston who was to become the first Roman Catholic to lead a theology department in a British university at the University of Kent in 1977.

At Durham, it was the study of English literature that guided and influenced Dan's religious development, and literature would remain at the centre of his later teaching in Delhi. Through James Thomson's long poem *The Seasons* (1726–30) and Wordsworth *The Prelude* (1805, 1850) he learnt to celebrate the beauties of the natural world. He also developed an abiding love of the poetry of George Herbert, William Blake and Gerard Manley Hopkins, finding in the world of English literature an ideal preparation for his later study of theology. During his first two years at Durham, the College chapel and a Franciscan mission were important to him, but it was only in his third year that he started attending a daily service of Holy Communion in one or other of the Cathedral's chapels. At the end of this year, he began to explore possibilities for ordination training in the Church of England, perhaps at Cuddesdon Theological College, near Oxford.

After Durham, the possibility of postgraduate study in English literature at Oxford was ended by his call up for National Service. In the mid-1950s, this was compulsory for all able-bodied young men. It lasted for two years, and Dan spent much of them in Germany and the Netherlands as an artillery subaltern, with a glimpse of the tactical nuclear weaponry then being introduced. On a short leave, he met the Bishop of Durham at the time, Michael Ramsey, who helped him on his way to becoming an ordinand at Cuddesdon. The Principal when Dan arrived there in 1956 was Edward Knapp-Fisher, later to be elected Bishop of Pretoria, and it was under Knapp-Fisher's guidance that he established the habits of prayer that lasted a lifetime. At this time, he encountered the work of Bishop John Cosin (1594–1672) which formed the basis of his first serious academic study in theology.[4]

In his first term O'Connor's lived in Church Cottage with John Austin Baker[5] and Graham Midgley, Dean of St Edmund Hall, Oxford. A lively, at

---

[4] For one of Dan's later essays on Cosin see below, Chapter 1 pp. 27–37.
[5] Later a Canon of Westminster Abbey and Bishop of Salisbury.

times even militant, student community was governed by the somewhat severe Knapp-Fisher. But Dan's troubles were rooted elsewhere, for in his first year his father became terminally ill, followed subsequently by the serious illness of his sister Kath. Yet if lectures, with the exception of those by John Austin Baker, were dull, the countryside around Cuddesdon provided him with abundant pleasures, not least for pursuing his love of horse riding. On the whole, however, the opportunities at Cuddesdon for theological study proved to be sadly unrewarding, despite visits from such eminent theologians of the day as Eric Mascall and Austin Farrer. In addition, reading in the writings of such thinkers as William Temple, R. H. Tawney, John Macmurray and V. A. Demant, as well as a group associated with Charles Raven, reinforced a leftist tilt in Dan's thinking that was to last his whole life.[6]

However, it was an encounter with Bishop John Cosin's *Collection of Private Devotions* of 1627 that really fired his imagination. The nature of the *Devotions*, bringing together Cosin's learning in the western devotional and liturgical traditions together with the book's literary beauty, resonated with Dan's need to develop theologically together with his great love for English literature. At that time, there was little written on Cosin despite his central role in the creation of the 1662 Book of Common Prayer, and Lars Hanson, Keeper of Printed Books at Oxford's Bodleian Library, readily assisted Dan, sharing with him the 1627 editions of the *Devotions* in the Bodleian. Thus a work of Anglican Christian devotion that is both learned and beautiful became a major landmark in Dan's theological journey.

As his time in Oxford as an ordinand drew towards its close, Dan was drawn back to his home country in the north-east of England by the prospect of a curacy in St Peter's, Stockton-on-Tees. There, too, he met Juliet Wood, who was in due course to become his beloved wife. But it was while he was at Cuddesdon and through the agency of MECCA,[7] the Church Assembly's agency co-ordinating the interests of the Church's missionary societies, that Dan's interest in work overseas

---

[6] In retirement in Scotland, Dan has been a staunch member of the Labour Party.

[7] Missionary and Ecumenical Council of the Church Assembly.

was sparked—and a future far beyond the diocese of Durham was already on the horizon.

Holy orders and holy matrimony

Dan was made a deacon by Bishop Maurice Harland in Durham Cathedral on Trinity Sunday, 1 June 1958 and began his ordained ministry in the industrial town of Stockton on the same evening. The vicar was Canon James McGill, an energetic Prayer Book Catholic who led a thriving congregation and was a strong supporter of the Society for the Propagation of the Gospel in Foreign Parts. Canon McGill, a product of the rigorous training of priests at Kelham Hall, was strict but kindly towards his young curate, though their time working together was short as the vicar was forced to retire early on health grounds. In the midst of a busy pastoral ministry, Dan still managed to maintain his research on Cosin, supported by day-off visits to Bishop Cosin's Library in nearby Durham.

The world was changing rapidly in the 1950s. Church attendance was beginning to decline while the new Teesside Industrial Mission, led by Bill Wright from 1959, was a far cry from Canon McGill's church and parish-centred ministry. Dan played his part in these changes and participated in a course for younger clergy led by an ICI management team, an introduction for the Church into the workings of a large industrial company. After Canon McGill's departure, St Peter's became a more relaxed and cheerful place as Dan was ordained priest by Bishop Harland on Trinity Sunday 1959.

It was just over a year later that Dan became engaged, on 29 September 1960, to Juliet Wood. Juliet's childhood and early life with Dan are recorded in her delightful book, luminous and at times painfully truthful, *A Stockton Childhood* (2018), which ends with their marriage and departure for India in 1963. Juliet was a devout and active member of the St Peter's congregation under Canon McGill with a talent for poetry and arts and crafts. Thus it was that, in 1960, she went to Matlock Teacher Training College in Derbyshire to study art, craft, religious knowledge and English, and as a result a long engagement ensued before Dan and Juliet were finally married on 17 August 1963.

By this time, Dan had moved on from Stockton and become curate to Father Gordon Defty at St Aidan's, West Hartlepool, while imagining that his future ministry with Juliet would be in one of the Durham pit villages. But work overseas beckoned, and a letter came from a Father Jourdain at MECCA reminding Dan of their earlier connections while he was at Cuddesdon. After some discussion about teaching and chaplaincy posts at one of the Asian Christian Colleges, it was suggested that Dan and Juliet consider going, with Dan as Chaplain, to St Stephen's College, Delhi, perhaps the most distinguished of the Asian Christian Colleges. Dan was interviewed at Cambridge by a committee chaired by the Master of Selwyn College, Owen Chadwick, and appointed, on the committee's recommendation, by Satish Sircar, the Indian Principal of St Stephen's, as Chaplain and a lecturer in the English Department. Juliet was placed on SPG's list of women missionary candidates, and was to teach at Queen Mary's School, Tis Hazari in Delhi, a mile away from St Stephen's.

From then things moved quickly. Apart from their marriage, Juliet had to complete her course at Matlock while Dan's work on Bishop Cosin was written up as an MA thesis in the University of Durham.[8] After a brief honeymoon in Edinburgh and Northumberland, on 7 September 1963, just 16 years into Indian independence, the young couple boarded the SS *Caledonia* in Liverpool for the twenty-day voyage to Bombay. A new life lay ahead of them in a bustling capital city still dominated by numerous equestrian statues of the rulers of the former British Raj.

---

[8] It was eventually incorporated in 1967 into a Clarendon Press edition of Cosin's *Collection of Private Devotions* with P. G. Stanwood of the University of British Columbia.

Chaplain, lecturer and writer at St Stephen's

Shortly before their departure for India, Dan had received a letter from Robert Runcie, then Principal of Cuddesdon and previously Secretary of the Cambridge Mission to Delhi. Runcie, together with Owen Chadwick, had visited India and he now offered some advice about St Stephen's College, Delhi. The College chapel, Runcie observed, had long been neglected and was poorly attended with morning prayers of a residual "English public-school type". Its revival should be centred on the Eucharist, and for this Dan was well prepared. On Dan's arrival in Delhi, the Principal, Satish Sircar, lost no time in introducing the new chaplain to his chapel, a building modelled on the chapel of Gonville and Caius' College, Cambridge, simple but deeply numinous. Dan quickly discovered how dire the weekday prayers were, sparsely attended by a handful of Christian members of staff and only the occasional student. The first thing, with the support of the principal, was to engender the culture of a Sunday Eucharist. In the context of the new Church of North India liturgy, Sunday worship took off surprisingly quickly, attracting a mixed congregation which also included staff and students from adjacent colleges. Students from other religious traditions attended the daily morning and evening prayers, and the chapel began to be an established part of the College's life. There was a Sunday school for the children of the office and kitchen staff, and as a result one year at Christmas the children performed a Hindustani Nativity Play in the College Hall before a large audience.

Dan quickly took an interest in the already established Student Christian Movement (SCM), initially with two Malayani students, John Philip and Ajit Ninan. This attracted a wide range of speakers to the College; a favourite was the great writer Nirad Chandra Chaudhuri.[9] At prayers for all undergraduates in the college assembly hall, the principal drew from Hindu and Muslim as well as Christian sources, while Dan organized a programme of "religious and moral instruction", which

---

[9] Nirad Chaudhuri (1897–1999) was also a well-known figure in Oxford, where he died at the age of 101. His masterpiece was *The Autobiography of an Unknown Indian* (1951).

involved members of staff from all religious traditions. Following the unification of ministries in India, Dan became a Presbyter of the Church of North India, which allowed him to assist as priest in several local churches in Delhi and beyond into Harayana and Rajasthan.

At the same time, both Juliet and Dan were teaching—Juliet at St Mary's School, where she was given charge of the Art Department, and Dan in the English Department of St Stephen's. Money was tight, and it was Juliet's earnings that furnished their house in College. In his work, Dan established friendships with two lecturers that were to endure long after their days in India, especially with Brij Raj Singh and Harish Trivedi,[10] and the department attracted a succession of extremely able students in English Honours.

Delhi was then a rapidly growing city of some four million people. Education was also expanding, and while St Stephen's College doubled its numbers to 1,200 in the 1960s, Delhi University, of which it was a constituent part, grew from under 40,000 to over 100,000 students, aided by massive overseas funding, not least from the USA. With such expansion came growing pains and the challenge to maintain standards, with the result that the later 1960s were disrupted with a series of strikes and protests. It was also the period of the United Nations' first Development Decade in India, connecting most obviously with India's programme of Five-Year Plans. From the Gandhian vision of village-republics, these Plans were intended to incorporate rural communities into large administrative blocks, although these were implemented only in selected regions, and this was to be incorporated alongside major industrial developments. The issue and practice of development, chiefly rural, was a major preoccupation of the churches. A book by a former missionary in Indonesia, the Dutch theologian Arend van Leeuwen, entitled *Christianity in World History* (1964), was of particular importance for theological reflection on the subject, and included pleas for dialogue with Marxism. Pope Paul VI's encyclical of 1967, *Populorum progressio* ("On the development of peoples"), was also significant and prompted a number of responses from India, not least from a Jesuit social

---

[10] The author of the Afterword of the present volume.

institute in Delhi[11] and the Christian Institute for the Study of Religion and Society in Bangalore, of which more will be said later. Most of the students at St Stephen's College were from urban, well-to-do middle-class backgrounds, but it was agreed during the famine of 1966, and especially in Bihar, that teams of students would go to affected areas and help with relief measures under local administrators. For many of them, this was a life-changing experience with long-lasting consequences.

Meanwhile life was becoming ever busier for Dan at St Stephen's College. He was invited to share in a consultation for a new department of religious studies at the recently established Punjabi University at Patiala, and his advice was that religious studies must not ignore current social realities.[12] The Christian Institute for the Study of Religion and Society (CISRS, better known as "scissors"), which had been established at Bangalore, South India in 1957, was important for Dan and many others. It was one of a dozen study centres created in Asia on the initiative of the World Council of Churches to promote inter-religious exploration and dialogue. CISRS was founded by two remarkable South Indian theologians, P. D. Devanandan and M. M. Thomas, and apart from publications and consultations it engaged in some pioneering work with Roman Catholics, the Jesuits bringing Paolo Freire to India for consultations. The religious ferment that was part of this period found an early response in the Cambridge Mission to Delhi's Teape exchange lectureship in memory of Bishop B. F. Westcott.[13] The first lecturer to travel from Cambridge to Delhi was Charles Raven in 1955 and the first from India to Cambridge was P. D. Devanandan in 1957.

In his teaching of English literature at the College itself, Dan found himself thrown in at the deep end. In his first week, he was teaching the plays of Christopher Marlowe to bright third year honours students, two of whom became lifelong friends—"Bhatto", Romesh Bhattacharji, and Gopal Krishna Gandhi, whose brother Ramchandra taught philosophy

---

[11] Vidyajyoti Insitute of Religious Studies, formerly St Mary's College, Kurseong.

[12] See below, Chapter 2, "The Study of Religion and Social Reality".

[13] A series of these lectures were delivered by Dan O'Connor himself in 1992 in Delhi, Calcutta and Bangalore under the title *Relations in Religion*. See below, pp. 61–82

in the College. Eventually settling into a survey course on literature from Chaucer to T. S. Eliot, Dan's aim was that students should learn to enjoy literature, and it was clear that some of them were formidable intellectuals. For example, in later years Nirupam Sen ran rings around his British and American equivalents when he became Permanent Representative of India to the United Nations. Rabindra Ray was to teach for years in the Department of Sociology at the Delhi School of Economics; his publications included a devastating demolition of Naxalite ideology.[14] Then there was Irwin Allan Sealy, to whom Dan introduced Laurence Sterne's *Tristram Shandy*, and who went on to become a distinguished novelist (notable for his first novel *The Trotter-Nama* [1988]), poet, artist and musician. He stayed in the UK for some time shortly before Juliet's death, cooking meals for Dan at that difficult time.

As a result of his teaching Dan published a fine study of Eliot's *Four Quartets* (1969)[15] in which he recognized "Little Gidding" as a clear and deeply Anglican link to his earlier work on Cosin's *Devotions*. Altogether his teaching load of 20 hours a week, added to his work in the chaplaincy, meant a busy life but a happy one, during which time he and Juliet had two sons, Aidan in 1965 and Tim in 1968.

For her part, Juliet, with a qualification in voice-production from the English Speaking Union, was becoming deeply involved in theatre, and particularly in costume and make-up, in St Stephen's College. Programmes survive from 15 productions, of which five were Shakespeare, between 1964 and 1971. She designed the sets and costumes for *As You Like It* and *The Comedy of Errors*, and, by way of contrast, *Henry IV, Part I*. Juliet's last Shakespeare play, in December 1971, was *The Merchant of Venice*, performed shortly before the O'Connors' departure from Delhi and return to Britain. There were many other productions besides Shakespearean drama, including light comedies like *Charley's Aunt* and more serious contemporary drama such as Camus' *Caligula* and Giraudoux's *Tiger at the Gates*. Of particular note, given the time of the development of the Naxalite Movement, was Mario Fratti's *Che*

---

[14] For more on the Naxalites, see below, Chapter 7, "Spring Thunder", pp. 129–48.

[15] See Bibliography.

Guevara (1968); Juliet's name in the programme, together with those of the actors and director Kapil Sibal, attracted the attention of the local police in Delhi.

Dan and Juliet had their one home leave in 1967, enjoying the westward journey, with days spent with Arab Christians and Muslim friends in the Holy Land, then sampling the joys of Greece and Switzerland. In England they were able to renew family ties, not least with Dan's sister Kath, newly married and with a son, Matthew. On her return to Delhi, however, Juliet wrote with relief at being back in their own home, preparing for the arrival of their second son, Tim, the following March.[16] She organized important work with the wives of the "college servants", welcoming them into her home and teaching them sewing and knitting as well as, through a doctor friend, providing advice on family planning and family wellbeing. It was remarkable, very largely hidden, work and a practical response to the poverty that was so widespread in Delhi.

But the time in India proved to be only one short decade. Dan's sister, Kath, was terminally ill, and so Dan and Juliet returned to England to support her and her young son. She died in 1972. Dan left India with a clearer and brighter Christian faith though it was also, he insisted, fuzzy at the edges. Later, when the West became more conscious of inter-faith dialogue, the hesitant came to learn that one effect of it was the firming up of one's own faith. Dan and Juliet had learnt this, living as they did amongst a handful of Christians, a few Jains and Buddhists, Jews and Parsees, together with many Muslims and Sikhs, countless Hindus of many varieties, and their own brand of Maoists—whom we shall come to shortly. Above all they had been granted the gift of lasting friendships; leaving St Stephen's was a terrible wrench, and in many ways Dan never got over it. India has a way of getting into one's soul, and as the essays in this book show so clearly, the country has always remained at the heart of his life.

---

[16] Dan edited Juliet's letters home to England in *Juliet's Letters from India* (Amazon, 2018). See further below, Appendix, pp. 183–5.

India: Glimpsing Westcott's dream

Now something must be said of Dan's theological work and development during his time in India.[17] Behind it lies the figure of Brook Fosse Westcott (1825–1901), bishop of Durham, and his dream of "a new Alexandria[18] on the banks of the Jumna". Westcott was the founder of the Cambridge Mission to Delhi with his vision of an Indian appropriation of Christianity, and St Stephen's College was an essential instrument of this. In his aim of a "further unfolding of the faith" in India, Westcott was disappointed that early Delhi missionaries did not teach in the vernacular. But things began to change in the early twentieth century, when S. K. Rudra, a Bengali Christian, was appointed as Principal of the College. Rudra and his colleague, the English priest Charles Freer Andrews (1871–1940) were both friends of Gandhi, and they offered a challenge to the pervasive racism of "British India", also demanding a "Church of India" to serve an independent nation. It was in collaboration with Rudra and Andrews that Gandhi planned the Non-Co-operation movement in the Principal's House at St Stephen's College.

The constitution of the St Stephen's College decreed that its Principal must be a Christian, but in almost all other respects the College was deeply and affirmatively pluralistic. As well as Christians on the teaching staff there were Muslims, Sikhs, Parsees and a wide range of Hindus, whilst among the students there were also Adivasis, Buddhists, Jews and a number who described themselves as "freelance". At the daily assemblies attended by all the undergraduates, the Principal read from the New Testament, adding prayers from Muslim sources and from the Nobel-prizewinning Bengali writer Rabindranath Tagore's poetry.[19] Dan added

---

[17] For a fuller account see Dan O'Connor, *Interesting Times in India: A Short Decade at St Stephen's College* (New Delhi: Penguin, 2005), excerpted below, Chapter 7, pp. 129–48.

[18] Alexandria in northern Egypt after the first century CE was the centre of a highly syncretic mix of Jewish theology and Greek philosophy to which was added Christian thought after Clement of Alexandria and Origen in the early third century.

[19] Tagore was a close friend of Andrews.

further inter-faith prayers to this mix. All the major faiths celebrated their festivals in college, and the chapel became so widely accessible as to sponsor, one year, a passion play, *Today is Friday*, in which not one of the participants was a Christian.

Such pluralism looked back to Westcott's dream for India, and in the Student Christian Movement and its Catholic equivalent there was a lively sense of Indian identity. Dan took his Christian students to the Golden Temple in Amritsar, and in the Christian staff study group he encouraged the study of Raimundo Pannikar's *The Unknown Christ of Hinduism* (1964). Wilfred Cantwell Smith (1916–2000), the distinguished scholar of comparative religion, was a neighbour in Delhi during 1963–4, before his departure for Harvard, and his book *The Meaning and End of Religion* (1962) was the subject of many conversations. In alternate years, the College hosted the Teape Lectures (referred to earlier), established in 1955 to explore the dialogue between Christian and Hindu religious thought. Sponsoring lecturers from both India and Britain, this exchange in honour of Westcott enabled the Delhi Mission to advance the bishop's dream.

Close neighbours of St Stephen's College in Delhi were the Cambridge Brotherhood, which was formed in 1877 in the Cambridge Mission to Delhi. One of its members, James Stuart, introduced Dan to his friend, the Benedictine monk Père Le Saux, a great explorer of Indian spirituality, who was to be better known as Swami Abishiktananda. Dan also became involved with the nearby Jesuit Vidyadyoti College of Theology, eventually contributing a chapter on C. F. Andrews and Munshi Ram to a book edited by George Gispert-Sauch SJ, *God's Word Among Men* (1973);[20] other contributors included Karl Rahner and Raimundo Pannikar. The World Council of Churches in India initiated new inter-religious programmes, not least under the leadership of the South Indian theologian S. J. Samartha. Altogether it was, for Dan and Juliet, a happy and creative time stimulated by numerous friendships with both Indian colleagues and a multinational array of missionaries including Roger Hooker, once a fellow curate in Stockton and now studying in the Sanskrit University in Varanasi. Another close friend

---

[20] See below, Chapter 3, pp. 47–60.

was the Roman Catholic artist Jyoti Sahi,[21] who sought to paint an Indian Christ in ways that inspired and sometimes alarmed his Church. He often painted a "dancing Christ", an image with profound Indian resonance, for divinity does indeed dance in Indian iconography.

It was another South Indian theologian, Madathiparompil Mammen Thomas (MM), who invited Dan to contribute to a series of books published by the Christian Institute for the Study of Religion and Society in Bangalore,[22] and the result was *The Testimony of C. F. Andrews* (1974) which examines Andrews' work with the two great figures of neo-Hinduism and the attainment of independent India, Rabindranath Tagore and M. K. Gandhi. Andrews was already the subject of a biography by Benarsidas Chaturvedi and Dan's Quaker friend in India, Marjorie Sykes,[23] but much work still needed to be done, not least on Andrews' theology and thought. The task took Dan to the National Archives in New Delhi and from his research he wrote a substantial Introduction to this selection of Andrews' own writings.[24] Further study of C. F. Andrews was to take up a great deal of Dan's time after he and Juliet left India and settled in St Andrews, Scotland, eventually resulting in a doctorate and a full-length study, *Gospel, Raj and Swaraj: The Missionary Years of C. F. Andrews, 1904–1914* (1990).[25] All this work reveals Andrews' (and Dan's) profound understanding of the phenomenon of Hinduism, especially neo-Hinduism and Indian spirituality.

It was notable that while all these vibrant realizations of Westcott's dream were taking place in India, almost nothing of it was known of in England where university libraries were woefully understocked with Indian material. All the more welcome, therefore, are Dan's later biographical contributions to the splendid volume *Love's Redeeming*

---

[21] One of his paintings adorns the covers of this book.

[22] The series was entitled "Confessing the Faith in India", and Dan's book was Number 10 in the sequence.

[23] Benarsidas Chaturvedi and Marjorie Sykes, *Charles Freer Andrews: A Narrative* (London: George Allen & Unwin, 1949).

[24] For an extract from this Introduction see Chapter 5, below, pp. 83–112.

[25] A later version of this book was published in India as *A Clear Star: C. F. Andrews and India, 1904–1914* (New Delhi: Chronicle Books, 2005).

Work: *The Anglican Quest for Holiness* (2001), edited by Geoffrey Rowell, Kenneth Stevenson and Rowan Williams, including notes on nine Indian Christians, among them K. M. Banerjea, N. N. Goreh, A. J. Appaswamy and (the only woman in the group) Pandita Ramabai Sarasvati. Dan's decade in India, with Juliet, was not spent in the task of "converting" people to Christianity but rather one of enjoying lasting friendships and engaging with the varied life and community of St Stephen's College, Delhi. One extraordinary privilege was when Juliet and Dan were presented to Prime Minister Nehru in October 1963. Nehru's death, some six months later, was a great blow to nationalist hopes. But two things at the time of Nehru's death are, perhaps, worth recording. Immediately on his death, a priest from the Cambridge Brotherhood, Ernest John, later a bishop in the Church of South India, was summoned to the Nehru household to share prayers with them. Then, a little later, as Nehru's body was about to be moved from the house to the place of cremation, Ernest John was again asked to lead prayers. Newspaper reports do not mention these events.

India: Nehru's nightmare

It will be useful to describe the political and social background in Delhi during Dan's time there. By the time that the O'Connors met Nehru in 1963 India had been independent for 16 years. Nehru represented all that was best in the new era—humane, progressive and a leading figure among the ex-colonial, non-aligned nations in the Cold War period. But by the early 1960s, there were many indications that things were not going well, and that Nehru was frustrated and distressed. India was a largely rural, deeply traditional society with entrenched power structures, and there were many specific, immediate issues to be faced, not least the Chinese invasion of 1962, which had been a terrible humiliation for India. It had led to Nehru's first and only defeat in a confidence vote in parliament. There were huge economic problems, the population was growing rapidly—and in 1963-4 the harvest failed. Nehru died in May 1964, but he passed his disappointed hopes on to his successors, briefly Lal Bahadur and then Nehru's daughter, Indira Gandhi. She was a tough politician, unlike her father whom she called "a saint who strayed into politics", but she was faced with enormous problems, not least through the failure of the monsoon in two successive years, 1965 and 1966.

Organizations like the Christian Institute for the Study of Religion and Society in Bangalore gave impressive service to the process of nation-building and the building of a post-colonial Church. On the other hand, Hindu communal politics resurfaced during the 1960s as an attempt to reverse the secular direction of Nehru's project, and the assassination of Gandhi in 1947 remained a bitter memory for many. Towards the end of 1966 a united front of Hindu revivalists was formed, and one of its leaders explained that "the perverted policies of the Government and the blind emulation of Western ways of living are responsible for the current deplorable state of affairs". During the 20 years of Congress' rule, "India's ancient culture has been destroyed". There were, of course, strong political elements in this Hindu fundamentalism, which at times suggested that the liberal, pluralistic consensus of Nehru was under pressure.

And yet, "dialogue" between religions remained a possibility despite all such rumblings. Not least there was the influence of the Second Vatican Council, followed by Pope John Paul II's visit to India in 1986, when he instructed the bishops to do everything possible to promote inter-religious dialogue as part of the apostolic ministry. The World Council of Churches also played its part in the process. But the question remained as to how much of this dialogue was more a Christian concern for contextualization than an answer to the questions which Hindus were asking, and it gave the impression that that it related primarily to India's high culture, which the poor majority of India's Christians regarded as a permanent mode of oppression.

The famine in 1967 coincided with a violent uprising of the dispossessed in West Bengal, in particular in a district called Naxalbari, followed by similar revolts in most parts of poor, rural India. These were accompanied by new political alignments, specifically the creation of a new Communist Party of India, its members often known as Naxalites or Maoists. For some of the students in St Stephen's College who had been volunteers in Bihar[26] during the famine, this party and its policies

---

[26] Bihar is in north-east India, adjacent to West Bengal, and is amongst the poorest of Indian states.

seemed a proper response to the questions raised by their experiences amongst the rural poor. There was also an urban aspect to the rural Naxalite upheaval, beginning in Mumbai in the 1960s and linked to the Dalit community, the majority of whom were Christian.[27]

Within university life, there was a growing commitment to revolutionary Marxist ideology and some 15 students from St Stephen's College and others, including some from women's colleges, abandoned their studies to join the new Communist Party of India (Marxist–Leninist), and they went underground mostly to agitate and organize in rural areas. Among them were some of Dan's students, and for them, at the time at least, the Cultural Revolution in China was a beacon. A Naxalite slogan appeared one night on the College tower, reading "China's Path is our Path, China's Chairman is our Chairman". As the college Chaplain, Dan admired the principled position of the three *naxals* whom he knew well, but he could hardly openly encourage them. Yet inequalities in Indian society were so profound and poverty so extreme, that, as a young priest, he could not but treat seriously the ideals of these bright young students who were sacrificing their own promising careers for their principles. Some of them were prepared to hold conversations with him. One of them urged him to read Edgar Snow's *Red Star Over China* (1937), which he did, concluding that it was a sort of Acts of the Apostles for the moment, opening a door to a discussion with some of the students on the significance of the Taiping Rebellion in nineteenth-century China, important for Mao and with fascinating, if extremely odd, Christian strands. One of Dan's English Honours students, Rabindra Ray, a Hindu who went underground, later went on to publish his Oxford doctorate under the title *The Naxalites and Their Ideology* (1988). The movement collapsed in 1971 both in India and elsewhere in South Asia. Dan's "three musketeers", Arvind Narayan Das, Rabindra Ray and Dilip Simeon, all went on to pursue successful and creative lives, all three at one time and another coming to stay with Juliet and Dan in the UK.[28]

---

[27] Dalits were previously known as "untouchables", being from the lowest stratum of the Indian caste system. They were excluded from the fourfold *varna* system of Hinduism.

[28] See below, Chapter 7, "Spring Thunder", pp 129–48.

"The auld grey toon beside the northern sea": St Andrews and Edinburgh

Dan and Juliet left India in 1972 as we have seen for family reasons, and Dan became Anglican chaplain to the University of St Andrews, its chilly climate and ancient university a stark contrast to the heat, and heated politics, of India. Juliet became a part-time teacher at St Leonard's School, then only admitting girls. Dan and Juliet became involved in what was at the time called the Campaign for Homosexual Equality, then fiercely opposed in Scottish law, and Juliet opened their home for discrete meetings of men fearful of the law. Dan also became active in the Scottish Episcopal Church, then a politically energetic and creative body. It was not long before students from India found their way to the O'Connors' door, and India was never far from their minds. Accordingly, Dan registered as a PhD student at the university, carrying forward his work on C. F. Andrews and specifically exploring the decade in which Andrews turned from empire-enthusiast to devoted friend of Gandhi and Tagore. Dan's study, begun in Delhi, was enriched by the availability of archives in London and Oxford. He also became a member of the Labour Party, getting to know Gordon Brown. But the time in St Andrew's was short, and five years later Dan and his family were on the move again.

It was Alastair Haggart, bishop of Edinburgh, who called Dan, not altogether willingly, to parish ministry in Edinburgh in the parish of the Good Shepherd, Murrayfield. Episcopal clergy, then and indeed now, were hardly well remunerated and by then Juliet was suffering from arthritis; life was not easy. But old students and friends from Delhi found their way to Edinburgh as they had to St Andrews, and it was here that Dan's PhD thesis on Andrews was completed, examined by Professor Duncan Forrester. But it was not long before another move was mooted, and to a place far more appropriate for Dan's missionary experience and passions.

Global village and the "Selly Oak Century"

Two posts were advertised at about the same time: Dean of Mission in the Federation of Selly Oak Colleges in Birmingham, and Principal of the USPG College of the Ascension within the same Federation. Dan applied for both jobs, was shortlisted for both, and was appointed to the latter. Juliet was later to be appointed as a college tutor. The post of Dean of Mission went to a Roman Catholic, Sister/Dr Marcella Hoesl of the Maryknoll Missionaries, joining a number of other Catholics on the staff of the Federation.

Dating back to 1903 and the founding of Woodbrooke College by George Cadbury of the Society of Friends, the five colleges of the Selly Oak Federation in the 1970s and 1980s were at the heart of ecumenical debates. Dan's College of the Ascension was founded in 1923, initially to train women for the "mission field", and in some ways it stood apart from the rest of the Federation colleges at the high church end of Anglicanism. Some years later the more evangelical Church Missionary Society (CMS) provided a degree of balance, and by 1970 four mission colleges—two Anglican (USPG and CMS), one Baptist and United Reformed (St Andrews), and one Methodist (Kingsmead), combined with a Department of Mission with a co-ordinating Dean of Mission.

When Dan arrived in 1982, the Federation was close to its zenith in terms of institutions and people involved. As Principal of the College of the Ascension, he welcomed students from all over the world, the majority sent by USPG, many of whom ended up in positions of leadership in the worldwide Anglican Communion. Many of the students were sent into English parishes during the vacations—often as much a steep learning curve for the hosts as it was for the students. One Malaysian Tamil, studying for a PhD, described the Church of England as like a decrepit old lady who never listened to her grandchildren. He had a point. There was also a dwindling number of men and women selected by USPG to work in the Church overseas, and they came to the College to prepare for their ministry, an important educational process in a Britain that was increasingly consumerist and, sadly, racist. From the central admissions office of the Federation came a flow of international students and visitors, one of these being Kirill, then Archbishop of Smolensk and Vyazma, sent to improve his spoken English for service in the World Council of Churches. He has subsequently become better known, and perhaps notorious, as Patriarch of Moscow and All Russia. Juliet was his tutor. A later letter from Dan to Kirill in Moscow never reached him. The chaplain at the British Embassy in Moscow, Patrick Irwin, a friend of Dan, was told by the Patriarch's gatekeepers that Kirill had never been to England—and they declined to receive any letter.

In 1987, Juliet joined Dan as a published author. Under the pseudonym "Beth Collier"[29] she published, with SPCK, *Beyond Words: Prayer as a Way of Life*.[30] Its publication came as a complete surprise to Dan who was fully aware in his own life of one reviewer's wisdom, who remarked, "Fortunate is anyone who has Beth Collier as a spiritual director." At about the same time, a family bequest to Juliet made it possible for the O'Connors to buy their first house, the former Episcopalian rectory at Elie in Fife, in preparation for their eventual retirement. For his part, Dan had the great good fortune to get to know Rasiah Saccidananda Sugirtharajah and his wife. "Sugi" was a doctoral student at the University of Birmingham, working on the use of the Bible in liberation theology. He went on to become a professor at Birmingham and pioneer of postcolonial biblical hermeneutics. Sugi and Dan became, and remain, close friends.

There was also a return trip to India on behalf of USPG, though this time Dan travelled without Juliet. It was made also on behalf of Archbishop Robert Runcie who was due to make a trip to India himself and needed someone to prepare information for him. Beginning in his old home St Stephen's College, Dan went on to visit Kathmandu in Nepal, Calcutta, and then south to the diocese of Nandyals. On the way, he was able to stay with his old friends Jane and Jyoti Sahi at their Art Ashram outside Bangalore. The visit ended in Mumbai.

Dan had not lost touch with the Christian Institute for the Study of Religion and Society in Bangalore, and now they asked him to write another book for their *Confessing the Faith in India* series, this time on

---

[29] Juliet's great-great-great grandfather was Admiral Sir George Collier, and his son was Admiral Sir Francis Augustus Collier.

[30] See Appendix, below, pp. 186–6.

Verrier Elwin (1902–64). Like Andrews before him, Elwin had been a rebel, anti-imperial missionary, thrown out of the Church by his bishop, a friend of both Gandhi and Nehru, and in time a distinguished anthropologist, ethnologist and activist on behalf of India's tribal peoples, the Adivasis. The result was Dan's edited selection of Elwin's writings, *Din-Sevak: Verrier Elwin's Life of Service in Tribal India* (1993).[31]

Dan's time at Selly Oak was busy and absorbing. Not only was he Principal at the College of the Ascension, he also represented the College within the Selly Oak Federation, in the Department of Mission, which he chaired, and in the USPG. He once described his job as the best in the Church of England, as it was within an endlessly stimulating community yet semi-detached from anything too "churchy"—part, indeed, of a vibrant global village. But such were the pressures that by 1990 he began to look for a move, and this was to take him back to Scotland.

Scottish Churches House, Dunblane

In mid-1990 Dan and Juliet moved from Selly Oak to the little Perthshire town of Dunblane near Stirling, where he was to be Director of Scottish Churches House. Dunblane was a far cry from the multicultural bustle of Birmingham; it was situated in a long row of old houses in the shadow of the medieval cathedral which had long since become the Church of Scotland parish church. The House was a conference centre serving the ecumenical movement under the auspices of Action of Churches Together in Scotland (ACTS). His relationships with the Roman Catholic Church were particularly happy; it had recently, joined the Orthodox, Reformed and Anglican churches in the World Council of Churches. Having encountered Roman Catholic friends at pretty well every stage of his ministry, this was an encouraging moment for him.

But the time at Dunblane was not altogether easy. The whole enterprise was a task waiting to be done, but Dan had neither the contacts nor the appetite for such networking. Although he was called Director, it was not very clear what he was supposed to direct. Furthermore the

---

[31] See below, Chapter 6, pp. 113–28.

prospectus for the post changed without warning just before he arrived—and it took three years to extricate himself from this uncomfortable and rather unhappy position. But there were some compensations, not least his connection with Professor Andrew Walls, founder of the Centre for the Study of Christianity in the Non-Western World (later World Christianity) at New College in the University of Edinburgh, where Dan became an honorary research fellow. At New College, he was able again to teach and supervise research theses. Connections with India remained strong, and his interest in and writing on the life and work of Verrier Elwin continued. There was also another visit to India to deliver the Westcott (commonly called Teape) lectures for 1992, and this time both Dan and Juliet were able to travel. The lectures were delivered in three locations—St Stephen's College, Delhi, Bishop's College, Calcutta, and the United Theological College, Bangalore. Following such distinguished predecessors in the Teape lectureship in India as Charles Raven, Owen Chadwick and Robert Runcie, Dan felt free to deliver a wide-ranging consideration of his topic: "The Upanishads and Catholic theology". His lectures were published with the title *Relations in Religion* (1994) under three headings, Friendship, Solidarity, and Ecumenism.[32] It was a glorious, and not quite the final, visit back to Delhi and India.

But a removal from Dunblane was inevitable, and so in January 1993 Dan and Juliet packed up their belongings and moved back to England, to a canonry at Wakefield Cathedral.

Canon of Wakefield

In the cathedral at Wakefield, Dan's stall was dedicated to Alcuin of York, another northerner, who was both a poet and a theologian. The West Yorkshire town of Wakefield is not on the usual tourist routes, and the diocese dates only from the nineteenth century. Dan enjoyed the liturgical life of the cathedral, but his true ministry thrived amongst the large Muslim population of West Yorkshire which had been attracted in the 1960s by the work available in the textile mills. There was a large

---

[32] For the text of the second lecture, "Solidarity", see below Chapter 4, pp. 61–82.

group from Mirpur, a poor area of Pakistan, and others from Gujerat in India. A few miles away in Dewsbury was what was then reputed to be the largest mosque in western Europe. Encouraged by the bishop, Nigel McCulloch, Dan found his way into the Muslim community and into the Dewsbury mosque, with its 300 boys preparing to become imams. A remarkable renewal movement, known as Tablighi Jamaat, also provided Dan with an opportunity to practise his long-rusty Urdu.

In addition to advising the bishop, it was clear that the local clergy and laity needed help to function in such a multi-religious context. Several parishes had Church of England schools in which the vast majority of children were Muslim. Dan enlisted the help of a new friend, the learned Mufti Faheem Mayet. Brought up in North India, he was acknowledged in the Muslim community as a distinguished scholar. Growing Muslim-Western hostility made it an especially important time to build good local interfaith relationships.

In 1995, Dan and Juliet made their final trip to India when Dan was invited to give the eighth Verrier Elwin memorial lectures at the new North-Eastern Hill University at Shillong in Maghalaya. This university was established to serve the tribal hill states of North-East India, a region where Elwin himself had worked among the tribal people. The trip ended with one last visit to St Stephen's College, Delhi. On their return to Wakefield, Dan was struck down by ill health—routine surgery was followed by a heart attack—and early retirement was advised. And so, after only three years in Yorkshire, the O'Connors returned to their house in Elie, Scotland and a happy 20 years of retirement together.

Retirement in Fife

For Dan, there was a great deal of writing to be done. In September 1997, he was asked, at the suggestion of Adrian Hastings, to write the history of the USPG for the Society's tercentenary in 2001.[33] Juliet's response was characteristic: "Well, it may kill you, but you'll die happy!" It was finally agreed that Dan would write the bulk of the book, a general

---

[33] Histories of USPG had earlier been written in 1901 and 1951.

historical survey of 300 years, while the rest would consist of 14 essays on agreed topics by other writers, both men and women, from around the world. One new aspect of the book was Dan's concentration on the first century of the Society, when it had sent hundreds of missionaries to North America, a period largely ignored by earlier "evangelical" writers, for whom mission from Britain began with William Carey in India a century later.[34]

This task took two years, involving research visits to the Society's archives in Oxford and London. These were revealing of the change in attitudes from the beginnings in 1710, when the Society was given two plantations in Barbados together with 300 slaves by Christopher Codrington, through to the determined anti-slavery movement by the end of the eighteenth century. Dan persuaded a distinguished Barbadian scholar to write of that particularly sensitive topic. The completed book, *Three Centuries of Mission*, was launched at St Paul's Cathedral and later, on 30 March 2001, a leather-bound copy was presented to the Society's patron, Queen Elizabeth II, at Buckingham Palace. There was one major further after-effect of the book: the editors of the *Oxford Handbook of Anglican Studies* (2015) asked Dan to write a section on "The Geography of Anglicanism", later described in the *Church Times* as "masterly".[35]

On the domestic front, 2000 brought a move from the house in Elie to Strathkinness, a village one mile west of St Andrews. The generations were shifting, and Juliet's mother died at Stockton in 1999, while Dan's mother died in Darlington in 2003. There was also another book, *Interesting Times in India: A Short Decade at St Stephen's College* (2005), recalling Dan and Juliet's happy years in Delhi. Then there was one more move, to a bungalow in Balmullo, also not far from St Andrews, where both Dan and Juliet continued to write. Some of Juliet's work was published after her death, edited by Dan, notably *A Stockton Childhood* (2018) and *Juliet's Letters from India* (2018). Dan also wrote *The Chaplains of the*

---

[34] William Carey (1761–1834) was a Baptist minister who went to India in 1793 and founded the Serampore University which became the first degree-awarding institution in India. He has been described as "the father of modern missions".

[35] For a full text of this essay, see below, Chapter 9, pp. 161–81.

East India Company, 1601–1858 (2012). India never left either of them, as is so often the case with those who have lived and worked in that remarkable country. That book was followed by a chapter on India in the second volume of *The Oxford History of Anglicanism* (2017), drawing particular attention to the work of Bishop Thomas Fanshawe Middleton (1769–1822), the first bishop of Calcutta and one of Dan's heroes.

In 2007, Dan delivered the Teape Seminars as a guest of Selwyn College, Cambridge, a link in more ways than one to his life in India, for it was Owen Chadwick, then Master of Selwyn College, who had interviewed him so many years ago, before his time in St Stephen's College, Delhi. Owen, aged 91, attended the seminars, and monopolized Juliet at a private dinner party one evening. Dan reported that he was as lively and entertaining as ever.

On 3 March 2016, Juliet died peacefully. At her funeral, a requiem was celebrated in the Episcopalian church of St James the Great at Cupar, a few miles from Balmullo. The celebrant and preacher was Bishop David Chillingworth, the Primus of the Scottish Episcopal Church. In his sermon, he summed up Juliet beautifully, for she spoke as with "the voice of a contemplative—a person who is spiritually strong because she has somehow absorbed her illness and pain and made it part of the journey". The burial was at Kilconquhar, just a mile from Elie, where the O'Connors had first had a house of their own.

And Dan—his journey has continued, not without its griefs, including the further loss of a grandson who died of an aneurysm in March 2021, but still living in the same bungalow in Balmullo and sharing his wealth of experience in the church and in India during the long and eventful journey from Stockton to Fife via Delhi. Dan's writings that follow represent moments from his long life and his immense contribution to scholarship, the life of the Church, and our understanding of the religious and cultural life of modern India.

The Writings

1

John Cosin: A Collection of Private Devotions, 1627

Daniel O'Connor was drawn to the writing of Bishop John Cosin when he was studying as an ordinand at Cuddesdon Theological College, Oxford, in the late 1950s. His interest and research continued during his time as a curate in Stockton-on-Tees, when he was able to return to his old university of Durham, where Cosin had been bishop between 1660 and 1672. Dan's work was eventually presented as an M.A. thesis in Durham in 1963 and found a public readership in the magnificent volume of Cosin's *Collection of Private Devotions*, edited by O'Connor and P. G. Stanwood of the University of British Columbia, Vancouver, and published by the Clarendon Press in 1967.[1] The essay printed here is a much later work by Dan, an edited form of a lecture given by him at a conference held in Durham on 2–4 July 1993, as part of the celebration of the 900th anniversary of the completion of the great Romanesque cathedral, where Cosin had been bishop, and in commemoration of the 400th anniversary of Cosin's birth. It was later published in a collection of essays on Cosin, edited by Margot Johnson, in 1997.

In his unpublished autobiographical writings, Dan tells us that his interest in Cosin was sparked by a chance encounter in a second-hand bookshop with five volumes of his works in the Library of Anglo-Catholic Theology series, added to later by the two Surtees Society volumes of

---

[1] Dan was responsible for the Introduction and Notes, clarifying the Anglican via media as well as Cosin's artistry as a writer. Dan also wrote two contributions on Cosin in *Notes and Queries* in October 1965 and November 1970.

Cosin's correspondence, and finally Percy Herbert Osmond's *Life of John Cosin, Bishop of Durham* (1913). He was especially drawn to the *Collection of Private Devotions* (1627), for both its profound devotional value and its beauty and artistry as a work of literature. He notes that there was little written on Cosin at that time,[2] but the *Devotions* became deeply meaningful for his own developing theology. Dan wrote that "at that time I used the terms 'Laudian' and 'Caroline'; for what Cosin represented in his *Devotions*. More recently we have favoured the notion of an Anglican Counter-Reformation. In this context, Cosin's *Devotions* is a classic.... [It] was something of a landmark in my theological journey."[3] We see here not only Dan's developing theology, looking back to the Laudian High Church tradition, but his deep and continuing love of English literature, which was to continue during his later teaching years in St Stephen's College, Delhi.

Bishop John Cosin was educated at Caius College, Cambridge, and as a young man served as librarian to two bishops—Lancelot Andrewes (Chichester, Ely and Winchester) and Overall (Norwich). He was a friend of Archbishop Laud and close to King Charles I; the *Private Devotions* were complied, as we shall see, for Queen Henrietta Maria's English maids of honour to encourage them in their devotions. Cosin was elected Master of Peterhouse, Cambridge in 1635, but ejected from this office in 1644 by the Long Parliament. He escaped to France and returned to England at the Restoration when he was elevated to become Bishop of Durham. The Cosin Library in Durham is one of his great memorials. As Secretary of the Savoy Conference in 1661, Cosin was a major influence on the 1662 revision of the Book of Common Prayer.

In Dan's more recent comments about the 1993 conference on Cosin in Durham, a slight note of caution is sounded. History has portrayed the work, and indeed life, of churchmen like Cosins and Andrews as scholarly and beautiful, but it tends to erase their embeddedness in the assumptions of class and privilege at the court of King Charles and Queen Henrietta, and the often barbaric treatment of their Puritan opponents.

---

[2] Geoffrey Cumings' *The Anglicanism of John Cosin* was published in 1975.
[3] From an unpublished manuscript in the papers of the late Ann Loades.

The beauties of literature and spiritual writings may have a darker side in the wider context of the society of their times.

Nevertheless, it remains appropriate to begin this collection of Dan's writings, otherwise devoted to his writings on India and the history of missions, with his lifelong concern for a classic of Anglican devotional and spiritual writing, just as it is equally appropriate to end it with excerpts from the spiritual writings of his wife, Juliet.

* * *

"Next to the various versions of the Prayer Book itself ... the most important Anglican liturgical compilation since the Reformation"—thus wrote a leading American liturgical scholar some 40 years ago, of Cosin's *Collection of Private Devotions*, and I guess that is still the case.[4] The *Devotions* have the added distinction of being the only extended liturgical text compiled by Cosin alone....

.... The immediate occasion of their compilation in the later part of 1626 and early in 1627 is described in an entry in the diary of John Evelyn, after he had visited the exiled Cosin in Paris in 1651. Cosin told him that:

> ... the Queene [Henrietta Maria] coming over into England, with a great traine of French ladys, they were often upbraiding our English ladys of the Court, that, having so much leisure, trifled away their time in the antichambers among the young gallants, without having something to divert themselves of more devotion; whereas the Ro: Catholick ladys had their Hours and Breviarys, which entertained them in religious exercise. Our Protestant ladys, scandalized at this reproach, it was complained of to the King. Whereupon his Majesty called Bishop White to him, and asked his thoughts of it, and whether there might not be found some forme of prayers amongst the antient Liturgys proper on this occasion ... [and] immediately commanded him to employ

---

[4] H. B. Porter, "Cosin's Hours of Prayer: A Liturgical Review", *Theology* (February 1953).

some person of the Clergy to sett upon the work, and compose an office of that nature. The Bishop presently named Dr. Cosin, (whom the King exceedingly approv'd of)...[5]

The relatively young Cosin, in his early thirties, already making his mark both as a career churchman and as a liturgist, was an obvious choice for the task, and he plainly went about it with energy and urgency for it was completed in three months, the book being licensed by the Bishop of London on 22 February 1627.

Cosin makes no reference in his Preface to the occasion of the compilation of the *Devotions*. Instead, he gives four very general reasons why such a collection of "DAILY DEVOTIONS AND PRAYERS... after the... manner and DIVISION OF HOURS" should at this time be published:

> The first is to continue & preserve the authority of the ancient *Lawes*, and old godly *Canons* [customs] of the Church, which were made and set forth for this purpose, that men before they set themselves to pray, might know what to say, & avoid, as neer as might be, all extemporall effusions of irksome & indigested Prayers...
>
> The Second is to let the world understand that they who give it out, & accuse us here in ENGLAND to have set up a *New Church*, and a *New Faith*, to have abandoned *All the Ancient Formes of Piety and Devotion*... doe little else but betray their owne infirmities...
>
> The Third is, That they who are this way already religiously given, and whom earnest lets & impediments do often hinder from being partakers of the *Publicke*, might have here a Daily & Devoute order of *Private Prayer*...
>
> The last is, That those who perhaps are but coldly this way yet affected, might by others example be stirred up to the like

---

[5] *The Correspondence of John Cosin*, edited by G. Ornsby, Surtees Society, 52 (London, 1869), I, p. 284, quoting an extract from Evelyn's Diary for 1 June 1651.

heavenly duty of performing their *Daily* & Christian *Devotions* to Almighty God ...⁶

In fulfilment of this commission, there lay to hand for Cosin to develop an entire tradition, namely that of the Primer, the traditional Western book of private devotion, "the fruit of generations of accretion and selection ... [with] a tradition of flexibility and adaptability".⁷ The *Hours* of the French ladies at the Court were, of course, unreformed Primers. There is plenty of internal evidence in the *Devotions* that Cosin was familiar with a number of these, but he is careful on his title page to make clear that his particular models are taken from the reformed Primers of the Church of England; the title page reads: "A COLLECTION OF PRIVATE DEVOTIONS ... CALLED THE HOURES OF PRAYER. *As they were after this manner published by Authoritie of Q. Eliz. 1560* ... ", published as he emphasizes in his Preface, "by high and sacred authority". There is not the time on this occasion to look at this interesting tradition, or at the Elizabethan models that Cosin used, but simply to note what he made of the tradition, how he used and modified it in the light of his own gifts and knowledge, and of his own Laudian churchmanship and conviction.⁸

The core of the Devotions, then, is Cosin's version of the Offices for the seven canonical hours of prayer as these had evolved chiefly in the Primer, though the Breviary is also influential here and there. His first Office, "THE MATINS, OR MORNING PRAYER..." is very substantial, a good deal longer than Morning Prayer in the Book of Common Prayer, though following it in general arrangement. His prayers at the Third, Sixth and Ninth Hours, and "PRAYERS AT THE VESPERS, OR TIME OF EVENSONG", all follow a much simpler pattern, with the Third very distinctively an Office of the Holy Spirit, the Sixth of the Passion, and the Ninth emphasizing the Passion as a revelation of the divine love and

---

6   John Cosin, *A Collection of Private Devotions*, ed. P. G. Stanwood, with the assistance of Daniel O'Connor (Oxford: Clarendon Press, 1967), pp. 11–15.
7   H. C. White, *Tudor Books of Private Devotion* (Madison, WI: University of Wisconsin Press, 1951), p. 8.
8   *Private Prayers put forth by Authority during the Reign of Queen Elizabeth*, edited, W. K. Clay (Cambridge: Cambridge University Press, 1851).

mercy. Compline is to be followed by a set of "FINAL PRAYERS TO BE SAID BEFORE BED-TIME", not in the form of an Office but plainly intended to be a provision for the seventh of the canonical Hours.

Accompanying these hours is a considerable amount of other material, as was the case of course with the earlier Primers. A preface, calendar and various tables, with a collection of catechetical material, corresponding to what was usually known as the "A.B.C." or "Articles of the Faith" in the earlier Primers, precede the Hours. Typical Primer elements following them include the Seven Penitential Psalms, the Litany, a set of Collects, another of Eucharistic devotions (much fuller and more formal than was usual), prayers for the Sovereign in the form of a votive Office, Embertide prayers (as in one of the Elizabethan Primers but here, seemingly uniquely, in the form of an Office), Offices for the sick and the visitation of the dying, and a concluding set of "Prayers and Thanksgivings for Sundry Purposes".

Almost the entire form of the *Devotions*, then, follows the precedent of and stands firmly in the Primer tradition. We are bound to ask therefore as to its originality. There are four main aspects to this.

First, there is the sheer richness and quality of so many of the prayers, from the delicate beauty of the very brief "At the washing of our hands" to the grandeur and dignity of the "Prayer and Thanksgiving for the whole estate of Christ's Catholic Church". Cosin uses the entire armoury of rhetorical devices to capture what he calls in his Preface "the grave and pious language of Christ's Church". The sources are immensely varied, but perhaps most striking is the bold and ample use of the Scriptures; the prayer for the Ember Week in September, to take one example, includes eight allusions to the Psalms and the New Testament.

Next, two features of the prayers deserve to be noted separately. One of these is the stress upon the Passion. Where in the original of a prayer we may find "that precious death", or "Thy Passion" or "His blessed passion", Cosin will expand these into "this Thy most precious death", "that blessed Sacrifice which once Thou madest for us upon the Cross", and "His most precious Passion and Sacrifice". One feels very much in reading and using the prayers in the *Devotions*, the centrality of the Passion in Cosin's own faith. Equally striking is the frequent affirmation of the goodness and bounty of God and the joyful potentialities of life, whereby, for example, out of his "blessed providence", we receive "the blessings of heaven above, and the blessings of the earth beneath". This is on such a scale in the prayers that we cannot but be in touch with an aspect of Cosin's own faith and outlook.

Third, an unusual feature of the *Devotions* is the large amount of prefatory material that Cosin includes. In addition to the Preface itself, "TOUCHING PRAYER, AND THE FORMES OF PRAYER", there are "Of the Calendar", "OF THE ANCIENT AND ACCUSTOMED TIMES OF PRAYER in generall", "AN ADVERTISMENT CONCERNING THE DIVISION OF THE HOURES" following, a separate note on "THE ANTIQUITIE..." or "THE ANCIENT USE..." of each separate Hour, a note on the Litany, and a dozen or so notes introducing and explaining the days and seasons of the church's year, accompanying the Collects, together with one prefacing the Ember Prayers. These prefatory passages are packed with scriptural and patristic allusions and quotations (there are some 126 patristic references, with many quotations, most of these being, I think, in Cosin's own translation), and with references to the Councils of the Church, the Book of Common Prayer, Canons and Royal Injunctions, to liturgical authorities and, on several occasions, to Richard Hooker's *Of the Lawes of Ecclesiasticall Politie*. This all no doubt reflects Cosin's concern to anticipate puritan objections, but it also discloses his love of order and his care for the tradition of the Church, while the individual prefaces give us a series of most attractive, learned and lucid expositions, eloquently encouraging the devout life.

Finally, the *Devotions* also provide us with a wonderfully wide-ranging demonstration of the particular character of Laudian theology and ecclesiology. In addition to the veneration for tradition, and confidence in the authority of the reformed Church of England, its doctrine and discipline being (in the words of Cosin's friend Richard Mountague) "Ancient, Catholick, Orthodox, and Apostolicall",[9] which we have just noted, there is the claim, echoing Laud himself, and soon to be repeated by George Herbert, of a uniquely favoured reformation. With regard to the use of the canonical Hours, this was for Cosin neither merely antiquarian nor necessarily Romanizing; the Elizabethan Church, had,

---

[9] Richard Mountague, *Appello Caesarem* (London, 1625).

after all, authorized them, while in Cosin's own time Laud observed them, as did the community at Little Gidding, and Lancelot Andrewes (whom Mountague called "our Gamaliel"), and the anonymous *The Whole Duty of Man* recommended their use.[10] On this point, we need to note Cosin's emphasis on the public liturgical obligation of the Christian, these private devotions being offered as essentially a private complement to common prayer, to that obligation "to give God a solemn and a public worship in the congregation of His saints". A great deal more of the character of the Laudian ideal is disclosed in the *Devotions*, the encouragement of outward signs of reverence, the frequent reference to the sacraments (and to the doctrine of baptismal regeneration, the Eucharist as a re-presentation of the merits and power of Christ's sacrifice, and the value of sacramental confession "for better preparation thereunto"), episcopal ordination as "the ordinary custom of the Church", prayers for the dead, and so on. So comprehensive an illustration of the Laudian ideal do the *Devotions* afford, in fact, that it is not unreasonable to describe Cosin's work as the typical Laudian text.

Those are the four main points that I would want to bring out about the distinctiveness of the *Devotions*.

We have seen that in preparing his book, Cosin seems to have tried to anticipate the criticisms of the Puritans. The onslaught to which he and the *Devotions* were subject was, nevertheless, ferocious in the extreme, making Cosin the first victim of the Long Parliament, and indeed reverberating in continuing attacks upon him throughout the years up to his withdrawal to Paris in 1643.

Official pressure seems to have been placed upon him to revise the second edition of 1627, but his response did nothing to relieve the pressure. The full force of the Puritan attack becomes evident in two pamphlets, both published in the earlier part of 1628. One of these was by William Prynne ("Marginal Prynne" as he was memorialized by Milton for his relentlessly pedantic style), and entitled *A Briefe Survay and Censure of Mr. Cozens Couzening Devotions. Proving both the forme and matter of Mr. Cozens his booke of private devotions, or the Houres of Prayer,*

---

[10] *The Correspondence of John Cosin*, I, p. 70, R. Mountague to Cosin, 23 May 1625.

lately published, to be meerely Popish ... *etc*. It is a long pamphlet, over one hundred closely printed pages, full of citations of pre-Reformation and Roman Catholic texts, but it is the wide divergence of his general attitude as a religious radical from that of the conservative Cosin that is at issue as the credibility of the religious settlement crumbles. Henry Burton's pamphlet, *A Tryall of Private Devotions* ... , also over one hundred pages, is a much more literary piece than Prynne's both in its vigorous and colourful style and its dialogue-structure. The provision of "Houres of Prayer" suggests the return of "Monkerie", and Burton is preoccupied with the fear of the return of papal power and influence in England. Both pamphlets are important as illustrations of the puritan position in its religious aspect as the country moves towards the Civil War. They were also effective, leading to Cosin's being summoned before the 1628 Parliament or one of its committees, the King's haste in proroguing Parliament to save Buckingham from impeachment serving also to let Cosin off that particular hook. The reassembled Parliament of 1629 proposed that the *Devotions* (along with some of Cosin's friend Mountague's books) be burned, and their authors "condignly punished", the dissolution of Parliament again saving the situation for Cosin. Over the following years, Prynne continued to attack Cosin and his book in his pamphlets. Meanwhile, Peter Smart, who had referred to the *Devotions* in his sermon of 27 July 1628, and to Cosin's "speculative and theoricall popery" therein, took up a number of Prynne's and Burton's points in a legal charge against Cosin and others, a further illustration of the success of the two pamphleteers with those who shared their views. Looking at all this, it is probably fair to state that Cosin's initial default in compiling the *Devotions* first confirmed the Puritans in that opposition to him which finally led to his flight to the Continent.

With his flight, expressions of disapproval of the *Devotions* came to an end. In contrast, evidence of a more favourable estimate of Cosin's book can be found over a far longer period. The evidence takes a variety of forms; the 19 editions that have been published; its influence on the revision of the Book of Common Prayer and on later books of devotion; and the testimony of various individuals. We can only touch upon these very briefly.

Three further editions in 1627, one at least a large one, followed the small first edition. Peter Heylyn makes the observation that:

> ... for all ... [the] violent opposition, & the great clamours made against it, the Book grew up into esteem, & justified itself, without any Advocate; insomuch that many of those who first startled at it in regard of the title, found in the body of it so much Piety, such regular Forms of Divine Worship, such necessary Consolations in special Exigencies, that they reserved it by them as a Jewel of Great Price and Value....[11]

The 1630s, which saw the Laudian church continue to flourish under royal protection, saw also two further editions. During this period also Cosin's Hours were in use at Little Gidding. Interestingly, there was a further edition between the execution of Charles I and the Restoration, in 1665, evidence perhaps for "the persistence of a Laudian viewpoint among the harrassed and scattered clergy ... [and] the re-emergence of a strong and determined High Church party".[12]

Further editions after the Restoration, in 1664, 1672, 1676 and 1681 are perhaps corroboration of the claim that this was "in a measure the brilliant period of Laudianism" with two further editions in 1693 and 1719 suggesting the persistence of the tradition.[13] The revival and partial reshaping of the High Church tradition effected by the Oxford Movement, which was, in its beginnings at least, self-consciously and deliberately a recovery of Caroline or Laudian Anglicanism, saw a renewed interest in the *Devotions*, five further editions appearing in the nineteenth century. There is also a good deal of evidence of Cosin's Hours in use in that period. More recently, the only edition, published by the Clarendon Press in 1967,[14] was a significant publisher's and printer's event. This beautiful

---

[11] P. Heylyn, *Cyprianus Anglicus* (London, 1668), III, p. 174.

[12] R. S. Bosher, *The Making of the Restoration Settlement* (London: Dacre Press, 1951), p. 4.

[13] Y. Brilioth, *The Anglican Revival: Studies in the Oxford Movement* (London: Longman, Green & Co., 1933), p. 16.

[14] That edited by O'Connor and Stanwood.

edition won a prize at the Hamburg Book Fair and earned a number of favourable reviews in specialist journals . . .

It remains to say a brief word about the *Devotions* and later editions of the Book of Common Prayer. The considerable number of traces of its influence in the *Durham Book* support the view that in 1660 Cosin wanted to go on where he had left off 20 years previously, and that his outlook before the Civil War and after the Restoration were not appreciably different. However, the forces of compromise that prevailed in the official stages of the revisions of the Prayer Book, virtually excluding all that was distinctively Laudian in the proposals of the *Durham Book*, ensured that only comparatively undistinctive elements from the *Devotions* found their way into the Prayer Book of 1662. Let me mention just two items. First, some ninety-five small explanatory details in the Calendar are from the *Devotions*, only two of them by way of the *Durham Book*, a nice reminder of Cosin's great love for the ordered and full observance of the liturgical year as what he would have called a "Provocation to . . . piety". Secondly, his fine version of the *Veni Creator*, first hand-written into a copy of the service which it is believed Charles I had himself held on the occasion of his coronation (at which the young Cosin had been Master of Ceremonies), and subsequently included in his "PRAYERS FOR THE THIRD HOURE", so strikingly an office of the Holy Spirit, becomes a fixed and much-loved element in the Ordinal, its exceptional quality even ensuring its crossing over from the Book of Common Prayer to the *Alternative Service Book* of 1980.These are two, among many other points from the *Devotions*, which Cosin's meticulous care forbids us to call mere details . . . The *Devotions* is indeed a jewel of a book, recalling us to "that true devotion wherewith God is more delighted, and a good soul more inflamed and comforted, than with all the busy subtilties of the world".

* * *

Edited and slightly abridged, from *John Cosin: Papers Presented to a Conference to Celebrate the 400th Anniversary of His Birth*, ed. Margot Johnson (Durham: Turnstone Ventures, 1997), pp. 194–205.

2

The Study of Religion and Social Reality

During the year before Dan left Delhi in 1972, a book of essays entitled *Approaches to the Study of Religion* was published by the Guru Gobind Singh Department of Religious Studies of the Punjabi University, Patalia, edited by Harbans Singh. Harbans Singh (1921–98) was a remarkable scholar, best known perhaps for his great *Encyclopedia of Sikhism*, published posthumously in 1999. Like Dan, Singh's scholarly interests spanned literature and religion, and he was also a visionary educator and administrator. In 1960, he was the Secretary of the Punjabi University Commission which led to the creation of the Punjabi University and what Dan calls its "new space-age campus". Here Singh played a vital role in, and was the founding chair as professor of Sikh Studies of, the establishment of a department of Religious Studies—among the first of such departments in an Indian university.

Through the good offices of Professor Margaret Chatterjee, professor of Philosophy at Delhi University and expert on the religion of Gandhi as well as a member of the St Stephen's College chapel community, Dan was invited to attend and speak at a seminar in the new university which was, in Professor Singh's words, "planned to help define the scope and methodological and curricular procedures for the study of religion as a scholarly enterprise". He was concerned that the papers read, including Dan's, should do more than present "any orthodox or definitive viewpoints [but] raise some very basic and pertinent points".[1] The seminar was held on 15–17 January 1971. There was only one other non-Indian speaker apart from Dan, and that was the Welsh theologian and philosopher H.

---

[1] Harbans Singh, Preface to *Approaches to the Study of Religion* (Guru Gobind Singh Department of Religious Studies, Punjabi University, Patiala, 1971).

39

D. Lewis. Lewis' contribution entitled "Truth in Religion", can hardly be called a paper as the notes indicate that it was "prepared from Professor H. D. Lewis' extempore observations".[2]

Dan's contribution, reprinted here in a slightly abridged form, primarily to omit certain historical references that are no longer relevant, sought to engage the study of religion with contemporary realities, and he drew attention to the then newly published and widely acclaimed study by the Nobel Prize-winning Swedish economist, Gunnar Myrdal, *Asian Drama: An Enquiry into the Poverty of Nations* (1968). He drew attention to Myrdal's astonishing number of references to religion, the great majority of them suggesting that India was fundamentally inimical to development and modernization, representing a tremendous weight of social and political inertia. This was, in fact, a widely held view in "progressive circles" at that time, though later it would come to be called "neo-colonialist".[3] Dan's paper is also notable for the number of literary references, from Jonathan Swift to Alfred Lord Tennyson, reminding us that he was a teacher of literature at St Stephen's College. It was written when Naxalite activity was at its height in Indian universities.[4]

The chair of the seminar referred to Dan's paper as the most significant contribution to the event—a notable accolade, given the academic distinction of many of the other contributors. Dan also recalls that he shared a room with the Jesuit scholar G. Gispert-Sauch, who was about to move from Darjeeling to Delhi, and whom we shall encounter once again in the next essay of the present book.[5] On the staff of the new department of religion was another Roman Catholic, Dr Pancras Christanand, a former teacher at St Stephen's College, Delhi. At a Mass celebrated in his house and in a generous ecumenical gesture, the two Roman Catholics asked Dan to be the celebrant.

Harbans Singh's description of the plans for the new department may teach us something today:

---

[2] *Approaches to the Study of Religion*, pp. 170–6.

[3] See unpublished manuscript by Dan O'Connor among the papers of Ann Loades.

[4] See further below Chapter 7, pp. 129–48.

[5] See below, pp. 47–60.

One concrete outcome [of the seminar] is that our scheme for the introduction of a teaching-cum-research course for the degree of M. Litt, has been finalized. This will be a two-year course after a Master's degree in a subject like Religious Studies, Philosophy, Linguistics, Literature, or History. Field work and comparative study will be encouraged. A student in this programme will have to acquaint himself with at least one religious tradition besides his own. He will also have to take up a course in the canonical language of his area of specialization.[6]

★   ★   ★

It was somewhere in the Gulf of Tonkin, as you may recall, that a renowned European traveller of the eighteenth century, having fallen among pirates, found himself being rescued from a barren deserted island into an extraordinary flying island called Laputa. Even more extraordinary, you will recall, were the ruling occupants of the flying island:

> Their Heads were all reclined to the Right, or the Left; one of their Eyes turned inward, and the other directly up to the Zenith ... I observed here and there many in the Habit of Servants, with a blown Bladder fastened like a Flail to the end of a short stick, which they carried in their Hands. In each Bladder was a small quantity of dried Pease, or little Pebbles. With these Bladders they now and then flapped the Mouths and Ears of those who stood near them ... It seems the Minds of these People are so taken up with intense Speculations, that they neither can speak, nor attend to the Discourses of others, without being rouzed by some external action upon the Organs of Speech and Hearing; for which reason, those persons who are able to afford it, always keep a *Flapper*, in their Family, as one of their Domesticks ... And although they are dexterous enough upon a Piece of Paper, ... yet in the common Actions and Behaviour of Life, I have

---

[6] Preface to *Approaches to the Study of Religion*.

not seen a more clumsy, awkward and unhandy People, nor so slow and perplexed in their Conceptions upon all other Subjects, except those of Mathematicks and Musick . . . The Wives and Daughters lament their Confinement to the Island, although I think it [Lemuel Gulliver concludes] the most delicious Spot of Ground in the World.[7]

Our Indian universities are still, at least some of them and at least in some respects, delicious Spots of Ground—but increasingly, it is to be observed, the world presses in upon us. "Slowly comes a hungry people, as a lion, creeping nigher",[8] and even within our gates there are those who are troubled and confused as they try to accommodate themselves to the tension of such a situation. I do not wish to propose a narrowly utilitarian function for our universities, but at the same time I want to say that the links between our academic work inside the university and the realities of existence outside should neither be so subtle nor so tenuous that we will fail to persuade our fellowmen that they are actually there. And this goes for the study of religion as for any other study. Perhaps more so for there is a sort of secularism abroad in our Indian universities which sees any religion in a wholly negative way and its study as academic in only the pejorative sense of the word. I do not for a moment suppose, of course, that those who are actually engaged in the study of religion could be as naive as this, or so dichotomizing, as to suppose that religious history is not relevant to the mundane and vice versa—but this is an attitude with which we have to contend. Fortunately, we have in India a very positive incentive to make some connections, for the life and work of Gandhiji exhibits a remarkable fusion of the religious and the mundane. "To a people famishing and idle"—he said—"the only acceptable form in which God can dare to appear is as work and promise of food as wages" (—though I think the idea was put more interestingly by a Russian

---

[7] Jonathan Swift, *Gulliver's Travels* (London, 1949), pp. 254–5, 259, 261.
[8] Alfred Lord Tennyson, *Locksley Hall* (1842), line 135.

theologian who said that, though earning one's bread might be a material problem, securing bread for one's neighbour was always a spiritual one).[9]

What has induced me to make the point I am trying to make—over and above the sharing in the tension of which I spoke earlier—is an observation in Gunnar Myrdal's *Asian Drama*, that monumental and already almost canonical "Inquiry into the Poverty of Nations". Having made a distinction between "the interpretation of old scriptures and the lofty philosophies and theologies developed over centuries of speculation" and "a ritualized and stratified complex of highly emotional beliefs and valuations that give the sanction of sacredness, taboo, and immutability to inherited institutional arrangements, modes of living, and attitudes", Myrdal goes on:

> Understood in this realistic and comprehensive sense, religion usually acts as a tremendous force for social inertia. The writer knows of no instance in present-day South Asia where religion has induced social change. Least of all does it foster realization of the modernization ideals ... From a planning point of view, this inertia related to religion, like other obstacles, must be overcome by policies for inducing changes, formulated in a plan for development. But the religiously sanctioned beliefs and valuations not only act as obstacles among the people to getting the plan accepted and effectuated but also as inhibitions in the planners themselves insofar as they share them, or are afraid to counteract them.[10]

Of course this begs a lot of questions, and indeed Mydal himself proceeds to make a series of qualifications:

> Not all elements of that system are necessarily irrational from the point of view of the modernization [of] ideals. Some beliefs and

---

[9] It has not been possible to recover which Russian theologian Dan is referring to here. (Eds.)

[10] Gunnar Myrdal, *Asian Drama: An Inquiry into the Poverty of Nations* (London: Allen Lane, 1968), Vol. 1, pp. 103–4.

practices undoubtedly represent a pragmatic accommodation to actual conditions and are in accord with rational considerations in planning. For example, the ritual washing of the body... the vegetarian diet... indigenous systems of medicine.[11]

However, Myrdal returns to his basic contention that the "combination of attitudes, institutions, and customary modes of living and working, sanctioned by popular religion, creates a tremendous weight of social and political inertia, which planning for development must try to lift".[12]

If our Indian institutes for the study of religion are not to be mere flying islands (and how long would the Flappers be prepared to work for us?), perhaps Myrdal could provide us with a programme. At least, we are challenged to make some discriminations, to show in what respects he is correct and in what he is not. And in fact, he himself *asks* for a number of clarifications. For example, after remarking that "an examination that confines itself to what is verbalized and explicit can convey only an inkling of the social significance of traditional attitudes and beliefs, some of which are very important inhibitions and obstacles to development", he goes on to call for an "intensive empirical investigation of these attitudes and beliefs in different strata of the population and their influence on behaviour. At present"—he adds—"solid knowledge about this highly relevant matter is scanty".[13] Myrdal makes a number of appeals of this sort, and we do not ourselves necessarily have to accept his value premises, or "modernization ideals" as he calls them, *in toto* before we can see that some pressing questions are asking for answers which students of religion might well be helping to provide.

In addition to the questions which Myrdal here poses, a number of others come to mind. Perhaps one of the biggest of these concerns our understanding of the modernizing process itself. Are its ideals simply those of the European Enlightenment, as Myrdal proposes, or are they part of the much longer religious history of the West? Do different religious groups accommodate themselves to the process in different

---

[11] Myrdal, *Asian Drama*, p. 110.
[12] Myrdal, *Asian Drama*, p. 111.
[13] Myrdal, *Asian Drama*, p. 94.

ways, and what is left of their differences as the process advances? What is it that gives the process its seeming inevitability so that "For him who has once eaten of the tree of Western civilization there can be no turning back"?[14] How do we conceptualize the belief that the building of a dam in India can only be adequately seen as "a development within Hindu and to some extent Muslim religious history"?[15] And then there is a whole range of subsidiary but equally pressing problems about, for example, religious values and family planning, about the interaction of traditional ethical norms and the relational demands of an industrial culture, and about the impact upon the inarticulate (or at least unlistened to) masses of new and sometimes anti-religious ideologies.

All this is to say nothing about the problem of human religiousness as it is being experienced so acutely in the West. Perhaps Indian institutes for the study of religion will enjoy—like the developing countries themselves—the historical advantage of the late-comer, but late-coming will only *be* an advantage if the Indian student of religion is using one ear to listen to the present groaning of the human spirit (and to the songs of hope) in other parts of the world.

It is a measure of the kindliness and openness of the sponsors of this seminar that they have invited a non-specialist to take part in it; I have no qualifications at all to speak on the relative importance of the different approaches to the study of religion, but as a priest who just happens to work in an Indian university it struck me that it might be worthwhile to make the point that I have tried to make, that there are questions crucial to human wellbeing in the present phase of history to which the student of religion must help to find answers through the various approaches which are at his disposal. Wilfred Cantwell Smith has said that the real secret of a valid and valued study of religion is the presence of "a haunting question" to which there is a strongly felt need for an answer.[16] Is there not a whole cluster of haunting questions in this area to which I have,

---

[14] Arend Th. Van Leeuwen, *Christianity in World History. The Meeting of the Faiths of East and West* (London: Edinburgh House, 1964), p. 14.

[15] Wilfred Cantwell Smith, *Study of Religion in Indian Universities* (Bangalore, 1967), p. 82.

[16] Cantwell Smith, *Study of Religion*, p. 83.

with Gunnar Myrdal's help, alluded? If so, then the function—or at least a function—of a study of religion, if it is to be legitimately at the centre of a modern university, is a very important one: so to discern and define what is happening to all as to enable us to make more free and more responsible decisions than we would otherwise be able to.

*　*　*

Edited and abridged from, Harbans Singh (ed.), *Approaches to the Study of Religion* (Patalia, Punjabi University, 1971, pp. 103–7.

3

Dialogue as Communion: C. F. Andrews and Munshi Ram

The life and work of Charles Freer ("Charley") Andrews (1871–1940) lie at the very heart of Dan O'Connor's writings and preoccupations. After reading Classics at Pembroke College, Cambridge, Freer was ordained into the Church of England, becoming Vice-Principal of Westcott House Theological College in Cambridge in 1897, before joining the Cambridge Mission to Delhi in 1904, teaching at St Stephen's College. His close relationship with Indian colleagues and friends outside the Christian community is movingly explored in this early essay by Dan, published the year after Dan left India in a volume of essays in honour of Fr Joseph Putz SJ, *God's Word Among Men* (1973), edited by G. Gispert-Sauch SJ. Much of the original essay, here much reduced, reproduced the words of Andrews and Munshi Ram themselves.

Mahatma Munshi Ram Vij (1856–1926) was drawn away from his youthful atheism when he met Swami Dayananda Sarasvati, the founder of the Arya Samaj, and in 1902 founded a Gurukula which drew Andrews to him.[1] Andrews first visited the Gurukula in Kangri near Haridwar in January 1913. Dan explores the two men's deep and spiritual relationship, Andrews finding a new language which drew him away from the imperial

---

[1] The Arya Samaj (literally "Noble Society") was founded in the 1870s, a monotheistic reform movement within Hinduism based on the authority of the Vedas, the four ancient sacred books of the Hindus. A Gurukula (literally, from the Sanskrit, "home of the teacher"), in ancient India, was an educational institution in which the students live with the guru in the same house. The manner of life was essentially monastic. (Eds.)

and missionary world of Delhi, Munshi Ram's language of the Divine Mother.

When Andrews later became a close friend and confidante of Gandhi the question of conversion was a recurring theme in their relationship. In his recent essay on Andrews and his "plural life" in Joel Carpenter and Rebecca Shah's book *Christianity in India* (2018), Bernado Michael writes of Andrews' "willingness to be undone" in relation to others.[2] During his first ten years in India, Andrews began the process of "unpacking his paternalistic imperialism and ignorance about his racial privilege". As he moved away from Delhi, developing a critical attitude towards European and British racial attitudes in India, he began to grow also in a larger religious vision which is beautifully articulated in his relationship with Munshi Ram as described by Dan in this essay. The articulation of the process of change and growth as his Christianity encountered the complex world of Hindu and Indian spirituality is described beautifully in Dan's essay. The theme of "unity", in an India which was increasingly being drawn towards the spirit of nationhood, is also important

When he returned to Scotland in 1972, Dan's preoccupation with the life and work of Andrews had only just begun. In 1974, he published a lengthy introduction to a book of extracts from the writings of C. F. Andrews, published by the Christian Institute for the Study of Religion and Society in Bangalore as part of their Confessing the Faith in India series. Part of this Introduction forms Chapter 5 below.[3] More extensively he undertook research for a doctorate, focusing particularly on the years 1904–14 in Andrews' life in St Stephen's College, Delhi.[4] It was published in 1990 as *Gospel, Raj and Swaraj: The Missionary Years of C. F. Andrews,*

---

[2] Bernado A. Michael, "A 'Willingness to Become Undone' in relation to Others: The Plural Life of C. F. Andrews", in Joel Carpenter and Rebecca Samuel Shah (eds), *Christianity in India: Conversion, Community Development, and Religious Freedom* (Minneapolis, MN: Fortress Press, 2018), Chapter 3 (Kindle Edition).

[3] See, below, pp. 83–112.

[4] St Andrew's University, PhD. Diss, 1981.

1904–14, and later republished in a more elegant format in New Delhi (2005) as *A Clear Star: C. F. Andrews and India, 1904–14*.[5]

*   *   *

When the Society of Jesus in India recently moved its Institute of Religious Studies, Vidyajyoti, to Delhi,[6] it moved it to a city which has thrilled many with its historic associations, among them Bishop Lightfoot of Durham, one of the founding fathers of the Cambridge Mission to Delhi, who had this to say of it:

> Delhi! What associations do not gather about the name? Delhi, the immemorial centre of Hindu tradition, the chief stronghold of Muhammadan power, the capital of the descendants of Timur, the seat of the most splendid, if not the most powerful, of Oriental monarchies, the city of many sieges, Tartar, Persian, Mahratta, English—Delhi the beautiful, the cruel, the magnificent, the profligate. And a name, too, not of less absorbing interest to the Christian than to the Englishman. The Delhi Mission was still in its infancy when the Mutiny broke out.[7] The Delhi Mission was baptized in blood. It was literally murdered. But here, as elsewhere, the blood of the martyrs was the seed-plot of the Church. The work of evangelization has revived.[8]

Delhi is a fascinating city still, breathing history and the ambivalent hopes of the future, earning even a paragraph in Harvey Cox's *The Secular City* (1965).[9] Among the city's recent acquisitions, replacing a squat and seemingly imperishable statue of Queen Victoria in the great Chandni

---

[5] Full details of all these publications are provided in the bibliography.

[6] It was previously in Darjeeling.

[7] The Indian Mutiny took place in 1857–8. (Eds.)

[8] J. B. Lightfoot, from a sermon preached at Cambridge on 30 November 1876, quoted in S. Bickersteth, *Life and Letters of Edward Bickersteth, Bishop of South Tokyo* (London: Sampson Low, Marston, 1899), pp. 42–3.

[9] Cox's *The Secular City* was one of the most widely read religious books of the 1960s. It stands alongside such books as John Robinson's slightly earlier

Chowk, is a new statue, the inscription in Hindi. Mahatma Munshi Ram, as he was known until he adopted the name of Swami Shraddhanand in 1917, lived from 1856 until 1926, and it is he who now presides in quiet dignity over the ever-crowded "moonlight market".

In his youth, Munshi Ram had come under the influence of the founder of the Arya Samaj, Swami Dayananda Sarasvati, and in 1902, at the age of 46, he founded at Hardwar, where the Ganges leaves the hills, a Gurukula which in a short time was to become the "centre and crown of the educational effort"[10] of the more conservative wing of the Arya Samaj.

The Arya Samaj was a growing force in the Punjab and the United Province in this period, and a focus and inspiration for the surging nationalist aspirations which the outcome of the Russo-Japanese war had helped to trigger.[11] The Samaj's reputation as narrowly Hindu and virulently anti-Muslim and anti-Christian had not deterred non-Hindus from visiting and being deeply impressed with the Gurukula and its founder. Among the earlier visitors were the Reverend W. E. S. Holland, Warden of the Oxford and Cambridge Hostel at Allahabad, who published an account of his visit in the June 1907 issue of *The East and the West*, and, in 1910, C. H. C. Sharp of St Stephen's College, Delhi, who visited the "Academy" with a party of his students, one of whom subsequently wrote an account of their visit in the College magazine.

It could have been from either of these men, or indeed from any of his numerous students or from other Indian friends who were sympathetic towards the Samaj, that C. F. Andrews[12] first heard of the Gurukula and its leader.

Honest to God (1963) in arguing for the positive effects of secularity and that God is present in both the secular and the formally religious realm. (Eds.)

[10] J. N. Farquar, *Modern Religious Movements in India* (New York: Macmillan, 1915), p. 126.

[11] 1904–5. (Eds.)

[12] Andrews joined the Cambridge Mission in 1904 as a teacher at St Stephen's College. The fullest account of his life and work is Benarsidas Chaturvedi and Marjorie Sykes, *Charles Freer Andrews: A Narrative* (London: Allen & Unwin, 1949). This biography has been overtaken by O'Connor's own subsequent work and writings on Andrews. (Eds.)

However he first heard of it, Andrews approached the Arya Samaj, as, indeed, he approached everything Indian, in a spirit of religious expectancy, for the Cambridge Mission to Delhi, of which he was a member, and whose "liberal catholic"[13] ethos he had deeply imbibed, had been founded on the great vision of its originators of a Christian engagement with Asia as significant and creative as had been the encounter with Greece embodied in the theological school of Alexandria. It was, in fact, in precisely such terms that Professor Westcott had conjured the vision of the Cambridge Mission's work, of creating "an Alexandria on the banks of the Jumna".[14]

We do not know when precisely Andrews first met Munshi Ram, but it was in Delhi, and probably late in 1912, after his memorable visit to England during which he had met the poet Rabindranath Tagore[15] for the first time. It was also—providentially, as it seemed to Andrews later— soon after he had entered into a surprisingly close relationship with the then Viceroy, Lord Hardinge. Andrews had already, in his book *The Renaissance in India*,[16] made an appreciative reference to the Gurukula, but only on the basis of the reports of "those who have visited the place", probably those of Holland and Sharp among others. That the Arya Samaj was a movement to be taken seriously he demonstrated in his book in a statistical appendix (p. 292), comparing its rapid growth by 1911 to some

---

[13] For some definitions of the phrase as used in the Anglican context, see, for example, A. M. Ramsey, *From Gore to Temple: The development of Anglican Theology between Lux mundi and the Second World War, 1889–1939* (London: Longmans, Green, 1960); A. Richardson, *The Bible in the Age of Science* (London: SCM Press, 1961); B. M. G. Reardon, *From Coleridge to Gore: A Century of Religious Thought in Britain* (London: Longmans, 1971).

[14] The original reference is not known, but S. K. Rudra quotes it in the *St Stephen's College Magazine* (April 1914).

[15] Rabindranath Tagore was a Bengali poet, playwright, and musician. Renouncing a knighthood which was awarded by King George V, Tagore was the first non-European to win the Nobel Prize for Literature in 1913. He was a fervent Indian nationalist and defender of the outcaste (Dalit) peoples. (Eds.)

[16] C. F. Andrews, *The Renaissance in India: Its Missionary Aspect* (London: London Missionary Society, 1912), p. 40.

quarter of a million members with the almost static and numerically insignificant Brahmo Samaj.

Andrews' first visit to the Gurukula was toward the end of January 1913, and we have a record of this in an article which he published in the March issue of the *Modern Review*. These extracts give some impression of his reactions:

> Here was the India that I had known and loved—the India of my day dreams and waking reveries of thought—the same India whose spirit had stirred me so profoundly at Benares and at Delhi; the India of the immemorial past venerated in song and art and worship by the souls of men and women who had lived and loved and died in each succeeding age; the India still cherished and revered by all her true children.
>
> But there was this striking difference. The spiritual presence which I had left at Benares and at Delhi, had a strangely sad effect upon me... There had been nothing in Delhi or Benares of the Springtime...
>
> But here, on the contrary, was a new spirit... Here was the India that I had met not among the old-world pundits with their beautiful, ascetic faces, but in the throbbing and pulsing of young eager hearts ready to lay down life itself in devotion to the Motherland. I saw before me that Motherland, not worn and sorrowful, beautiful only in decay, but ever fresh and young with the spring time of immortal youth...
>
> ... If there was to be a Renaissance in India, a true rebirth, it was from sources such as these that it would spring. Here character would be formed in harmony with the genius of the country, not against it.
>
> I came to know and love in the days that followed the founder of the Gurukula, Mahatmaji Munshi Ram. He told me of his ideals and of the difficulties which had been overcome...

In his concluding paragraph, Andrews fits his new experience into the expansive framework which is to become so distinctive of his developing theology:

Stone by stone, line by line, the foundations of the New India are being laid. Sometimes the experiment ends badly, and what appeared to be solid granite is found to be mere rubble. Much useless debris, also, has to be cleared away before the bed rock on which to build is ultimately reached ... In spite of that which tells of human failure and short-coming, in spite of the folly, pride and sinfulness of men, we can trace through all the hand of the great Artificer, making all things new.[17]

Andrews' coming "to know and love" Munshi Ram during that visit was the beginning of a deep and fascinating relationship in which both the Christian and the Hindu were profoundly changed. Some 180 letters, mostly written by Andrews to Munshi Ram, were recently given to the National Archives of India by Shri. Benarsidas Chaturvedi, who was, with Miss Marjorie Sykes, Andrews' principal biographer. They provide us with the means of studying this Hindu-Christian encounter in some detail.

Before, however, looking at some of the letters, a further brief description of Andrews and Munshi Ram together at Hardwar is available to us. It occurs in the first chapter of J. S. Hoyland's *C. F. Andrews: Minister of Reconciliation*.[18] Hoyland, a Quaker, had gone out to India as a missionary late in 1912, and spent his first few months staying with Andrews, in the household of S. K. Rudra, Principal of St Stephen's College. In March 1913, Andrews took Rudra's son, Sudhir, and Hoyland, to the Gurukula for a week. Hoyland's account is most perceptive:

At the Gurukula C. F. A. identified himself, in the first place, with those whom he had come to serve. He became an Indian amongst Indians. He has not as yet adopted Indian dress (this was to come later); but he ate Indian food: he adopted Indian customs: above all in his attitude he gave evidence, moment by moment, of his humble-spirited desire to learn from and to understand the Indian point of view. The head of the Gurukula at that time was Mahatma Munshi Ram ... It was immensely instructive to listen

---

[17] *Modern Review* XIII:3 (March 1913), pp. 330–5.
[18] Published, London: Allenson & Co, 1940.

to a conversation between these two great men. Munshi Ram was a magnificent figure of a man, with a thin ascetic face, and a huge hooked nose. He looked like an Afghan. Many, indeed most, of his ideas were poles asunder from those of C. F. A. He was very emphatic, sometimes definitely dogmatic, in his statement of his views. But C. F. A. listened patiently, made no comment on what was repellent but took pains to bring out by further questioning and discussion what was of permanent value. In those conversations one could see "that of God"[19] in the intellectual and spiritual outfit of Mahatma Munshi Ram being reached, emphasized, developed, by the quiet and humble fashion in which C. F. A., ignoring the less worthy parts of his friend's views, asked for further information on and implied his deep interest in the more worthy parts. The two personalities acted and re-acted in each other in a remarkable way. Munshi Ram's personality was by far the more striking and in a sense "effective". C. F. A. was content to take a very secondary place, to sit back and listen most of the time, now and then throwing in a suggestion or asking a question which strengthened "truth" in his friend. In this way was vindicated and established, not Indian "truth", or British "truth": not Hindu "truth", or dogmatically Christian "truth", but a new universal Truth . . . [20]

This [. . .] spirit pervades Andrews' letters to Munshi Ram, though prior to all "dialogue" in their relationship was something more profound, more personal, for which "communion" is perhaps the appropriate word. A letter written [by Andrews] between these two first visits to the Gurukula sets the tone:

> I am praying for you every day . . . You have won my love, dear Mahatmaji; it is quite instinctive with me (as with you also) to pray for those I love.[21]

---

[19] A phrase revealing of Hoyland's Quaker background (Eds.)
[20] Ibid., pp. 14–16.
[21] The letters are described as "Correspondence with Munshi Ram" among the Chaturvedi letters in the NAI New Delhi. This and subsequent

Soon after his return from the second visit, the relationship assumes the language of communion:

> I cannot tell you, dear Mahatmaji, how I love you, but you know it without words. I cannot tell whence it has come, this great love, except from God, and I thank Him for it, for it is one of the greatest gifts I have ever received at His Hands.[22]
>
> I think it was then I came to know you and love you with all my heart, when I saw you with your children, especially the little ones. I can understand how the presence of God must come into your life in and through them, and it is that above all else which draws me to you ... Your love for me, receiving me with open arms into your heart and confidence, has been a new discovery to me of the nearness of that presence.[23]

Soon Andrews is using, seemingly without contrivance, Munshi Ram's language of the Divine Mother:

> ... when your letters ... came ... I knelt down and poured out my whole heart to God in thankful prayer. It is beyond all I dared to hope that this great love of yours has been given to me. I do not deserve it. It is indeed, as you say, the Loving Mother herself who has joined our hearts together and no human instrument will be able to separate them ... Only with two friends has there been anything approaching it, one is Sudhir's father and the other is Rabindranath Tagore. In each case it has been the Divine Mother herself drawing us together ...[24]

Only a few months before, Andrews had been advocating in *The Renaissance in India* a reclamation by the Church of the concept of the

---

    quotations will be described as "Correspondence", with the appropriate date. Correspondence, "Sunday, 1913".
[22] Correspondence, 20 April 1913.
[23] Correspondence, 24 April 1913.
[24] Correspondence, 26 April 1913.

Mother inasmuch as "in any religion which is to become acclimatized in India this ideal of motherhood must have a prominent place".[25]

... There is throughout the correspondence a recurring preoccupation with "keeping the world out of the heart", with the attainment and preservation of "Shanti".[26]

> The Gurukula—which means you yourself in your own dear home of peace—has taught me more than anything else since I came to India the need of the daily practice of shanti and receiving it from the Divine Mother herself... I feel more and more that here is our great need in this country, to get back to the sacred peace of the Rishis. I do not of course mean a cessation from active life... but a calmness and quietness of spirit in which the soul has time to grow deeper and deeper instead of being merely ruffled and agitated by every superficial wind that blows... [27]

Certainly for Andrews "a cessation from active life" was inconceivable, [yet his] own particularly "activist" role made the need for such a disposition seem the more important:

> Do you know I have been finding the Gita[28] such a wonderful help in my life up here... there comes the wonderful message of the Gita about doing works without attachment: and that strengthens me and guides me... We can be at peace amid the ceaseless play of forces, with a quiet calm of spirit which is (in God's hands) the very highest and deepest force of all... I can see now how wonderfully the Gita applies to those whose duty calls them to a public life, the life of a kshatriya.[29]

---

[25] Correspondence, 26 April 1913.
[26] Literally, "Peace". (Eds.)
[27] Correspondence, "1913".
[28] The Bhagavad Gita. (Eds.)
[29] Correspondence, 21 May 1913.

There is, finally, Andrews' groping after a unifying principle in his experience. The spirit behind this is well illustrated here:

> I have been thinking very much what you were saying to me one day about India being the sacred land of the world's surface from whence religious truth has flown and from whence it springs up again and again—the very home of faith and devotion. That is true, undoubtedly, beyond words, and I have felt it almost instinctively and feel it more and more. My whole life has changed since I came to this country and all the deep convictions of my early days have been still further deepened and strengthened and also in many ways transformed . . . . .[30]

The fullest statement of this quest for a principle of unity among the letters comes in one written in October 1913, just a month before he was to sail for South Africa to assist Gandhi, an action whereby he became, he felt, "a child of Aryavarta not merely in name and thought, but in deed and act":[31]

> I agree wholly and entirely with you that the world today is still making *force* instead of Truth, the ultimate criterion; and the ideal which Hindu India has stood for all these centuries seems to be ruthlessly brushed aside and overwhelmed by the rising forces of worldly power. I feel, to put it this way, that Hindu India still, in spite of decay, is far more Christian than the so-called Christian countries of the West in this matter—if Christianity is to be judged by the standard of the Sermon on the Mount . . . .. Oh! How I long to be able to work all this out in my own dim and confused mind, which is groping towards a unity—and every now and then a gleam of light comes and shows me what is in the distance![32]

---

[30] Correspondence, 13 July 1913.
[31] Correspondence, 5 April 1914.
[32] Correspondence, 28 October, 1913.

Throughout the letters, in one way or another, one can see Andrews seeking to bring what he called "fresh light and a new point of view" into the relationship [with Munshi Ram].

There is much more that one could wish to draw out of these letters. There is the continuing reconciling work at the political level, culminating in a meeting between Munshi Ram and the Viceroy (and, rather more improbably, between Munshi Ram and Sir Michael O'Dwyer!);[33] there is the growing sense of incompatibility between Andrews' "fixed" role as a missionary—confided unreservedly to Munshi Ram—and "the call of the sanyasi";[34] there is the concern to draw together the diverse and, at this time, unconnected forces of the National Movement:

> My friend here, Mr. Gandhi, is winning his way into my heart and he has found me out! I talk all day about you and tell now about the Gurukula and now about Shantiniketan and now about Sushilat Delhi, and he smiles as my words always come back to these three fixed points.[35]

Historically, this was perhaps one of the most important achievements, adumbrated in letters such as this last, a process which drew Gandhi and Tagore together, made Rudra a sympathetic assistant in such matters as the drafting of the Khilafat claim and the conception of Non-co-operation,[36] and drew Munshi Ram deeply into the central events of the Movement

---

[33] Sir Michael O'Dwyer (1864–1940) was Lieutenant Governor of Punjab between 1913 and 1919. During his period of office, the Jallianwala Bagh massacre occurred in Amritsar on 13 April 1919. As a result, O'Dwyer's actions are often considered highly significant factors in the rise of the Indian independence movement. (Eds.)

[34] Correspondence, 5 May 1913.

[35] Correspondence, 20 January 1914.

[36] The Khilafat Movement among Indian Moslems began in 1919 and was an effort to revive the Ottoman Caliph as a symbol of unity. It initially drew support from Gandhi's non-co-operation movement. (Eds.)

as, in Gandhi's words, "an esteemed co-worker",[37] who could declare, at the Amritsar Congress in the immediate shadow of the Jallianwala Bagh massacre,[38] "We must conquer the English with our love."[39]

Finally, to revert to the original theme of this paper, the relationship between Andrews and Mushi Ram, [there is] a unique letter in the collection, one of the few surviving from Munshi Ram to Andrews, written on 25 April 1913, Arya Samajist to Christian missionary:

> My dear Mr. Andrews,
>
> Your letter of the 21st instant has made me feel what I have not felt for the last 28 years. I had been an atheist of some 9 years standing when the vision came to me which poured a balm into my lacerated soul. I had laid my doubts before the great Dayananda thrice and had been silenced in discussion, but I was not convinced. And when I repeated this a third time the great Yogi said "You asked questions and I have replied to them. I never had the presumption to say that I would convince you. It is *He* alone who can convince you of *His* reality." And the time came and I was not only convinced but felt the Presence and a calm which I cannot describe. And then I had to struggle and struggle in the Arya Samaj. Ah!
>
> The Divine Mother alone knows how many times this heart of mine has been hit hard during the last 28 years. I thanked the Divine Mother for this new blessing for I felt that I had not lived in vain. As regards your trouble with those who cannot see things

---

[37] Evidence before the Disorders Enquiry Committee, 9 January 1920, included in *Collected Works of M. K. Gandhi*, 98 volumes (New Delhi, 1960).

[38] Otherwise known as the Amritsar Massacre, this took place on 13 April 1919. A peaceful crowd was gathered at the Jallianwala Bagh in Amritsar to protest against the Rowlatt Act, which gave the police almost unlimited powers of arrest, and the detention of pro-independence activists. On the orders of brigadier general R. E. H. Dyers, troops fired on the crowd. Some estimates put those killed at 1,500. Britain has never formally apologized for the massacre. (Eds.)

[39] Quoted in *Young India*, 7 January 1920.

with your eyes—I thank our Divine Mother for having given you the strength to act with true Aryan (in other words Christ-like) patience. You think that portion of your letter has made it rather gloomy. Oh! My dear friend, believe me, when I assure you that it has filled me with hope and faith in the Love of God instead. With the Divine Mother's blessings and under her guidance, I and you, sinners as we are, will in the end be able to convince our brethren that the Mother belongs specially to no country or sect and that Her loving arms were open for all her children, irrespective of colour and creed at all times.

I cannot write more. It is difficult for me to pour forth my whole heart to you in writing for I am master of no single civilized language. But I am convinced that my heart has already found a response in your own. I believe that the Loving Mother has herself joined our hearts which no human instruments will be able to rend asunder. There is no time of day when I do not think of you.

Believe me my dearest friend
Yours every affectionate
Munshi Ram.[40]

Theologically—and we have indicated only very lightly the theological character of the encounter of Andrews and Munshi Ram, wishing to let the letters speak for themselves—this final letter could stand as a conclusive witness to the effectiveness of the approach in which witness to the Revelation in Christ is borne within a context of communion, of Christian solidarity with the non-Christian.

* * *

Abridged from, G. Gispert-Sauch, SJ (ed.), *God's Word Among Men: papers in Honour of Fr. Joseph Putz SJ* (Delhi: Viyajyoti, Institute of Religious Studies, 1973), pp.73–83. Explanatory footnotes have been added to Dan's original notes by the editors.)

---

[40] Correspondence, 25 April 1913.

4

Solidarity

It was when Dan O'Connor was leaving Selly Oak in 1992 and moving back to Scotland that he received an invitation to deliver the Westcott, or Teape, Lectures in India. The lectures were endowed by William Marshall Teape (1862–1944), an Edinburgh-born clergyman, who intended that they should be named the Westcott Lectures in memory of his teacher, Bishop Brooke Foss Westcott. They were founded to facilitate a yearly exchange between Britain and India to further the relationship between the Christian and Hindu traditions.

In his Introduction to his published Westcott Lectures, *Relations in Religion* (1994), Dan recalls the portrait of Bishop Westcott, the founder of the Cambridge Mission to Delhi, hanging in the main entrance to St Stephen's College, Delhi. His lectures, delivered in Delhi, Calcutta and Bangalore in 1992 have three titles—Friendship, Solidarity and Ecumenism. An edited form of the second lecture—Solidarity—is reprinted here. Although it now shows some signs of its age—a brief reference to a young Robert Mugabe as a disciple of Gandhi might grate a little today—it offers a valuable portrait of C. F. Andrews drawn at the close of the twentieth century to match the previous essay and its images of Andrews and Munshi Ram, many of them through Andrews' own letters, in the early years of the same century.

In each paper, the same theme continues: Andrews' ability to move beyond the boundaries of his own culture and religion, his "willingness to be undone", here in his friendship with Gandhi and espousal of the cause of Indian nationalism.

In addition, we are introduced to another figure among the British in India: Verrier Elwin (1902-64)—whom we shall see much more of later.[1] Elwin, like Andrews, was an Anglican priest who embraced a life with the tribal people of Central India, standing thereby outside the authority of his bishop, Alexander Wood, Bishop of Nagpur, who denied him a licence as a clergyman. He was, in Dan's later phrase, abandoned by the Church. But Elwin, who became a friend of Nehru, went on to live a life of remarkable, selfless service to the tribal people and to India, and to be recognized for outstanding work in the field of anthropology.

Looking back on his Teape lectures over some 30 years, Dan notes that he had not at that time come across the notion of solidarity in an inter-religious context and likes to think that at the time this was something of an innovation. However, the notion of solidarity as a moral and social virtue was very much in the air in Roman Catholic social thought and in the Polish political struggle around the Lenin Shipyard at Gdansk, where the trade union known as Solidarity had been founded in August 1980. The Polish Pope John Paul II had played a major part in the Catholic engagement with it. This certainly must have played a powerful if indirect part in Dan's thinking on the subject.

More recently, Dan has written about his sense of solidarity through inter-faith encounters and experiences:

> Most contemporary cases I picked up in encounters and conversations—for example in my getting to know Swami Agnivesh,[2] whose "Vedic socialism" chimed with my own Christian commitment. One of his collaborators was a Church of South India Bishop Azariah—it helped perhaps that he was a compulsive rule-breaker! The collaboration of Christian and Buddhist Dalits I learned from a Delhi Church of North India priest. In England, there was the case of an Anglican priest administering to an Asian community's temple. This was my

---

[1] See below, Chapter 6, pp. 113-28.

[2] Swami Agnivesh (1939-2020) was a social activist and cabinet minister in the state of Haryana. He is perhaps best known for his work with the Bonded Labour Liberation Front, which he founded in 1981.

former College of the Ascension student, Michael Ipgrave and his ministry among the Jains in Leicester. He went on to write a learned thesis on the Trinity and inter-faith activity.[3]

* * *

There is a second strand in inter-religious relationships, that I suggest we call solidarity. This is, of course, a word that has a variety of meanings—above all, there is what is sometimes called primordial solidarity, our solidarity with our own specific origins. That, surely, is what Gandhiji had in mind when he said. "I must restrict myself to my ancestral religion ... the environment wherein we were placed at birth by God."[4] It is this primordial solidarity with his own kinsfolk that Arjuna had to struggle to overcome with Krishna's help on the Field of Dharma. But this primordial solidarity is very far from what I have in mind today in speaking of inter-religious solidarity, which is a moving *out* from that sort of thing, a moving beyond such restriction, across frontiers, in order to stand beside, to identify with the other.

Curiously, I have always thought of the word "solidarity" as belonging to the world and discourse of politics, but I have consulted several dictionaries of politics in vain. The term simply does not appear. Interestingly, and I believe, significantly, the fullest consideration of the idea that I have come across is in a religious context, in a recent Roman Catholic document, *Sollicitudo Rei Socialis* ("Concern for social matters"). Section 38.4 of this papal teaching begins:

> It is above all a question of interdependence, sensed as a system determining relationships in the contemporary world in its economic, cultural, political and religious elements, and accepted as a moral category. When interdependence becomes recognized in this way, the correlative response as a moral and social attitude,

---

[3] Adapted from personal correspondence with the editors.
[4] Cf. "One must work out one's own salvation in the religion of one's own forefathers", Gandhi to I. Bamlet, 22 May 1927. *Collected Works*, Vol. XXXIII, p. 353.

> as a "virtue", is solidarity (that is,) . . . a commitment to the good of one's neighbour with the readiness . . . to "lose oneself" for the sake of the other.

Solidarity, then, like friendship across the religions, can be a religious event in itself, not least because it is motivated, as it almost *has* to be, by love, by a sense of justice, or by a vision of human unity. A simple example would be the way in which at Gandhi's Tolstoy Farm in South Africa, the Hindus, Jews and Christians kept the Ramadan fast with their Muslim comrades, thus expressing their solidarity as comrades in faith as well as in the struggle. And of course Gandhi's life is full of examples of this solidarity across the religions. Indeed, the cause of Hindu–Muslim unity in particular was so crucial and yet so difficult that he saw as early as 1909 that someone would probably have to die in expressing that particular solidarity.

C. F. Andrews is, of course, another such example. His going to South Africa at Gokhale's[5] request marked the beginning of an ever-deepening solidarity with his Hindu friend in a common cause. This story is well known, too well known for us to chronicle it again today, but well worth looking at from this angle of inter-religious solidarity.

In this case, the solidarity preceded the friendship, for Andrews went to South Africa as a sort of independent commission of enquiry, on behalf of Gokhale. The friendship, however, seems to have been instantaneous—"We simply met as brothers," (Gandhi later recorded) "and remained as such to the end"—the end being some 26 years later, with Gandhi at Andrews' deathbed in Calcutta, clasping his hand.[6] (What

---

[5] Gopal Krishna Gokhale (1866–1915) was a leading figure in the Indian independence movement, and a mentor to Gandhi. He visited South Africa in 1912 at Gandhi's invitation. At the end of 1913, Andrews met Gokhale in Delhi, who said to him, "We need you in South Africa. When do you start?" Andrews arrived in Durban on 1 January 1914. It was the beginning of his friendship with Gandhi. See Benardsidas Chaturvedi and Marjorie Sykes, *Charles Freer Andrews: A Narrative* (London: Allen & Unwin, 1949), pp. 92–3. (Eds)

[6] *Harijan*, 19 April 1940.

an opportunity lost, incidentally, in the 1982 Attenborough film on the life of Gandhi, along with other gaps such as the invisibility of Ambedkar! Andrews was dropped after one year's story-time, whereas in fact, as I have just said, Gandhi and Andrews worked together for a quarter of a century—a real test and a real authentication of both their deep friendship and their solidarity.) And yet, even on his deathbed, Andrews' recorded words point not so much to friendship as to solidarity, as the dying Charlie turned to Gandhiji and said, "Swaraj is coming, Mohan."[7] In the intervening more than a quarter-century of comradeship, there were a number of important facets to their relationship.

It was, first of all, of course, a solidarity in political commitment. Before they had met, Andrews recognized in Gandhi what he called "a saint of action", while he later testified that his own activism was reinforced—"To be with him . . . gave me a high courage, enkindled and enlivened by his own."[8] In some respects, their political solidarity had its complementary aspects. Thus, the indentured labour issue was one in which the British imperial and colonial authorities were implicated, and so it was one that Andrews could very properly take up, as indeed he very effectively did. The issue of untouchability, on the other hand, was one that Gandhi tried to keep Andrews out of. Presumably, Gandhi's insistence that this was a question for the Hindu community to deal with reflected his own interpretation of the problem, (and we might regret the absence of the objectivity of an outsider's view that Andrews might have brought into that situation), but it did also make for a sensible, complementary deployment of forces. It certainly took nothing away from their solidarity in political commitment, so that on Andrews' death in 1940, Gandhi bore witness to the "innumerable deeds of love he performed so that India might take her independent place among the nations of the earth".[9]

---

[7] Sykes and Chaturvedi, *Charles Freer Andrews*, p. 317. "Swaraj" means self-rule or self- government. (Eds.)

[8] C. F. Andrews, *What I Owe to Christ* (London: Hodder & Stoughton, 1932), p. 223.

[9] M. K. Gandhi, "The Legacy of C. F. Andrews", *Collected Works*, LXXI, pp. 408–9.

Gandhi also described the relationship between himself and Andrews as "an unbreakable bond between two seekers and servers".[10] Those two words, "seekers" and "servers" point to the invariable religious dimension of their solidarity. On the more straightforward side of this solidarity, there are of course many things that could be said.

In an early article of Andrews', soon after the two had met in South Africa, he explains the origin of Gandhi's understanding of *ahimsa* as "the principle of 'passive resistance', taken originally from Tolstoy's writings' on the Sermon on the Mount, but drastically remodelled and re-interpreted in the light of Hindu religion".[11] While he enthused at the practical application of the teaching of Jesus in Gandhi's *satyagraha*,[12] he was always careful to acknowledge in this way the latter's Hindu heritage. He deals with Gandhi's understanding of the "supreme reality of the *atman*" in a similar way—"The message of the Upanishads, that man's deliverance comes through realization of the *atman*" had assumed for Gandhi "a new and living meaning". This new meaning affirmed the dignity of the human person over against the denials implicit in South African racism and oppression. Despite Andrews' insistence that Gandhi's practice was on the basis of these reshaped Hindu teachings, they amounted to nothing less than "the fulfilment in action of those ideals which,"—Andrews said that he—"as a Christian longed to realize".[13]

But the grounds of their solidarity went even deeper, and this comes out particularly in what Andrews wrote about the great Delhi Fast of 1924. Throughout this, he had ministered with two old friends, Hakim Ajmal Khan and Swami Shraddhanand,[14] to Gandhi's needs during his hunger strike. In the course of doing so, he wrote, he had known more deeply, in his own personal life, "the meaning of the cross".[15] At the same

---

[10] Gandhi, "The Legacy of C. F. Andrews", p. 408.

[11] *Modern Review*, May 1914.

[12] *Satyagraha* is a Sanskrit word meaning "truth force". It refers to a form of non-violent resistance. (Eds.)

[13] *Modern Review*, July 1914.

[14] Munshi Ram. (Eds.)

[15] C. F. Andrews, *Mahatma Gandhi's Ideas* (London: Allen & Unwin, 1929), p. 313.

time, he quotes at length a passage from the Katha Upanishad about those rare beings who can realize the Divine Light within, and with a song that was sung as Gandhi was about to break his fast, the song of the true Vaishnava "who knows and feels another's woes as his own". Part, then, of this solidarity involved an acknowledgement of Gandhi's Hindu roots and inspiration, but, along with that, the claim that he had seen in Gandhi something profoundly Christ-like.

There was also a common bond in their understanding of the service of the poor. Both saw this as an essentially religious task. Gandhi, after going to South Africa, had discovered in his involvements there in the plight of the Indian community that "God could be realized only through service".[16] He went on to elaborate on this (no doubt aware of Vivekananda's earlier exposition of this idea) as being a question of serving God in the poor, of serving God as *Daridra Narayan*.[17] Not surprisingly, he came to love, and to use in his prayer meetings, Song no. 10 from Tagore's *Gitanjali*, "Here is thy footstool ... among the poorest and lowliest and lost." But Andrews also knew this poem and said that its message represented "the strongest belief ... (that he had) in the world"—it was fundamental to his Christianity.[18] This is very important. Both Gandhi and Andrews speak of this aspect of their commitment in particular emphatic ways. For Gandhi, it is a matter of God being realized "only" through service of the poor, for Andrews that this is a matter of his "strongest" belief, that God is to be worshipped and served in "the poorest and lowliest and lost". Here, they share their deepest religious conviction, but deriving from their quite separate and distinct religious traditions, and this shared religious conviction undergirds their solidarity in the national movement.

There were, of course, issues on which they differed, and at this point it seems appropriate to introduce the notion of "critical solidarity". They were united but did not hide their differences. Some of these were not

---

[16] M. K. Gandhi, *An Autobiography: The Story of My Experiments with Truth* (Ahmedabad, 1927), p. 198.

[17] *Daridra Narayan* is a nineteenth-century axiom of the Indian sage Swami Vivekananda that service to the poor is equivalent to service to God. (Eds.)

[18] Andrews to Tagore, 2 March 1914 (Santiniketan).

related specifically to their common endeavour within the national movement—the matter of taking vows (including vows of celibacy), for example, and the matter of religious conversion—but others, such as the matter of burning foreign cloth, for example, and some of Gandhi's fasts, were, and their disagreements were sharp. In the case of the former, Gandhi had declared the wearing of foreign cloth a sin, and Andrews questioned this, suggesting that a campaign on these terms would encourage both racism and self-righteousness, the latter in particular pointing to perhaps a deep difference in their understanding. With regard to Gandhi's fasts, for the most part Andrews gave very strong support, but he saw the danger of the method, that it could be "used by fanatics to force an issue which may be reactionary instead of progressive".[19] He also admitted that, insofar as it could be seen as an act of suicide, it instinctively repelled him. Underlying Andrews' reservations on these and other matters were important issues between the religion of the two friends, and in particular Gandhi's rejection of the body and all matter as the source of all selfishness, which Andrews could not accept. They aired these differences in long and careful letters to one another, and often subsequently in print. Andrews summed up his thinking on the whole question of their differences when he wrote:

> I feel that there are clear-cut distinctions between Christians, Hindus and Muslims which cannot today be overpassed. But I do not think we need to anathematize one another in consequence. We should rather seek always to see the best in one another, for that is the essential feature of love ... That seems to me to be a fine way towards peace in religion, without any compromise, syncretism, or toning down of vital distinctions.[20]

It proved to be a fine way also to solidarity, but to the *critical* solidarity that proved to be an inescapable aspect of their relationship.

---

[19] Letter to Gandhi, 1932, quoted in Sykes and Chaturvedi, *Charles Freer Andrews*, p. 264.

[20] Andrews to Gandhi, 1936, reprinted in *Guardian*, 4 March 1948.

In their solidarity, then, their 26 years together in a common human cause, for all the misunderstandings and mistakes, as in any human project, their most profound religious convictions were engaged, were challenged, reshaped and renewed. And through it all, the solidarity remained a constant.

I am sure there is something for us here. Out of Gandhi's own role in the national movement, in spite of the very understandable reservations that many in India have today about aspects of it, a worldwide symbol of non-violent struggle for justice has been forged. It is a symbol that seems to radiate amazing energy, and I have been fascinated and moved at how it continues to retain this energy and inspiration—across the continents, in Zimbabwe, where Robert Mugabe (a Roman Catholic Christian) was for long under Gandhi's influence,[21] and in South Africa, where Hindu and Muslim colleagues of Mandela at least until very recently described themselves as Gandhians; in the United States, where not only Martin Luther King (a Protestant Christian) but also the most recent Christian opposition to the national security state takes Gandhian notions of *ahimsa* and *satyagraha* as a hermeneutical key for reading the Gospel of St Mark;[22] in Latin America, where Archbishop Helder Camara proposed the Gandhian methodology as the "only alternative to the spiral of violence"; in the Philippines, during the movement (chiefly among Roman Catholics) that overthrew Marcos; and even as recently as May 1992, in (predominantly Buddhist) Thailand in the People's Alliance for Democracy protests, the example of Gandhi is held up as a beacon of freedom and human dignity. It is perhaps as important now as when it all happened that we should know that this is a story, most emphatically, of non-violent struggle, but also of inter-religious solidarity.

But before we turn to the issue of inter-religious solidarity today, I should like to look at another recent historical case, because it, too, has its own relevance. It is a less well-known story than that of Gandhi and

---

[21] One needs to remember that this essay is now more than 30 years old. (Eds.)
[22] Ched Myers, *Binding the Strong Man: A Political Reading of Mark's Story of Jesus* (Maryknoll: Orbis, 1988).

Andrews, and the solidarity takes a different form. I am thinking of the story of another rebel missionary, whose name was Verrier Elwin.[23]

Although much less well known today than Andrews, Elwin was known and respected around the world in his time, and an honoured figure in India in the decade before and the two decades immediately after independence. The French writer of the period, Romain Rolland, put it like this: "In Africa, Albert Schweitzer, the philosopher, in India, Verrier Elwin, the poet."[24]

Elwin's life and work in India fall into four distinct phases, and we must concentrate on the third phase for our concern with the matter of solidarity, but must sketch in the earlier two briefly, to set the scene, and to note the fourth.

Elwin first came to India in 1927, a bright young Oxford graduate, to join the ashram at Pune known as the Christa Seva Sangha. He came with a desire to make reparation for the imperial role of some of his ancestors, and also to identify with the poor.

His first steps in identifying with others took a rather rarefied form. In his first three or four years in India, while he remained at the Pune ashram, he devoted himself to study and writing, in a field that I would call inter-cultural spirituality. He was interested in prayer and contemplation, and wrote a series of studies at this time looking for commonalities and comparisons between Hindu and Christian texts on contemplation. These studies are still worthy of consideration ... but we need only to note today how they indicate Elwin's willingness to venture openly and appreciatively into other people's religious worlds.

While still at Christa Seva Sangha, however, Elwin was already feeling his way out into contemporary India and its concerns. This represents the second phase of his Indian life, as he came into close contact with Gandhi, turned the Christa Seva Sangha upside down with spiritual hartals, spinning and the like, and even went on a secret mission on

---

[23] See Elwin's autobiographical *The Tribal World of Verrier Elwin* (London: Oxford University Press, 1964); also Daniel O'Connor, *Din Sevak: Verrier Elwin's Life of Service in Tribal India* (Bangalore, 1993).

[24] Romain Rolland, "About This Book", in Elwin's *Leaves from the Jungle: Life in a Gond Village* (London: Oxford University Press, 1936), p. 7.

behalf of the Congress to the N. W. Frontier to make contact with Khan Abdul Ghaffar Khan, and to write a report on the situation there. This represents a second step towards the solidarity he was seeking, and it was secured by a touching friendship with Gandhiji himself. Elwin carried into this phase, too, his literary interests and gifts, and wrote three books on Gandhi and the national movement, and a series of interesting interreligious essays. One of these latter was on what he called "Religious and Cultural Aspects of Khadi", and it included an interesting exploration of Gandhi's understanding of *Daridra Narayan*; another tried to relate the theory and practice of *satyagraha* to the Christian understanding of the Cross, a piece entitled "Calvary Satyagraha". Most substantial, though, was a long essay published in the *Modern Review* on "Mahatma Gandhi's Philosophy of Truth", a study in which he drew on his by now considerable knowledge of mysticism both eastern and western, and which contains the remarkable comment: "It is as though we have heard the voice of Plato on the banks of the Sabarmati."[25]

There were two long-term effects of this phase of Verrier Elwin's life. The first of these was that he ran into trouble with both the imperial and also the ecclesiastical authorities: the British government permitted him to remain in India only on condition that he abjured politics, which he agreed to do; in his ecclesiastical troubles, his bishop virtually drove him out of the Church over the next few years. The second consequence was that in his search for a form of solidarity with the poor, he took the advice of Gandhi, Patel and others, and committed himself to work with India's tribal people. This led into the third phase of his Indian life, the phase of a profound solidarity.

For the next more than 20 years, from 1932 to 1953, this brilliant, witty, life-loving Oxford graduate lived in tribal village India, a life of great simplicity, often of considerable poverty and hardship. It was also a life of ever-deepening solidarity across the vast religious and cultural

---

[25] Verrier Elwin, "Mahatma Gandhi's Philosophy of Truth", *Modern Review*, August–October 1933.

gap that would appear to separate such a person from the Indian *adivasi*[26] world.

Before we look more carefully at this as a case of inter-religious solidarity, there are three points to make. First, Elwin did not go into *adivasi* India alone. He was accompanied by a Maratha friend, Shamrao Hivale, and he constantly testified to the importance of this friendship for all that he was able to do there. Second, his motivation was deeply religious, he would "follow the Crucified among the crucified", to use his own phrase;[27] although his own abandonment by the Church, in the early 1930s, left him almost completely cut off from his own community, there can be no doubt of his original motivation, to identify with the poor as a special place of God's presence, nor can there be any doubt as to his persisting underlying faith in God, in what at the end of his life he called "a greater love and a greater reality than we can know in our ordinary lives".[28] Third, this immersion in the life of the tribal poor, though full of hardship, was also a source of immense happiness to him, and he often spoke of the happiness it brought him.

It is impossible to catalogue here his life during these 20 years. He took with him into tribal central India his scholarly gifts, and became a pioneer anthropologist, writing over 20 major monographs. These have been described variously as "perhaps the greatest thing of its kind that has yet been done", "a *tour de force* in anthropological literature", and so on.[29] He received the Padma Bhushan from the President of India[30], and a D.Sc from his own University of Oxford. Indeed, it was said of him that "No other anthropologist, either British or India, has made as massive a contribution to our knowledge of Indian tribal

---

[26] *Adivasi* is the Hindi for "original inhabitant" and refers to the ethnic tribal groups regarded as the original inhabitants of India. (Eds.)

[27] Verrier Elwin, *The Supremacy of the Spiritual* (Madras, 1993), p. 3.

[28] Verrier Elwin, *The Tribal World of Verrier Elwin* (London: Oxford University Press, 1964), p. 346.

[29] M. C. Pradhan, "Verrier Elwin as Anthropologist", in M. C. Pradhan (ed.), *Anthropology and Archaeology* (Bombay, 1969), p. 8.

[30] The Padma Bhushan is the third highest civilian award in the Republic of India. (Eds.)

societies as Verrier Elwin."[31] Much more importantly to Elwin himself, though, his anthropological work was always dedicated to the welfare and advancement of the tribal people, and he preferred to call what he was engaged in "philanthropology" (bringing together the two words, philanthropy and anthropology in an ingenious way). This led to a friendship with Jawaharlal Nehru, who affirmed that he had learned a great deal from Elwin, and who, at the end of Elwin's 21 years in the forest, appointed him, in now independent India, "to advise the Government on the whole tribal problem in India".[32] In this latter role, which represented the fourth phase of his Indian life, Elwin had a major influence upon the very enlightened official policies that emerged under Nehru with regard to the tribal people.

But behind all this and as the foundation of it was his remarkable twenty-one-year venture in inter-religious solidarity. Not that Elwin and Hivale entered into this with any very clear idea of what they were going to do, beyond doing what good they could, and a sense of calling to live among the poor, a decision, as Hivale later wrote, "fraught with years of deprivation and suffering".[33] Their intentions were clarified when they named their enterprise the Gond Seva Mandal, with its associated Ashram of St Francis. During the first few years, they learned and practised some elementary medical skills, and aspects of rural development, and started some small schools. Their funds came entirely from friends, including Gandhiji, and were entirely devoted to the work, while they themselves lived in what Elwin called "apostolic discomfort".[34] Subsequently, as their anthropological and philanthropological interests developed, they called their base the Tribal Welfare and Research Unit, the research being always accompanied by concern for tribal welfare, the welfare always based on sound research.

It is quite clear that they entered into a remarkable, perhaps uniquely, close and affectionate relationship with the tribal people. Elwin was, from

---

[31] Christoph von Fürer-Haimendorf's obituary of Elwin in *Man*, LXIV (1964), pp. 114–15.
[32] Elwin to his mother, 12 December 1953 (India Office Records).
[33] S. Hivale, *Scholar Gipsy: A Study of Verrier Elwin* (Bombay, 1946), p. 40.
[34] Circular Letter, 6 January 1937 (Elwin Papers, India Office Records).

all accounts a very attractive personality, with a gaiety and élan and a rich sense of humour that helped them to relate, but also a lively, enquiring mind about everything that he encountered in this new, tribal world. It is also the case, of course, that he approached the *adivasi* people from such an immense social and cultural distance that he was almost free of the sort of preoccupations and prejudices that those who had always lived somewhat nearer to them had developed. There was also the essential mediatory role that Hivale played. Above all, though, he and Elwin were appalled at the depth of suffering and oppression and deprivation that they encountered, and the dedication to easing this suffering undoubtedly was the motivation of their solidarity. We need to say more, in the particular case of religion, about how closely Elwin entered into the tribal world, and simply note here that his entering successively into two marriages, the second a great and enduring success, is a further measure of the quality of the personal and social identification that was entailed.

Very early in Elwin and Hivale's entry into this world, new interests were breaking in. They began to discover the tribal people amongst whom they lived as people with a living culture. The first fruits of this were in their jointly edited *Songs from the Forest* (1935). Strikingly, they note that most of the songs in this first collection came from four women of one household, the house of a leper. "Two of the women are the leper's wives, one his sister, the fourth a niece, herself married to another leper." Out of such humanly desperate material, beautiful and moving evidence of a culture was secured. At the same time, they saw a further importance in these songs thus collected. They were "the villagers' own book about themselves".[35] Thus Elwin and Hivale had begun to discover a new role, that of being a voice for the voiceless.

That, I think, is as good a way as any to describe the fruits of this deep solidarity with the tribal poor. The immense and immensely impressive body of writing that Elwin and Hivale produced during his 21 years in the forest served to advance the cause of the tribal people. It did so in a number of ways. For example, by analysing and exposing particular injustices in a responsible and scholarly way, they were able to promote a

---

[35] Elwin and Hivale, *Songs of the Forest: The Folk Poetry of the Gonds* (London: Allen & Unwin, 1935), p. 11.

whole series of reforms in legislation and administration. This amounted in the end to little less than *A New Deal for Tribal India* (to quote the title of one of Elwin's later books).[36]

Secondly, by publishing a vast corpus of tribal poetry and song, and many related studies, it was possible to convey to educated people the message of a common humanity:

> The forest-tribesman ... with his strange knowledge and weird customs, his utter poverty and ignorance, is interested in the same essential things as the rest of the world.[37]

There was, indeed, in tribal life, a practical wisdom and a fine understanding of community and an often sensitive harmony with the natural order, that were important contributions towards the common life of the nation. This was something that Nehru acknowledged that he had learned from Elwin.

Along with this, Elwin's work disclosed, in W. G. Archer's words, "the Indian sensibility in some of its most truly indigenous and spontaneous forms".[38] Here we need to note Elwin's treatment of the relation of tribal religion to the great, Sanskritic tradition. His early contact with the tribal people led him into a sharp reaction against Hinduism insofar as he saw it as the religion of the tribals' oppressors. Gradually, however, he seems to have come round to a more benign view, at least to the extent of recognizing that if the tribal people were to find an honoured place in Indian society, some sort of relationship to the great tradition would need to be acknowledged. For this reason, he drew attention on several occasions to sympathetic references to the tribal people in the great tradition. For instance, he recalls the story in the *Ramayana* of Rama's encounter with an aged ascetic, a tribal woman called Sramana

---

[36] Verrier Elwin, *A New Deal for Tribal India. Abridgement of the 10th Report of the Commissioner for Scheduled Castes and Scheduled Tribes for the Year 1960–61.* Ministry of Home Affairs, 1963.

[37] Ibid.

[38] W. G. Archer, Preface to Elwin's *Folk Songs of the Chhattisgarh* (Bombay, 1946), p. xxxiv.

Savari, an encounter notable for Rama's tenderness towards the tribal, and culminating in his giving her permission to depart from the world, whereupon in his presence she goes into a fire and ascends into the heavens while all the sky is lit by her glory. Elwin repeated this piece in several of his books in order, as he says, to overcome a "national antipathy" towards the tribals fostered by the *Vishnu Puranas* and the *Mahabharata*.[39] At the same time, while he recognized that there was much in tribal teaching that had "borrowed from the common sub-Puranic and Epic tradition that pervades the whole of village India", he demonstrated that many Hindu elements were very recent intrusions, so that it was indeed correct to speak, as he did, of "tribal theology".[40]

For Elwin, though, this tribal religion was more than a body of teaching. His book on *The Religion of an Indian Tribe* (1955), and some of his accompanying comments in his autobiographical *Tribal World*, show that he entered into tribal religious life with an extraordinary openness and sensitivity. He describes how, for example, during the best part of a decade, he visited all the main Hill Saora villages and there witnessed, and even more unusually, *assisted* "over and over again" at many of the ceremonies, "particularly the funerary rites and sacrifices designed to heal the sick". He even, when he was himself sick, submitted himself to the ministrations of shamans and shaminins. He found himself dreaming of the Saora gods. Here is solidarity in a unique key! He says that "knowledge of the people gradually sank in until it was part of ... (him)".

> There comes a moment when everything falls into place and you suddenly see the life of a people as a harmonious whole and understand how it works.

He says this can only be achieved after arduous study, and "is one of the greatest achievements that a scholar can have".[41] In all this, though,

---

[39] Verrier Elwin, "The Tribesmen in Ancient India", *Tribal Welfare and Research Unit Newsletter*, No. 4, September 1952.

[40] Verrier Elwin, *Tribal Myths of Orissa* (London: Oxford University Press, 1954).

[41] Elwin, *Religion of an Indian Tribe* (Bombay, 1955), p. 193.

Verrier Elwin was more than a scholar. The compassion that first led him and Hivale into the forest was a deeply religious compassion, and I would submit that only his own persisting compassionate faith enabled him to enter as he did into the religion of an Indian tribe. For this reason, he prefaced his *Myths of Middle India* (1949) with a quotation from Winternitz:[42]

> In all our investigations into the origins of customs, we are standing on holy ground ... at the psychological source of all that is highest and noblest in man.

Even more strikingly, he pierced through the squalor and poverty to which the tribal people had been reduced, to ultimate, and ultimately theological, realities:

> To the stranger's eye ... (the shamanin) may be just one more dirty old village woman; but to the Saora whose life is broken by tragedy, she may well be an angel of strength and consolation.[43]

Only Elwin's own profound and compassionate entry into the life of the tribal people in their suffering but also in their faith could have permitted him to write thus.

In considering the case of Elwin, there is, of course, a difficulty, the difficulty that he had been outlawed by the Church by this time. A careful reading of the evidence, however, suggests that he remained a Christian in intention at this time, and that we have in his 21 years in the forest a remarkable example of inter-religious solidarity. Certainly, his old friends in the Congress saw him as pursuing a Christian vocation in the *adivasi* world. It was one which they admired, for it was at this time that they began to call him *Din-sevak* (servant of the poor).

Here, then, are two different types of inter-religious solidarity. In the one, that of Gandhiji and C. F. Andrews, two religious people out of

---

[42] The Austrian Sanskritist and colleague of Max Müller, Moriz Winternitz (1863–1937). (Eds.)

[43] Ibid., p. 171.

different communities and traditions, and intending always to be faithful to their own community and tradition, nevertheless find sufficient common ground to be able to unite in the closest of life and action for over a quarter of a century in pursuit of a common human vision, in their case, the vision of *swaraj*. In the other, Elwin and Hivale, the former in particular, inspired by their own religious tradition, enter into and share in the life of another community, a suffering and oppressed community, and enter into it so deeply and compassionately as to be able to be an effective voice for the voiceless.

Of course, times and circumstances change, but I believe that this notion of inter-religious solidarity is not less suggestive for us now than it was in earlier decades. In Britain, for example, where there is a persisting racism in both society and the churches, the situation is complicated by the fact that the racially oppressed minorities are also, in fact (in all except one case) what are called in Britain people of other faiths, Muslim or Hindu or Sikh. In the face of this, though, some striking cases of inter-religious solidarity are to be found here and there. In the early days of immigration into the Southall area of London, when the incoming Muslims were very hard up and could not afford their own meeting place, the local parish church made accommodation available for the children's Qur'an class, and also made their church building available for large meetings of the Sikh community. More recently, the Jain community in Leicester, needing local expertise to help them establish their own identity and presence through a cultural centre, appointed a local Christian priest as their part-time administrator, with his bishop's permission and support. As I wrote these lectures, the churches in Scotland were being encouraged to contribute to an aid fund established by Scotland's Muslims in support of the welfare of their co-religionists in the former Yugoslavia. There are an increasing number of such stories. They present a counter-model of inter-religious solidarity in a society in which attitudes of religious antagonism inherited from the colonial past and racial prejudice are liable to mutually reinforce each other. Such models of solidarity are very important in that context. Those involved explain them in different ways, as the Christian duty to love the stranger, or quite explicitly in some cases to counteract racism, or as part of the search for common concerns or shared values in the interest of common citizenship.

No doubt your circumstances here offer different opportunities for the exploration of inter-religious solidarity.[44] I was moved to read the accounts of young people, certainly Hindus and Christians among them, who did relief work in the refugee camps for Sikhs in Delhi and other places in November 1984. Many of them, I would guess, would not have much interest in religion, would perhaps want very little to do with religion at all, certainly made no reference to it in the reports that I read, and yet their humanity, compassion and courage were put to work to reach across a religious frontier and be in solidarity with their Sikh neighbours.

A much more explicitly religious and inter-religious case of solidarity is recorded by a friend of mine in South India. The story involved the liberation of some 200 families of bonded labourers, and coming together in this, in an extraordinarily providential series of stages in the story were an Arya Samaj swami, a Sikh local official, and a Christian theological teacher. No doubt they each found spiritual resources in their own tradition that enabled them to commit themselves to this common project. This particular swami, we know, finds his inspiration in his re-reading of Dayanand's exposition of the Vedas, in particular the passages in the *Satyarth Prakash* dealing with the duties of a ruler, as a form of what he calls "Vedic Socialism", the Christian in his rereading of the Gospel of St Matthew from the perspective of the interests of the Dalits. Many others came to be involved in various ways, and the account I have suggests that the experience of liberation was varied and enriching to many who were drawn into the episode—a group of lawyers, journalists, local people who helped: above all, of course, the liberated labourers, of whom the account suggests that they "found their freedom not physically only, but spiritually as well in a measure, for they had to muster up great courage and learn to stand together". Noteworthy, too, however, in relation to our theme, was the recurrence of the word "solidarity" in my friend's account, the "strength of the solidarity ... between the Sikh sub-collector and his new Hindu Punjabi friend", the swami, and that too which the Christian experienced in working with these two. I recently had the privilege of meeting the swami concerned,

---

[44] This lecture was delivered in India, in Delhi, Calcutta and Bangalore in 1992. (Eds.)

in London, and he spoke warmly of the Christian friends he has made in the work he does. Incidentally, his published writings on his Vedic Socialism disclose interestingly another liberative strand . . . for he often refers, when the average male writer will speak of man and mankind, to woman and with the bonded labourers. The Christian theologian who was involved in this summed up his account, "What has happened *ad hoc* needs to become the order of reality if the degree of freedom and solidarity experienced is to find complete fulfilment."[45] That is no doubt a dream still awaiting its realization, but the testimony to inter-religious solidarity in such a cause is a story for our times.

It brings us, however, to a particularly acute difficulty with the possibility of Hindu-Christian solidarity in India today. You will recall the Bishop in Andhra whom I quoted in the first lecture,[46] who said that he and his people, as victims of centuries of "caste terror", found the idea of inter-religious dialogue very hard to swallow. And the fact is, of course, that the majority of Christians in India, perhaps 70 per cent or more, come from the most oppressed sector of society. It is hardly surprising, therefore, that as the Dalit consciousness develops, Christians from that same sector, or at least the more articulate and educated among them, are increasingly voicing what they call a Dalit Theology. It has, of course, its relevance to the Dalit experience in the Church as well as in the wider community. It needs to find a creative relationship with the also nascent tribal theology that is emerging in India today. It also relates them to comparable developments in Christianity around the world, to liberation theology, black theology, feminist theology, minjung theology, and so on—areas of exceptional religious vitality in the Christian movements in our time,

---

[45] Dhyanchand Carr, "Social Action and Communicating Christ", *Anvil* 4:2 (1987), pp. 161–74.

[46] The bishop is not named but described in the first lecture in this way: "He was a highly educated man, with impressive qualifications from Chicago but also with a deep love for his own culture, of which there seemed to be a positive renaissance going on in his own church. He and the many thousands of Christians in his diocese were all from one of two groups, the Malas and the Madigas, at the very bottom of the Hindu social structure." Daniel O'Connor, *Relations in Religion*, p. 17. (Eds.)

which are displacing the older, long-dominant theologies of the West, and recovering neglected, some would say, essential features of the teaching of Jesus and Christianity. Thus, the Bishop of Madras writes, "That feeling of being God-forsaken is at the heart of our dalit experience in India. It is the 'dalitness' of the divinity that we see in the Cross of Jesus."[47] But this fledgling Dalit theology faces very special problems in the Indian context. Where is it to find support in the wider community? If it has allies, they are most obviously among other Dalits, such as those who see the Buddha,

> Speaking and walking
> Amongst the humble and the weak
> Soothing away grief
> In the life-threatening darkness
> With torch in hand
> Going from hovel to hovel.[48]

It is interesting that India has recently witnessed the first national consultation, at Nagpur, of Buddhist and Christian Dalits together, under the title, "Dalit Solidarity".

Where else might the Dalits hope for the support of solidarity? They see India's classical, Sanskritic religious tradition as a gigantic edifice of oppression, devoid of any redeeming feature. But that, of course, is not the complete picture. There is the reinterpretation of Advaita by Vivekananda, and its renewal in practical life—C. F. Andrews wrote of how he had seen this in the way Ramakrishna Mission workers in cholera camps and famine areas had learnt to identify themselves with

---

[47] Source unknown. But see: "He died on the Cross as a true *Dalit*, crushed and broken while yet being innocent ... the *Dalit* Christ who is the Resurrected Lord, must be encountered in the *Dalit* experience in our day. It is this encounter with God of the Oppressed in the suffering of the oppressed *Dalits* in our land that has to be articulated and formulated as *Dalit* Theology." M. Azariah, "Doing Theology in India Today", *National Council of Churches Review* 108:2 (1988).

[48] Dayar Powar, "Siddhartha", quoted in *Journal of African and Asian Studies* 15 (1980), p. 38.

the sick and the suffering, and he went on, "I would ask you... to practise in your own daily life such faith in Advaitam ... When the outcaste comes to you, the untouchable, the *namasudras*, say to yourself the same thing, "Tattvamasi"— "Thou art that!" There are also respected Christian voices in India today, those of Stanley Samartha, for example, and M. M. Thomas, reminding us of this strong prophetic tradition against social injustice within the Hindu household of faith. But this is a debate that the outsider like myself can take little part in. Thomas sees the emergence of "a new composite culture, ... in its dominant framework Hindu, but drawing into it, partly in an incoherent mixture, partly in a more dynamic synthesis, the values and spirit from other religions and secular ideologies".[49] Samartha concludes his case by advocating that people should join together in common struggle against evil.[50] That that is possible is what my story about the solidarity of Swami Agnivesh and his Sikh and Christian companions, together with their bonded labourer companions, suggests. It is one of the fundamental principles of liberation theology that the renewed understanding of God and experience of God's grace follow from the praxis of justice and peace. We need to treasure the stories and experiences of inter-religious solidarity that we know, for they surely witness to the only credible forms that our separate religious traditions can hope to sustain into the future, those that are compatible with a shared vision of a human future...

* * *

From Daniel O'Connor, *Relations in Religion*, The Westcott Lectures, 1992 (New Delhi: Allied Publisher Ltd. 1994), pp. 18–36. Some explanatory footnotes have been added by the editors.

---

[49] "The Role of Religion in the Struggle Against Poverty in India", in P. Mathew and A, Muricken (eds), *Religion, Ideology and Counter-Culture: Essays in Honour of S. Kappen* (Bangalore, 1987), p. 112.
[50] S. J. Samartha, "In Search of a revised Christology: A Response to Paul Knitter", *Current Dialogue* 21 (December, 1991).

5

Some Distinctive Features of Andrews' Thought

During Dan's years teaching in Delhi, he writes of the work of a group of South Indian theologians and Christians in the field of inter-religious study. They were S. J. Samartha, M. M. Thomas[1] and P. D. Devanandan. In Bangalore, they established, under the auspices of the World Council of Churches, a prolific think-tank called the Christian Institute for the Study of Religion and Society (CISRS), which between 1955 and 1975 set up an extraordinary programme of conferences and meetings, drawing on peoples of all faiths from across India. They also published extensively, and it was in their series *Confessing the Faith in India* that Dan published (No.10) his first extensive work on C. F. Andrews.

The Testimony of C. F. Andrews, from Dan's Introduction of which this chapter is drawn, is largely extracts from Andrews' own writings. It includes an autobiographical piece, letters to Indian friends, including Munshi Ram, Rabindranath Tagore and Gandhi. Given the time when these were written, in the earlier part of the twentieth century, Christian contempt for Indian religions was the standard imperial attitude, making Andrews' anti-imperial, indeed post-colonial, stance all the more remarkable. There are also essays on the development of the Church in India, on Christ and other religions, particularly Hinduism, and finally some poems and comments on the theme of Christ and oppression.

---

[1] M. M. Thomas, with whom Dan corresponded for many years, later became Chair of the Central Committee of the World Council of Churches and Governor of Nagaland. Thomas' book *Acknowledged Christ of the Indian Renaissance* (1969) also provides a useful sketch of Andrews' thought.

Andrews was not a great poet, but he could write with profound feeling for the suffering of others and the place of Christ in a world of pain and misery. For example, there is a short poem entitled "The Indentured Coolie":

> There he crouched,
> Back and arms scarred, like a hunted thing,
> Terror-stricken.
> All within me surged towards him,
> While the tears rushed.
> Then a change.
> Through his eyes I saw Thy glorious face—
> Ah, the wonder!
> Calm, unveiled in deathless beauty,
> Lord of Sorrow.[2]

Dan wrote an extensive, sixty-page introduction to these writings, his first long piece on Andrews' life and work. The essay reprinted here is an edited form of one section of that Introduction, outlining some of the distinctive features of Andrews' thought and theology.

Dan notes that the book was published in India in 1974, two years after his own return to the United Kingdom, and the publication missed the centenary of Andrews' birth (1971) by some three years. It was indeed from the national celebration of Andrews' birth centenary that interest in Andrews grew and stimulated Dan's own work, which began at the end of his decade in Delhi in the early 1970s. The delay in publication did not seem to worry Dan's colleagues at CISRS, and the book was warmly welcomed in Indian theological institutions. In undertaking this considerable task, in addition to his duties as chaplain to the University of

---

[2] *The Testimony of C. F. Andrews* (Madras, 1974), p. 248. The historian Hugh Tinker, who wrote a book about Andrews, *The Ordeal of Love: C. F. Andrews and India* (1979), concluded that Andrews' almost single-handed demolition of the system of indenture throughout the British Empire was an achievement to equate with the abolition of slavery. See also, Tinker, *A New System of Slavery: The Export of Indian Labour Overseas, 1830–1920.* (1974).

St Andrews, Dan has written; "To me it was a good experience. Though Andrews wrote too much and could lapse at his worst in later years into the tone of a late Victorian oracle, at his best he wrote like an angel, and both reading and writing about him was something of a spiritual experience, and I found myself saying I did not know where he finished and I began."[3]

Dan describes his work on this book as "a stepping stone in my life as a writer on the rebel missionaries who played such a part in what Nehru called the country's awakening".[4]

* * *

For all his fine academic career, Andrews was not a systematic theologian. He was essentially a religious man of action, and he wrote most often not merely as a participant in an ongoing theological debate (although his writing is an important contribution to this), but in order to do things in the area of human development and relationships—to stem and reverse the denationalizing tendencies within the Indian Church, to advance the movement towards independence on what he judged to be the right lines, to enlist support and secure justice for Indians overseas, to advance the cause of the poor and the outcaste, to promote mutual understanding and respect between India and Britain, and between Hindu and Muslim, to encourage the practical expression of faith. And yet, no one can ever have been in any doubt as to the source and motivation of his concerns in the Christian faith. Nor did he shrink from the declaration of his mature conviction that:

> Human life would sink back incredibly far, beyond all recovery whatsoever, if it were not for this supreme miracle of grace which Christ's presence has brought to mankind.[5]

---

[3] Private unpublished correspondence with DJ.
[4] Private correspondence with DJ.
[5] C. F. Andrews, *What I Owe to Christ* (London: Hodder & Stoughton, 1932), p. 307.

It is possible, therefore, despite his own lack of interest in (or time for) systematic theological exposition, to identify distinctive and sometimes developing theological emphases.

Andrews' theology is from first to last incarnational, a Christology rooted, as was Westcott's, in the historic revelation. It is interesting to note in this respect how his early stress on the historical Jesus, in his prefatory notes on Stokes' *Historical Character of the Gospel* (1913), finds a late echo in a letter to C. E. Raven (1939). He only very rarely refers to the Old Testament, and in what may well be his only published venture in the field of what might be called comparative systematics, in an article on "The Creation Theory of the Universe",[6] his arguments are largely derived from points made by correspondents at Cambridge to whom he had referred the problem. On one occasion or another, he touches on most of the New Testament writings, but it is the historical Jesus as discerned in and through the four Gospels as "the Human Christ"[7] and "the Eternal Word",[8] who is the centre of his devotion and his thought.

The death of Christ is far from ignored, and Christ is "the Divine Redeemer from sin and death",[9] but characteristically when a chapter is added to the study of the Last Discourses, in *Christ in the Silence*, it is entitled "the Glory of the Cross"—and equally characteristically the chapter concludes:

> We must be ready at His word of command to go back into the midst of strife, where His brethren—the poor, the oppressed, the afflicted—are still suffering. For he is still there, suffering

---

[6] *Modern Review*, April 1909, pp. 336–9.

[7] *Register Containing Biographical Notes as Dictated by C. F. Andrews about Himself*. (Handwritten by Banarsidas Chaturvedi, 1920–21?) Chaturvedi Papers, National Archives of India, p. 103. (Hereafter, *Biographical Notes*).

[8] C. F. Andrews, *The Renaissance in India: Its Missionary Aspect* (London: London Missionary Society, 1912), passim.

[9] Andrews, *What I Owe to Christ*, p. 17.

with them in their midst; and in our love for them we show our love to Him.[10]

A conversation with "one of the noblest of Indian saints and teachers" (Dwijendranath [sic] Tagore?) adds further illumination on this matter:

> "... when some chapters of your Bible tell us of a God of wrath, who delights in blood and can only forgive after blood has been shed, we are inclined to turn away in disgust. For we have in our own ancient legends such blood-thirsty deities, and we are trying to expurgate them from our scriptures. Surely you, too, ought to do the same." I assured him that Christ's highest mission on earth had been one long endeavour to bring to an end such wrong conceptions of God and to reveal Him as the Father whose love is universal.[11]

To return to our main point, throughout Andrews' writings, "the Human Christ" and "the Eternal Word" is the standard of judgment and the justification for specific actions. Thus, "the meek and lowly Son of Man" is set over against the posture of the European races towards the non-European,[12] "the Word, within your heart, which enlightens every man" is a reason for supporting "complete and perfect independence for India",[13] "the homeless Christ", stripped bare of worldly power, is ill-represented by "the widespread external resources and the extensive material organization of foreign missions",[14] and Christ is "the great Emancipator" from the narrow bondage of special formulae:

---

[10] C. F. Andrews, *Christ in the Silence* (London: Hodder & Stoughton, 1933), p. 289.

[11] Andrews, *Christ in the Silence*, p. 67.

[12] From the sermon "Imperial Responsibilities", *Modern Review*, May 1913, pp. 571-4.

[13] *To The Students* (pamphlet, Madras, 1920).

[14] "Missions in India Today", *International Review of Missions* Vol. XXII (1933), pp. 189-200.

> ... while his wideness of outlook and largeness of heart never implied any lowering of the moral standards, it did imply a complete freedom from narrow, exclusive judgments, and a readiness at all times to stand by the side of the weak and the oppressed wherever they were to be found ... He is always and everywhere the Son of Man.[15]

This concept of "the Son of Man" recurs frequently in Andrews' writing, to express an understanding of the universal significance of Christ:

> Because Christ is Son of Man, Christianity must be all-comprehensive, larger far than the church of the baptized. The Christian experience must be one of an all-embracing sacrament in which Christ is seen and revered in all men.[16]

This surprisingly early statement of this idea (1910) is expanded illuminatingly in 1932:

> ... the supreme miracle of Christ's character lies in this: that he combines within Himself, as no other figure in human history has ever done, the qualities of every race. His very birthplace and home in childhood were near the concourse of the two great streams of human life in the ancient world, that flowed East and West. Time and place conspired, but the divine spark came down from above to mould for all time the human character of Christ the Son of Man. This is a tremendous claim to set forward. In all other ages of mankind, verification would have been impossible, because the world of men had not yet fully been explored. But in our own generation the claim may at last be made, and may be seen to correspond with the salient facts of human history. For those who, through intimate contact with other races, have

---

[15] "Jesus Christ", *The Guardian*, 22 September 1938, p. 597.
[16] "Christ in India" (*c.*1910), quoted in Benarsidas Chaturvedi and Marjorie Sykes, *Charles Freer Andrews: A Narrative* (London: George Allen & Unwin, 1949), p. 64.

> gained the right to be heard have borne witness that each race and region of the earth responds to His appeal, finding in the Gospel record that which applies specially to themselves. His sovereign character has become the one golden thread running through mankind, binding the ages and the races together.[17]

The references here to "all men" and to the binding of "the ages and races together" remind us of Andrews' strong stress upon human solidarity, expressed in his use of the term "the Body of Humanity". The *idea* is present throughout his earliest book, of 1896,[18] but this particular *phrase* we start to find only towards the end of the first phase of his theological development in India, and it recurs thereafter more or less right through his life. The term is used in two contexts. It is used to express a sense of the religious solidarity of man, an idea which ... had at one stage "vedantic" implications, and later a Christian-universalist meaning. It is used also to express a sense of the social solidarity of man, so that, for example, the effect of industrialization in British East Africa is seen as "a desecration ... among the weaker members of the Body of Humanity".[19] Behind the idea, as Andrews uses it, lies a universalist interpretation of the Pauline doctrine of the body:

> When we come to the second great factor of the national movement, we go for our direct teaching to St Paul's ideal of the body of humanity, of which Christ the Son of Man, is the head,—"Whether one member suffer, all the members suffer with it; or one member rejoice, all the members rejoice with it." In this idea of the Body of Humanity, there is the fullest possible scope for national development. It is indeed, the charter of national rights and liberties.[20]

---

[17] Andrews, *What I Owe to Christ*, pp. 153–4.

[18] C. F. Andrews, *The Relation of Christianity to the Conflict between Capital and Labour* (London: Methuen, 1896).

[19] C. F. Andrews, *Christ and Labour* (London: Student Christian Movement, 1923), Chap. 10.

[20] From the sermon "Imperial Responsibilities".

Such an interpretation is, of course, compatible with the patristic position, with which Andrews, as a good liberal-orthodox Anglican, was well acquainted, but he gives no clue as to whether he was recollecting any particular text, or was merely echoing the general patristic understanding of the corporate universal redemption by the Son who assumed not *a* man but *man*.[21] His interpretation is similarly, and not surprisingly, compatible with the universalist position of Maurice[22], who said that: "The truth is that every man is in Christ."[23] Maurice sustained his universalism by combining "an insistence upon the definite character of the signs of the Church's constitution with an unwillingness to define the Church's present boundaries".[24] This is not unlike Andrews' position. He too, as we have seen, spoke of a Christianity that must be "larger far than the Church of the baptized", and yet, in a book such as *The Good Shepherd*, based on a series of lectures in pastoral theology at Cambridge, he took for granted "the definite character of the signs of the Church's constitution".

The idea of human solidarity is a good starting point for an examination of Andrews' understanding of religions. In his early book, *North India* (1908), there is a certain ambivalence of attitude at times, as for example when he says: "Islam has a great contribution to make to the Christian Church."[25] In the same book he expresses more clearly the idea of fulfilment:

---

[21] For a specific reference, Hilary of Poitiers, *De Trinitate* 2:24: "He was made man of a virgin so that he might receive the nature of flesh: that the body of humanity as a whole might be sanctified by association with this mixture." I am grateful to Canon R. C. Walls of New College, Edinburgh, for this reference.

[22] F. D. Maurice (1805–72), Anglican priest and Knightsbridge Professor of Moral Philosophy at Cambridge. (Eds.)

[23] F. D. Maurice, *The Life of Frederick Denison Maurice: Chiefly Told in His Own Letters* (London: Macmillan, 1884), Vol. I, p. 155.

[24] A. M. Ramsey, *F. D. Maurice and the Conflicts of Modern Theology* (Cambridge: Cambridge University Press, 1951), p. 34.

[25] C. F. Andrews, *North India* (London: Mowbray, 1908), p. 134.

> What is needed is a clear Christian apologetic suited to the East, sympathetic and discriminating, showing the fulfilment in the Incarnation of the longing for the Presence of God manifest in the flesh, which Hinduism represents but fails to satisfy.[26]

One should recall here J. N. Farquhar's prefatory thanks in *The Crown of Hinduism* (1913) to Andrews, "who read the whole work in manuscript with extreme care and made many suggestions of great value".[27] It may have been at about this time that Andrews was writing:

> We may surely believe that the Eternal Word was the Light of Buddha and Tulsi Das in their measure, even as He was, in so much greater a degree, the Light of the Hebrew Prophets.[28]

At this time, too, much in the manner of Farquhar, he was saying that "Hinduism, great and lofty as it is, must die and be reborn before it can live in Christ".[29]

That Andrews soon moved beyond this carefully qualified position, under the influence of Tagore and Munshi Ram, we find substantiated first in the correspondence with the latter. He wrote to him that he sensed in Munshi Ram's love for him "the nearness of that presence", and that this made him "long to learn more and more ... the meaning of the unity of our spiritual natures one with another in the Divine".[30] An elaborate rationalization of this experience is to be found in the long essay "The Body of Humanity" (first version in *The Modern Review* for September

---

[26] Andrews, *North India*, p. 202.
[27] J. N. Farquhar, *The Crown of Hinduism* (London: Oxford University Press, 1913), p. 4.
[28] Andrews, *The Renaissance in India*, p. 167.
[29] "The Indian Missionary ideal", *The East and the West*, January 1911, pp. 46-7. See also Farquhar, *The Crown of Hinduism*, pp. 50-1: "In the philosophy and theistic theology of Hinduism there are many precious truths enshrined; but ... Hinduism must die in order to live. It must die into Christianity."
[30] Correspondence with Munshi Ram. Letters of 24 April and 12 June 1913.

and October 1913), with its view of "the different religions as forming together one organic whole".

Nicol Macnicol, in his study of Andrews, suggested that the basis of this view rested on a limitation in Andrews' understanding of Hinduism:

> When... Andrews speaks of Hinduism as he saw it in the religion of his two friends (Tagore and Gandhi) he is not really speaking of what we may call central Hinduism.[31]

Macnicol explains that by "central" he means monistic Hinduism. It is true that Andrews expressed "only a faint and distant sympathy" with the philosophy of Advaita Vedanta,[32] and that his appreciation of Hinduism (and of Islam, Buddhism and Sikhism) limited by a rather perfunctory grasp of Indian languages[33] was supported by the frequent reiteration of a very limited set of texts, illustrating, for example, "the principle of overcoming evil by the perfect submission and sacrifice of love",[34] but it would be wrong to suggest, therefore, that he had no knowledge, let alone appreciation, of "central" Hinduism. Probably Macnicol was unaware of Andrews' "dialogue" with Munshi Ram. This dialogue, as observed by a close friend, indicates a more subtle and sophisticated position:

> Many, indeed most, of his ideas were poles asunder from those of C. F. A.... But C. F. A. listened patiently, made no comment on what was repellent... One could see "that of God" in the intellectual and spiritual outfit of Mahatma Munshi Ram being reached, emphasized, developed.[35]

---

[31] N. Macnicol, *C. F. Andrews: Friend of India* (London: J. Clarke, 1944), p. 89.

[32] *In the Woods of God-Realization*, or *The Complete Works of Swami Rama Turtha, M. A., of Lahore* (Delhi, 1910), Vol. I, p. xxvi (Introduction by Andrews).

[33] I am grateful to Mrs. C. B. Young for this observation.

[34] "The Body of Humanity", later version, reprinted in *Visvabharati Quarterly* 36 (1970–1), p. 158.

[35] J. S. Hoyland, *C. F. Andrews: Minister of Reconciliation* (London: Allenson & Co., 1940), p. 15. See also above, p. 54.

Similarly, we may note that he found it possible to declare, as a delegate of the Cow-Protection Society of Calcutta, at a conference at Vrindaban in 1921, that he had for many years "taken a deep interest in the question of cow-protection".[36] The same visit to Vrindaban led to an expression of profound appreciation of "the Sannyas ideal" of the Vaishnava devotees: "This picture of utter loneliness with God had often impressed me in my reading of Christ's life in the Gospels."[37] Andrews' sense of an organic unity beneath the outward differences of religion, at this period, then, however else we may judge it, did not rest on a partial view of Hinduism—partial as any Westerner's or indeed any man's might be—but on a sensitivity to "divine beauty, truth and love"[38] wherever he identified these across the Hindu spectrum.

Andrews' understanding of Hinduism in the third phase of his theological development in India was modified, as we have suggested, by the recovery and expansion of his apprehension of the universal Christ, and by his developed capacity, in the light of his friendship with Gandhi, for objectivity with regard to the faith of his friends. In particular, as his paper on "The Hindu View of Christ" indicates, he came to see that what he called "the harmonizing tendency within Hinduism", for all his appreciation of it, could only function in the context of an almost entire lack of appreciation of what may be called the "historical sense". He spells out this issue elsewhere:

> ... in the Word made flesh, the Babe of Bethlehem, the Crucified, the Risen Saviour, we have only one concrete fact we need to focus all our dimly beautiful imaginings. We have the one central point from which all the crystallization of our highest thoughts about the eternal and infinite may begin. We have left the purely negative region of philosophical abstraction, and are back once more in the dear, lovable, concrete world of flesh and blood, of shape and form, of individual and personal existence. "Neti, Neti" ("He is not that, He is not that"), was the negative conclusion

---

[36] "The Protection of Cows in India", *The Leader*, 4 September 1921.
[37] "Vrindaban", *Modern Review*, October 1921, p. 463.
[38] Andrews, *What I Owe to Christ*, p. 153.

of the metaphysical mind of the East, but Tulsi Das expressed the deepest need of the human heart when he turned to the philosopher and cried, "Sir, show us the Incarnate!"[39]

At the same time, along with this more rigorous evaluation of Hinduism, we may note in this final phase a frequently repeated demand for a Christ-like sympathy with men of other faiths. Andrews' developed position, then, with regard to religions, was surprisingly close to that of other liberal-orthodox Christian thinkers in this period. One has in mind the British delegation to the Conference of the International Missionary Council at Jerusalem in 1928, which included William Temple, Charles Raven and Oliver Quick. Hallencreutz sums up their distinctive and "very significant" contribution on the relation of Christianity to religions as one "spoken of in terms of witness to the Revelation in Christ and of Christian solidarity with the non-Christian".[40] If Andrews' universalism seems to have taken him slightly beyond this position, it was certainly in a very similar direction that his later thought moved.

Andrews' understanding of evangelism and conversion is closely related to his experience and understanding of Hinduism. Two important factors were: the dislike of any approach by the Christian which implied an attitude of superiority, reminiscent of the "religious exclusiveness which so deeply offended Christ and called forth His severest condemnation";[41] and, more positively, "the indubitable *experience* of the presence of the Spirit of God among men who are not Christians".[42] His understanding of the question of evangelism and conversion was undoubtedly tempered by these factors.

---

[39] Andrews, *Christ in the Silence*, p. 180.
[40] C. F. Hallencreutz, *Kraemer Towards Tambaram: A Study in Henrik Kraemer's Missionary Approach* (Uppsala, Sweden: Gleerups Forlag, 1966), p. 192.
[41] Andrews, *What I Owe to Christ*, p. 253.
[42] Sykes and Chaturvedi, *Charles Freer Andrews*, p. 311.

An early expression of a view not dissimilar from that of William Miller and Bernard Lucas[43] is to be found in an article he wrote for Macnicol and Robertson's *The Indian Interpreter* of October, 1909:

> I am led more and more by missionary experience to regard the conversion of India, not as the aggregate of so many individual conversions, but far rather as a gradual process of growth and change in thought, idea, feeling, temperament, conduct—a process which half creates and half reconstructs a truly Christian religious atmosphere, Indian at its best, and Christian at its best ... This does not of course mean that I cease to believe in the conversion of the individual, but I seem to see other and more silent processes of the Spirit, which lead, it may be, to more distant, but no less important results.

A gloss on this idea is added by his remark in *India in Transition* (1910):

> If Christianity is to succeed, it must not come forward as an antagonist and a rival to the great religious strivings of the past. It must come as a helper and a fulfiller, a peace-maker and a friend. There must no longer be the desire to capture converts from Hinduism, but to come to her aid in the needful time of trouble and to help her in the fulfilment of duties she has long neglected.[44]

No doubt Andrews was encouraged in this view by Rudra, one of whose observations on the subject he records:

> I find it difficult sometimes to read St Paul's Epistles. He is like you Englishmen—always trying to force someone to his own point of view and "compassing sea and land to make one proselyte." Christ

---

[43] For an exposition of their "liberal" approach, see K. Baago, *Pioneers of Indigenous Christianity* (Bangalore and Madras, 1969), pp. 75–80.

[44] C. F. Andrews, *India in Transition*. Cambridge Mission to Delhi, unnumbered occasional papers (London: London Missionary Society, 1910), p. 12.

himself is free from such forceful methods to obtain success. His great parable is that of the seed growing secretly. The East understands that hidden growth.[45]

Andrews' famous, much later, letter to Gandhi on conversion shows that he never ceased to believe in the conversion of the individual, while he continued to maintain his Christo-centric universalism. Perhaps his most successful conflation of these two convictions is to be found in the preparatory paper that he wrote in 1938 for the Tambaram Conference of the I.M.C.[46] when referring to his experience of the Spirit of God among men who were not Christians, he continued:

> These very questionings drove me back to Christ Himself and the result was revolutionary. The scales fell from my eyes, and I saw with a thrill of joy how all outer names and titles—all man-made distinctions—were superseded in the light of the one supreme test, love to God and love to man. This was the Gospel, the good tidings—a gospel from God worth bringing down from Heaven. This is the vision of Him which impels His followers to go out to distant lands across the sea. We go out, not merely to quicken those who are dead in trespasses, but also to welcome with joy His radiant presence in those who have seen from afar His glory.[47]

It remains to say something of the theology underlying Andrews' social concerns.

First of all, the national movement. He saw, and expressed frankly his belief in the fundamental significance of the contribution of missions, and also of western imperialism, not least in its educational role, to the Indian awakening. However, as M. M. Thomas has pointed out, Andrews' understanding of the place education and missionary education had played, reflected "the sea-change taking place in the theological climate

---

[45] Andrews, *What I Owe to Christ*, p. 167.
[46] International Missionary Council. (Eds.)
[47] From a Tambaram preparatory paper, quoted in Sykes and Chaturvedi, *Charles Freer Andrews*, p. 311.

by the early decades of the twentieth century"[48] in that he saw the limitation of the older educational policy of substituting western culture for Hindu, and advocated rather a policy of Christian assimilation, which would utilize "the deepest springs of Indian national life", so that "the wealth of English literature, science and culture would be grafted on to the original stock of Indian thought and experience".[49] Going even further, in the light of his understanding of the Logos doctrine, he was able to say to his students in Delhi:

> You can never repeat the past, but you can learn noble lessons from it, lessons with regard to those great words that ring today in modern ideas, "humanity, liberty, freedom". You can learn these lessons, I repeat, not merely from the literature of the West, but here in India, here from the lips of your own Indian people, here from the history of your own Indian race, here from the lives of your own Indian fellow countrymen. You can trace those lives as they were lived in the past by Indian men and Indian women ... lived with many faults and imperfections, it is true, as all human lives are, but lived with a remarkable amount of freedom, humanity, unity, spontaneity.
>
> When you have learnt these lessons from the past, then go back to your own experience of India today and compare those earlier times, thoughtfully, carefully, scientifically, with your own and ask the question for your own practical life, "What present bonds of custom can I unloose, what chain of impeding habit can I unbind, in order to take my share in building up a new India not unworthy of the old?"[50]

And pointing to contemporary India, even to such an avowedly anti-Christian movement as the Arya Samaj, he claimed to discern the

---

[48] M. M. Thomas, *The Acknowledged Christ of the Indian Renaissance* (Madras, 1970), p. 254.
[49] *The Renaissance in India*, pp. 38, 39.
[50] "Indian History: Its Lessons for Today", *St Stephen's College Magazine*, November, 1908, p. 18.

providential guidance of "the great Artificer, making all things new".[51] Here, surely, in such perceptions, liberal orthodoxy provides a profound and meaningful dimension to "the theology of national renaissance".

Andrews recognized perhaps uniquely early the theological—and indeed human—significance of M. K. Gandhi. In an article in *The Modern Review* for December 1907 he was quoting an Indian friend to the effect that:

> In the East the idea is everything and advance is not made by material circumstances merely, but by personal devotion of multitudes towards the *guru* who sacrifices himself for the idea.

His visit to South Africa in early 1914, to assist Gandhi in the struggle for Indian rights there, disclosed for him the "guru" that the Indian situation demanded: "Mr. Gandhi has shown to the world, in practice, that which we have all been groping after—a moral equivalent for war."[52] This equivalent, as he immediately saw, was deeply Christian in spirit. In many places thereafter, he points to Christ-like aspects of Gandhi's actions. Nowhere does he push the Logos doctrine further than in his account of the Delhi Fast, with its cautious but unmistakable hints of analogies with the Atonement. At the same time, where he found grounds for disagreeing with Gandhi, and there were many—Thomas points out that "they revolve round Gandhiji's equation of the essential self of man with the *atman* and the consequent rejection of the body and all matter as the source of all selfishness"[53]—he was not slow to draw attention to them.

His three books on Gandhi are very important. Gandhi spoke many times of his close relationship with Andrews, "than whom I do not own on this earth a closer friend".[54] This gives them a uniqueness within the

---

[51] "Hardwar and its Gurukula", *Modern Review*, March 1913, p. 335.
[52] "Mr. Gandhi Vindicated", *Modern Review*, June 1914, p. 586.
[53] Thomas, *The Acknowledged Christ of the Indian Renaissance*, p. 226.
[54] C. F. Andrews, *Mahatma Gandhi's Ideas* (London: Allen & Unwin, 1920), p. 93. The three books referred to are, in fact, by Gandhi and edited by Andrews. The other two are *Mahatma Gandhi: His Own Story* (1930) and *Mahatma Gandhi at Work* (1931) (Eds.).

corpus of books on Gandhi. The clarification that they effected of the character and ideas of Gandhi was an attempt to dispel the profound distrust in England of Gandhi's integrity of purpose in a period of intense constitutional negotiation. That the attempt failed to a large extent tells us more about the reactionary nature of official British attitudes, both in India and Britain, than it does about the books themselves. They are extremely valuable books in a further respect. To say simply that Andrews "edited" them, conceals their significance as a disclosure of some of the chief features of Hindu-Christian dialogue as it has to be conducted: throughout, Gandhi's views are not merely quoted and described, but discussions with Andrews and others are recorded, and Gandhi's ideas are examined and analysed in the sympathetic light of Andrews' own Christian beliefs. The books, then, represent a standing illustration of dialogue on the Hindu-Christian frontier.

Another aspect of Andrews' thought on the national movement with theological implications was his interest in the arts, painting and poetry in particular. Not only did he set an example in a modest way with his own poems, but he also saw and drew attention to the important role of the arts in establishing specific moral and spiritual values in the process of nation-building, and in the assertion and expression of cultural identity.

Starting from his own knowledge of western literature—for example, Shakespeare, whom he sees in the context of "the triumph of English nationality over Spanish imperialism"—and arguing that "nationality, when it touches the heart of a great people, is itself a spiritual thing", he suggests that

> ... when a nation as a whole moves forward into higher freedom and self-consciousness, new spiritual powers are awakened and a new environment is fashioned, wherein the highest literature and art may flourish.[55]

Having thus established the "spiritual" dimension of the role of art in the development of a nation, it is not surprising to find him drawing attention to the riches of Indian art both past and present, particularly

---

[55] "Shakespeare and Nationality", *Modern Review*, July 1907, pp. 65–8.

among the latter "the delicate tender Eastern paintings of Abanindra, the music and poetry of Rabindranath Tagore",[56] and seeking to persuade his readers that "literature and art are ... mighty forces making for national development".[57]

It is worth noting also how energetically Andrews shared his appreciation of the work of Tagore, with the quite deliberate intention of inspiring respect for Indian culture, for example among the administrators at Simla and the ruling whites of South Africa, and so of undermining the prevailing attitudes of racial superiority. In Cape Town he noted, of his lecture on Tagore, that "many have said that this actually brought about the beginning of the change which led up to the passing of the Indian Relief Act".[58] He used this same lecture also as a means of inspiring Indian self-respect, for as soon as he had initially delivered it before the Viceroy and his party at Simla, he repeated it in the Arya Samaj Mandir in the lower bazaar, "the room ... crowded and the windows even ... full of people listening from the outside", an event which led to invitations to speak elsewhere in Simla, at the Bengali Kari-bari Club and the Brahma Mandir.[59]

Before Ezra Pound had made his memorable observation that "Tagore has sung Bengal into a nation",[60] Andrews was pointing out how through a whole group of writers in Bengal there was "a whole people awakening to self-conscious national life".[61] Not that he allowed his enthusiasm to obscure what were for him the wider implications of the national movement:

> Let India be true to herself, her own instincts, her own innate genius; let her bring forth her own treasures boldly, yet with simplicity, and the best minds everywhere will receive her into that noblest of all fellowships—the fellowship of the good and

---

[56] "National Literature and Art", *Modern Review*, November 1908, p. 365.
[57] "National Literature and Art", p. 366.
[58] *Biographical Notes*, p. 125.
[59] Correspondence with Munshi Ram, letter of 31 May 1913.
[60] In *The Fortnightly Review*, March 1913. (Eds.)
[61] "Toru Dutt: A Memoir", *Modern Review*, February 1911, p. 147.

wise. At the same time, let her throw all the energies of her new awakening into the uplifting of the poor. Then the whole people will advance towards a greater and larger life, and the new literary revival will not dwindle down to the selfish pleasures of a Palace of Art from which the cries of suffering humanity are excluded.[62]

Nor was Andrews slow to draw out the implications in all this for the Church. Reviewing in 1915 a book on western art, "a supreme witness to the spirit of Christ", he exclaims:

> What a revolution it would make in the Indian Christian Church if the spirit of this book could be assimilated and Beauty (as felt in painting, music and poetry) were allowed to have its true place in the newly awakened consciousness of young Indian Christians. How, with one breath of healthy fresh air, would all the ugly decorations and paraphernalia of our churches, along with all bad tunes and bad poetry of our hymn-books, be blown clean away ... never to return![63]

An aspect of Andrews' social concern which he interestingly links with the significance of art, music and poetry for both the national movement and the assimilation of Christianity in India, is the position of women in Indian society. He points out in an important chapter on "Indian Womanhood" in *The Renaissance in India*, that:

> It is in literature and philanthropy that the greatest triumphs of educated Indian women have been won ... Sarojini Naidu and Sarola Devi are names well known over all India for their interest in social reform and also for their literary power ... At the Calcutta National Congress in 1906, one of the most striking features was the assembly of Bengali ladies who led the singing of the songs of new Bengal.[64]

---

[62] "An Evening with Rabindra", *Modern Review*, August 1912, p. 228.
[63] *Young Men of India*, June 1915, pp. 297–8.
[64] Andrews, *The Renaissance in India*, pp. 209, 210.

He goes on to suggest that this represents in fact a reconstruction of a lost religious ideal enshrined in, for example, the *Ramayana*.

Turning to the important role of Indian Christians with artistic gifts, women like Aru and Toru Dutt, and Krupabai Satthianadhan, he expresses the interesting conviction that:

> The naturalization of the Christian message amidst Indian conditions of life and thought will take place through the medium of art, music, and poetry more than through the channels of controversy and hard reasoning.[65]

Andrews' own profound attachment to his mother and her memory, reinforced later by the powerful impression he received of the distinctive role of women in the struggle in South Africa, served to substantiate his belief in the importance of Indian womanhood in the Indian awakening, an importance such that he was led to the conclusion that the advance of female education represented "a great advance" in the national movement, in comparison with which the earlier stages were "but tiny steps",[66] and to his perspicacious observation that:

> If there is any country in the East about which it would be safe to prophesy that woman will take a leading part in the regeneration of society, it surely is India.[67]

Closely interlocking with Andrews' commitment to the struggle for Indian nationhood were other social concerns, each with an equally careful theological underpinning.

He saw the need to end the practice of indenture of Indian labourers very much as an aspect of the national movement, and so of the struggle for spiritual integrity and personal freedom. While his work in this field,

---

[65] Andrews, *The Renaissance in India*, p. 220.
[66] Andrews, *The Renaissance in India*, p. 232.
[67] Andrews, *The Renaissance in India*, p. 208.

"his greatest single service to the Indian people",[68] was very largely a matter of careful compilation and publication of statistics and persistent discussion with the British colonial authorities and what he called "the Capitalists", his initial inspiration lay in a vivid vision of a suffering Indian labourer in Natal as Christ.[69] Similarly, the necessity of extending the struggle was for Andrews a spiritual necessity: "Christ was calling me to go out to Fiji."[70]

Even before he learned of the specific injustice of indenture, indeed almost as soon as he had set foot in India, Andrews had become aware of the racist component of imperialism, and set about exposing it. Always he started from the identification of prejudice and set against it the contrary evidence of observation, and always the religious dimension is included. A good early example is the series of three essays, "Indian Character— An Appreciation", where the gifts and virtues of Indian character are presented to be regarded "with all thankfulness as precious treasures worthy to be brought within the City of God".[71]

His concern with racialism, however, was not confined to the treatment of the Indian people, but was a concern with racial prejudice in all its manifestations. This led him to remind his Indian friends that Indian well-being in Africa could not be achieved apart from the struggle for dignity for the African; it led him to concern himself with the plight of the African American in the United States, and to protest in Germany in 1937 against the persecution of the Jews; and when he spoke at the Tambaram Conference of the I. M. C., he chose the subject of "Inter-racial Reconciliation". Characteristically, he did not ignore the fact of racialism within the Indian social system; speaking to a student audience, he used terms to which they could respond: "The Upanishads tell us further that the Advaitam is also the Avarna—He is without colour, or

---

[68] A British administrator's estimate, quoted in Sykes and Chaturvedi, *Charles Freer Andrews*, p. 126.

[69] Andrews, *What I Owe to Christ*, p. 284.

[70] Andrews, *What I Owe to Christ*, p. 285. For the full poem, "The Indentured Coolie", see above, p. 84.

[71] *Delhi Mission News*, July 1905, p. 86; also October 1905 and January 1906.

caste distinction."[72] More frequently and more normally, his appeal was simply and unequivocally to the Jesus of the Gospels, born of a despised race and yet preaching and practising forgiveness, and to two favourite Pauline texts, Galatians 3:28 and Ephesians 2:14.

A final important aspect of Andrews' social concern—going back directly to the influence of Westcott, was with regard to the issue of rich and poor, capital and labour. Again, there was a strikingly practical side to his concern, well illustrated in his role in the 1920s as President of the All India Trade Union Congress at one of the most critical stages of its development. Specifically in the Indian situation, including here the case of the Indian indentured labourers overseas as a part of the Indian situation, Andrews' thought and action related almost invariably to the relationships of western capital labour, so that the problem interlocked with those of imperialism and racism. (It is not therefore surprising that a newspaper like *The Englishman*, in a leader of 24 June 1921, on "Indians and Strikes", after accusing Andrews' of emotionalism, remarked that "his utterances savour a good deal of communism"!) Because of the connections of this issue with those of imperialism and racism, and probably because of his early acquaintance with Keir Hardie and his reflections on the labour–capital conflict in Britain, and because of his theological presuppositions, Andrews was at heart an internationalist, moved by the instinctive internationalism of the poor:

> When I think today of the problem of the relation of India to England, I have no hope whatever for the upper classes. A few of them will be unselfish, but the great majority will be undoubtedly selfish and India will be exploited by them if she is not strong enough to stand out against them. My one hope for the poor of the world is that these poor people in every country... may in one way or another learn to sympathize with one another and help one another... There is more brotherhood among the poor of every race than among all the rest of the world put together.[73]

---

[72] Address to the Assam Students' Conference, 1924. Reprinted in *Vishvabharati Quarterly* 36 (1970–1).

[73] *Biographical Notes*, p. 71.

Just as he felt the solidarity of the poor to be a reality, so, too, he saw the solidarity of oppression:

> Mystically, the name of this new world city is still Babylon— Babylon the Great. But in modern history its name is London and Paris and Berlin, Calcutta and Tokyo, New York and Buenos Aires, Johannesburg and San Francisco, and many other names besides... It has become coterminous with the human race itself in its greed and rapacity, in its gigantic and crushing material organization, in its traffic for the souls of men.[74]

Andrews' interest in workers' movements was not limited to India, Britain and the British colonies. The Russian and Chinese revolutions were also noted, if with the caution of an outsider. In the Preface to *Christ and Human Need* (1937), a further variant on his original Burney Prize essay,[75] he writes of the relation of the Christian faith to communism, "as it has been expounded by Karl Marx and practised to a certain degree in Soviet Russia", as the most "urgent and exciting" aspect of the labour problem. In the same place, he points to "the most searching and difficult" lesson to be learned from a historical study of the labour problem: " ... the failure that always comes from the short-sighted use of violent means ... and the fallacy of short-cuts".[76] This is not to say that he could not understand and sympathize with those driven to desperate measures, "the uprising at last of the down-trodden peasantry of agricultural Asia against age-long tyranny and oppression":

> Owing to their untold miseries, whole provinces have cast off the central role of the Nanking Government, and ... are now in revolt. They have joined the Soviet Republics in a mass revolution born of despair and misery.

---

[74] *Christ and Labour*, Chapter 11.
[75] Awarded in the University of Cambridge in the field of philosophy of religion. (Eds.)
[76] C. F. Andrews, *Christ and Human Need* (London: Hodder & Stoughton, 1937), Preface.

In the light of this, Andrews reminds his readers of developments in India, "where the misery of the peasant remains almost unrelieved", developments which: " ... point forward to an epoch-making change of attitude in the future".[77]

If we are to reconcile this sympathy with those who go for rapid and revolutionary change with his rejection of "the short-sighted use of violent means", we are to find the reconciliation in the methods of Gandhi, in which Andrews had learned to see "the true significance of the Sermon on the Mount—not as an unpractical ideal, but as the most practical of all methods of overcoming evil in this world".[78] He claimed to have found an added theological validation of the message of Gandhi in Simkovitch's *Towards the Understanding of Jesus* (1921), where it is argued that:

> ... the great and fundamental cleavage (between Christ's method and that of both the Pharisees and the Zealots) was constituted by Christ's non-resistance to Rome.[79]

This is not to say that Andrews advocated or believed that Gandhi advocated non-resistance. On the contrary:

> The last memorandum that Andrews ever wrote was a protest against the impression which he felt had been given by one of the Metropolitan's broadcasts, that from the Christian point of view any resistance, even non-violent resistance, to injustice and oppression was wrong. "Our Lord", he wrote, "was in the direct line of the great Prophets. He made no secret of his own opposition to the Herodians. He challenged the State rulers in Jerusalem on the debased and corrupt form of their own

---

[77] "Asia in Revolution", *Modern Review*, October 1932, pp. 373–4.
[78] *Christ and Human Need*, Preface.
[79] V. G. Simkovitch, *Towards the Understanding of Jesus* (New York, 1921), p. 41.

theocratic rule. He fearlessly dealt, from first to last, with public affairs."[80]

At another level, however, he spoke with perhaps even greater conviction and out of even more profound personal experience:

> But pain that is futile and cruel; evil that is outrageous and monstrous—can any light be thrown here by the gospel of Christ? There are certain words of Christ and His apostles which speak of these sufferings themselves—so apparently meaningless and cruel—as being nothing less than the travail pains which have to be borne if the birth of the new order of mankind is not to be frustrated. Therefore they are to be welcomed, even with joy, as the messengers of good things to come ... Both in Man and Nature there appears to be the deep inscrutable need of some ultimate travail-pain, in which Christ Himself shares, some agony endured to the bitter end by voluntary surrender which almost takes the form of joy. Only thus can Man rise, by a supreme venture of faith, into his full spiritual manhood.[81]

Andrews' interest in spirituality was very practical. It was for him not a subject for academic study, but the very core of his life: " ... the inner life in Christ ... the fountain-head of outward speech and action".[82] He wrote a good deal on prayer and spirituality, his letters to Munshi Ram being the most interesting early pointers to his developing viewpoint, but undoubtedly *Christ in the Silence* (1933) is his most revealing and attractive work in this field. This is not surprising. It is based on the Last Discourses of our Lord, Chapters 13 to 17 of St John's Gospel, which he recalled devotedly from his childhood when he had listened to them in the Catholic Apostolic Church's Holy Week Liturgy in the church in Summer Hill Terrace in Birmingham. He describes them as far more familiar to me

---

[80] Sykes and Chaturvedi, *Charles Freer Andrews*, p. 315.
[81] Andrews, *Christ in the Silence*, pp. 253, 254, 257.
[82] Andrews, *Christ in the Silence*, p. 11.

than any other part of the New Testament",[83] their great sayings speaking to much as, in Hinduism "... the teacher whispers in silence some sacred text, or *mantram*, into the ear of the young initiate, which will remain in his mind as a lifelong possession".[84] Recalling, too, the stress which Westcott had placed on St John's Gospel as having a peculiar relevance to India, Andrews had stated his intention as early as 1909 of writing a devotional commentary on these chapters.[85] Throughout the book, he draws attention to the appeal that these chapters already held for Indians, among them P. C. Mozoomdar, to whom this Gospel spoke "in his own religious language, making him in the highest sense a Christian Bhakta,[86] a devotee of Christ".[87] It is precisely in these terms that Andrews, in the Introduction, describes his own spiritual life:

> It has been along this ... pathway of *bhakti* (devotion) ... as a Christian Bhakta, that my own inner life has found true unity and completeness in Christ.[88]

Elsewhere, in fact several times, he describes this experience as one of "Christ's friendship":

> Life itself would have been utterly different if the sense of Christ's presence had been absent and the joy of His friendship had been unknown.[89]

---

[83] Andrews, *Christ in the Silence*, p. 46.
[84] Andrews, *Christ in the Silence*, p. 57.
[85] *The S. P. G. and Cambridge Mission in Delhi and the South Punjab. The 31st Report* (1909), p. 29.
[86] In Sanskrit, Bhakta means "faithful" or "devoted". (Eds.)
[87] Andrews, *Christ in the Silence*, p. 102.
[88] Andrews, *Christ in the Silence*, p. 14. Andrews does not indicate that he was aware of Appasamy's work in this field.
[89] Andrews, *Christ in the Silence*, p. 240.

He is emphatic that this experience "cannot possibly be put down to imagination, for it has gone deeper into character itself and changed my whole nature. It is . . . a *moral* certainty."[90]

A number of other features of this book are of interest in a study of Andrews' theology. For example, he makes frequent reference to the dynamism of the West, which he sees in all its ambivalence:

> The thrill and excitement of this new speed of human activity . . . and faith in the future had clearly its own place in the Kingdom of God . . . But there was a strained look upon the faces where peace ought to have had its throne.[91]

Over against this, he contrasts Indian personalities, Christian and Hindu, whom he had come to know well:

> As with Sadhu Sundar Singh, so . . . I found in Rabindranath Tagore . . . a depth and stillness and quiet calm which I had never personally witnessed with such intensity before.[92]

But in making this contrast, he adds a distinction: "The East has its own dangers to the life of the soul . . . There is a deadly calm, like a miasma, over many lands in the East, altogether different from the living peace of Santiniketan."[93] In another place, still making the East–West contrast, he observes that

> This simple personal devotion to Jesus as the one living Way to God was the earliest and deepest loyalty of the Christian Church. Even before the word "Christian" was used, first at Antioch, the followers of Jesus were called the "people of the Way" . . . In the

---

[90] Andrews, *Christ in the Silence*, p. 131.
[91] Andrews, *Christ in the Silence*, pp. 28–9.
[92] Andrews, *Christ in the Silence*, p. 18.
[93] Andrews, *Christ in the Silence*, pp, 30, 267. Santiniketan is a district of Bolpur, a town in West Bengal established by the father of Rabindranath Tagore, under whose subsequent vision it became a university town.

> midst of the ever-increasing complexity of modern life, which binds us to formal routine both in Church and State, we long intensely to get back to this simple personal devotion as the centre and crown of our own lives. In the East this thought of the Way, with a personal leader to guide, is very well known. The Kabir Panth and the Dadu Panth offer examples of such a course, which the religious life of India instinctively follows. May we not learn from the East, where Christ and His disciples began their ministry of healing and blessing, to return once more to these simplicities rather than ourselves impose upon the East our own complex religious systems?[94]

In similar contradistinction from the "divided and distracted modern world", Andrews quotes two Christian hymns, one by Ellen Lakshmi Goreh, daughter of Nehemiah Goreh, the other a Delhi *bhajan*, which "give something of the atmosphere of India as it is felt in Christian worship".[95]

In another reference to Kabir, after suggesting common factors in all mystical experience, he goes on to add that that Christian spirituality, in the way that it takes suffering into account, is a uniquely comprehensive type:

> It is true also that far beyond the boundaries of Christendom the pure in heart, who seek God, find Him with serene joy according to His good promise. Kabir, that greatest of the Northern Indian saints, cries from the depth of his heart, "Joy for ever! No sorrow, no struggle! There have I seen joy, filled to the brim, perfection of joy!" We may thank God with all our hearts when we find how universal this note is in every mystical faith, and cherish every one of these great sayings of the saints. But there is found in Christ Himself, and in those who follow Him along the royal highway of the Cross, a strange and beautiful intermingling of suffering and joy that gives a new note in the glorious harmony of

---

[94] Andrews, *Christ in the Silence*, pp. 154–5.
[95] Andrews, *Christ in the Silence*, p. 269.

heaven's music; and this new note of joy in suffering, when once it has been learnt, can never be forgotten. It haunts the memory of mankind. It is surely the "new song" before the throne, which only those can sing who are "redeemed from the earth" and "follow the Lamb whithersoever He goeth".[96]

That Andrews did not regard baptism as delimiting the company of the redeemed, we have noted elsewhere, and his comment in the Introduction, that Gandhi had "interpreted through his actions" much that he had tried to write about at first-hand in this book, is a salutary reminder of this.

The place of suffering in Christian discipleship is presented elsewhere in *Christ in the Silence* in sacramental terms:

> ... we shall rejoice to be counted worthy to suffer with Him; and at each Communion of His body broken and His blood outpoured we shall renew the solemn sacrament and pledge, that we will "show forth the Lord's death until He come".[97]

Other uses of the term "sacrament" in the book relate even more directly to Andrews' concern for the practical, outward expression of the spiritual life. He writes of

> ... a dual realization of His gracious Presence, ever waiting to be fulfilled in my own life and ever ready to be made welcome. There was the sacrament of loving service in the outer world and the sacrament of silent communion in the inner chamber of the heart.[98]

Similarly:

---

[96] Andrews, *Christ in the Silence*, pp. 215–16.
[97] Andrews, *Christ in the Silence*, pp. 260–1.
[98] Andrews, *Christ in the Silence*, p. 22.

> It is equally clear that Christ's word, "Do this", with regard to the washing of the feet and the new commandment, is no less incumbent on us than the "Do this" of the Eucharist itself. For these acts are also a sacrament. In every fulfilment of the commands of humility and love, we "do show forth the Lord's death until he come". We keep Christ in remembrance. His humility is to be our humility. The love of Christ is to be our own love. The great words of the Gospel, "So God loved the world", must be illustrated by our example and set forth in our lives.[99]

There is, finally, an insistence on the necessary integration of inner and outer for the person who is "in Christ":

> In Christ ... love to God and love to my fellow-men become inseparably one. Thus the spiritual life, in all its many activities, finds its true goal. It becomes a unity where Christ is the one centre.[100]

Thus, the consistency between thought and action, theology and practical life, so central to an incarnational theology, finds further support at another, perhaps deeper level of personal being.

*　*　*

From, with some editing, Daniel O'Connor, Introduction to *The Testimony of C. F. Andrews*. (Bangalore: The Christian Institute for the Study of Religion and Society, 1974), pp. 32–53.

---

[99] Andrews, *Christ in the Silence*, p. 89.
[100] Andrews, *Christ in the Silence*, p. 81.

6

Karanjia

Dan O'Connor has written two major works on the life and work of Verrier Elwin, an extensive introduction to selected writings of Elwin in *Din-Sevak: Verrier Elwin's Life of Service in Tribal India* (1993), and his Verrier Elwin Endowment Lectures for 1995 under the title *A Liberating Force and a Friend* (1996). It is from the first of these that the essay here reprinted is taken.

Verrier Elwin (1902–64) was, like C. F. Andrews, an Anglican priest, though he attended Oxford university rather than Cambridge, where he gained a double first in English and theology from Merton College. Also like Andrews, he was quickly appointed vice-principal of an Anglican theological college, in his case Wycliffe Hall, Oxford (1926–7) during which time he was ordained.

In November 1927, he travelled to India and joined J. C. (Jack) Winslow's religious community, the Christa Seva Sanhai, at Pune in western India. The ashram was founded in 1920 and was devoted to the indigenization of Indian Christianity. An early meeting with Gandhi, and the ensuing friendship between the two men, led Verrier Elwin to Karanjai, the subject of the essay here, and to his life's work among the poor tribal peoples of north India. Here his closest friend was Shamrao Hivale, whom he had met at Puna. Elwin's association with Indian nationalists prompted the disapproval of the local bishop of Nagpur, Alex Wood, and with "the utmost sorrow", Elwin formally left the Church in 1935, though his Christian spirit shone brightly to the end. During his 20 years' work among the tribal people, Elwin carried out distinguished anthropological work and, as indicated by Dan in this essay, wrote a number of books on the life and culture of the people with whom he lived.

In 1954, Nehru asked Elwin formally to address the problems of the tribal peoples of north-east India as advisor for tribals to the North-East Frontier Agency, and he moved to Shillong in Meghalaya state, where he remained for the rest of his life, becoming the first foreign national to be granted Indian citizenship. His distinctions included a Fellowship of the Indian National Science Academy, the degree of DSc from his old University of Oxford, and the Padma Bhusan, the third-highest civilian award in the Republic of India.

For Dan, Elwin is outstanding as, like Andrews, he was a Christian priest who was far ahead of his time in many ways, and in the 1930s understood the need for the Christian to moved towards postcolonialism in British India. He was very different from Andrews, a person of great personal charm, marrying into the tribal culture to which he devoted his life. In the following essay, his humour, as well as his faith and humility, are quite clear. The section which follows this piece in Dan's Introduction is entitled "Abandoned by the Church". In Dan's words, "the most careful scrutiny of the evidence makes it clear that he was driven out of and abandoned by the Church".[1] Views in this differed among his contemporaries. Richard Acland, Bishop of Bombay between 1929 and 1947, regarded Elwin's withdrawal from the Church as "a self-imposed hardship to make his penance for the wickedness of Englishmen as thorough as possible".[2] Dan observes:

> In 1950, he assured his mother in a letter that he continued to observe Christmas and the other Christian festivals, adding, "I am only out of sympathy with official Christianity, and for that matter with official Buddhism, Hinduism and Islam." A couple of years later, in a Bombay newspaper, he is quoted as saying that he believed in "Christianity and the Christian way of life". In that same decade, he arranged for the baptism of his sons.[3]

---

[1] Dan O'Connor, Introduction to *Din-Sevak: Verrier Elwin's Life of Service in Tribal India* (Delhi, 1993), p. 59.

[2] Quoted in Introduction, p. 88.

[3] Introduction, p. 59.

* * *

A few months in the company of Gandhi, and a running discussion with Hivale, helped to make clear the next step for Elwin. He had reported to his friends in England back in July 1931 how his mind was working at that time.

> ... For the last eighteen months, I have been feeling an insistent urge to a life of closer identification with the poor. And the need to give myself to work for them. I have specially felt the needs of the untouchables. I know that I am quite unfitted for such work, but recently the pressure of the interior call has become unbearable, and the Sangha has now allowed me to begin to make preparations for starting a little Ashram specially devoted to the cause of the untouchables.[4]

Somehow, between this date and the end of the year, Elwin and Hivale had modified their plans, and the combined influence of the Congress friends, in particular of A. V. Thakkar, whom Elwin called "the first inspirer of this work", and of Jamanlal Bajaj, Vallabhbhai Patel and Gandhi himself, redirected their attention towards India's tribal peoples.[5] The advice was that they should work in Central India, and on the advice of the local bishop, the Bishop of Nagpur, they settled upon a Gond village called Karanjia....

....Here, on a little hill above the village where they had their "original shed", at the end of January 1932, they built the small huts of mud, bamboo and thatch which constituted the Ashram of St Francis, and its accompanying Gond Seva Mandal, while all around them, in those early days, "lay the vast mysterious forest, whose silence was broken at night

---

[4] Circular letter of Elwin, 2 July 1931. (cC)
[5] Letter to members of the Eremo, 8 November 1934. (cE) (Letters from Elwin to Sorello Amata and Nonna Speranza of the Eremo Francescano, Trevi, Italy.) The Indian National Congress was founded in 1885. Gandhi became its president in 1921. (Eds)

only by the roar of the tiger or the high melancholy call of the deer".[6] It was here, and in one or two similar places in central India, that Elwin and Hivale were to spend almost the whole of the next quarter century. It was an extraordinary venture for this immensely gifted Oxford graduate and his Mirfield trained Indian friend. The impulse and inspiration lay in their deep sense of vocation to an evangelical identification with the poor in their poverty...

... The story of these early years at Karanjia is wonderfully recorded, with great sensitivity and a hilarious sense of humour, in Elwin's *Leaves from the Jungle: Life in a Gond Village*, published in 1936 and largely made up of extracts from his diaries for these first four years. The conclusion of Romain Rolland's prefatory note gives some impression of the impact Elwin was making, and puts the venture into some perspective:

> In Africa, Albert Schweitzer, the philosopher: in India, Verrier Elwin the poet.[7]

....From the beginning, living "among these poorest of the poor", Elwin was moved and appalled by the plight of the tribal people: their "endless, limitless suffering" was "a cancer eating out ... (his) heart and giving no rest". Daily, he and Hivale had to "bear the terrible sight of utter poverty and desolation". Travelling further afield, on his first tour of enquiry and study among the Baigas, he wrote:

> Some of the things I saw keep me awake at night—the diseases and the hunger and nakedness, and the more than Satanic—the Beelzebubic—behaviour of the civilized world to these unhappy people.

---

[6] Verrier Elwin, *The Tribal World of Verrier Elwin* (London: Oxford University Press, 1964) (TW), p. 102. This autobiographical work was published posthumously, three months after Elwin's death. (Eds.)

[7] Verrier Elwin, *Leaves from the Jungle: Life in a Gond Village* (London: Oxford University Press, 1936), p. 7.

Such was the impact of all this that he was compelled to ask, "When will God visit his people?"[8] He was surprised that, in amongst the very favourable reviewing of *Leaves from the Jungle*, there was a criticism that it was too light-hearted and humorous.

> Our life here isn't nearly frivolous enough ... here where the poverty, disease, oppression and sheer stupidity is a constant nightmare that it almost crushes you, every chuckle is a spiritual triumph.

In the same way, he was stung by a remark at the outset of the Second World War about the fact that, at Karanjia he was far from all that:

> Remember that though a Great War might kill a million soldiers, malaria kills over ten million annually in India alone, and there are nearly a million lepers in India ... War, I know, carries off the youth of a country. But our people cannot expect, on an average, a span of life exceeding 20 years. Someone said to me, "You at least are safe." But what is more dangerous, the malarial plasmodia, the treponema pallidum, the lepra bacillus, or the bomb?[9]

Not that Elwin was content simply to bemoan the lot of his new neighbours. He described the Gonds as "one of the victim races of the earth", and clarified their poverty in very simple, direct terms:

> The other day the Sub-Inspector of Police told me that he had in his safe the sum of 4,000 rupees, which had been collected as revenue from the villages in our valley, that is, from people whose average *annual* income (after taxes have been paid) is from 10 to

---

[8] cE 7 February 1932, Letters to Family (cF) 1 July 1935.
[9] cC, 8 April 1937.

12 rupees. 4,000 rupees is, incidentally, the monthly stipend of the Bishop of Bombay.[10]

In a number of places, most strikingly in two short publications entitled *Children of Poverty* and *Loss of Nerve*, he spelt out in careful detail the causes of the suffering of the tribal people. It stemmed from a combination of official policies (both those of the British Government of India, and those of the local Congress), Hindu "reform" movements, missionary impositions, and private commercial exploitation. From this, there resulted, for the tribal people, loss of land, loss of freedom of the forest, banning of the ritual hunt, contact with alien and inappropriate legal and educational systems, economic impoverishment, and the collapse of tribal industries.

We shall look in more detail below at what in the long term Elwin set out to do in response to all this, but should note that from the beginning the ideal was service. The St Francis Ashram was established in association with the Gond *Seva* Mandal [sic], the Society for the Service of the Gonds. Although they began with very little relevant experience and technical knowledge, Elwin and Hivale's intention was to serve the poor. There are some glimpses of this both amusing and moving in his letters at this time:

> ... a lovely girl poisoned by a witch. The poor child was deadly cold, a chill sweat running from her, her eyes staring, in terrifying convulsions—Shamrao with mustard water, I desperately turning the pages of *Family Medicine*. All night her life was in the balance, but in the end she was saved ... Then there was the old sadhu, who died in such utter filth and misery. None of his Hindus would touch him, so I had to lay him out and wash him, and then we burnt his body in a lovely little glade of the forest. It was a beautiful sight, a symbol of immortality after the misery of the

---

[10] *Children of Poverty* (CP), p. 7. This short pamphlet was published while Elwin was in England in 1932. It is reprinted in *Din-Sevak*, pp. 211–19. (Eds.)

previous night, to watch the bright flames leaping up to greet the rising sun.[11]

But there was more than this entirely individual and personal service. A regular programme of rural reconstruction, based largely on the well-known work of F. L. Brayne of the Indian Civil Service,[12] was established. Hivale went off for training at the Bhil Seva Mandal. A leper home was opened, and Elwin took advice from missionary friends with long experience of caring for lepers. Similarly he was very concerned about the need for appropriate education. His description of an early anti-illiteracy programme during 1832–3 gives an indication of the liberative thrust to this:

> As we draw a real picture of their own lives, their faces beam with the joy of understanding themselves, and discovering this light which they have been carrying with them all the time. This is the cultural awakening of a people, that is slowly going on in this obscure place.[13]

In less than two years, they had opened seven schools in the locality, and one of their new colleagues, Srikant, was preparing textbooks, a Gond Primer and First Reader.

... Elwin was always looking for ways to widen the scope of the work. Thus, in 1933, at the Servants of India Society in Pune, he "had a long and very interesting talk with Srinivasa Shastri about the possibility of extending the franchise to our hill and forest folk, and how we could get them more adequate representation on the Councils". A little later he

---

[11] cE, 26 March 1936.

[12] Frank Lugard Brayne (1882–1952), an ardent evangelical Christian, served in the British Indian Army in the First World War after some years' civil service in the Punjab. After the War, he returned to the Punjab to become district officer of Gurgaon, not far from Delhi. His Gurgaon Scheme was an attempt to help the plight of poor farmers by encouraging and facilitating a programme of self-help. He wrote several books on the subject. (Eds.)

[13] cC, 16 April 1933.

indicated his intention of widening the scope of their work by renaming the project the Bhumijan Seva Mandal, the Society for the Service of the People of the Soil, "to include the other tribes and the poorer Hindu castes".[14]

Throughout these developments, Elwin remained himself committed with a most thoroughgoing sincerity and commitment to a life of poverty and identification with the poor amongst whom he lived. Leaving the Christa Seva Sangha had meant giving up any form of guaranteed financial support. It had been "a step of faith at midnight". He therefore had to work very hard to raise funds for the work he was initiating. Much depended upon his personal approach to individuals, and over the next 20 years, he was constantly writing to individuals—150 letters one week, while a little later he noted that there were "180 friends of the Ashram who must be corresponded with".[15] The supporters of this work were an extraordinarily varied lot of people. At the beginning, most of his support came from within India, much of it from Hindu and Parsee friends. Gandhi was among these contributors. The list widened to include several of his former Christa Seva Sangha colleagues, the Bombay Missionary Council, Sir Lancelot Graham, K. C. I. E., Secretary to the Legislature of the Government of India, Friedrich Heiler, Evelyn Underhill, Stanley Jones, even Lord Sankey, the former Lord Chancellor of England, and William Temple, Archbishop of York. He was very relieved when in 1937 the Sir D. J. Tata School of Social Studies[16] appointed him a Research Associate. But all of this was strictly for the work, and for more than 20 years he himself had to live on the small amounts he was able to earn from writing, struggling along in what he called "Apostolic discomfort".[17]

In this regard, we need to note that he entered into this with a strong sense of vocation. "The yearning for real poverty" was so great in him that he felt driven to fulfil it. The impulse, of course, went back to his

---

[14] cE, 20 July 1933, cC, 20 August 1938.
[15] cE, 8 September 1934.
[16] Founded in 1936 as the Sir Dorabji Tata Graduate School of Social Work and now the Tata Institute of Social Sciences (TISS), a multi-campus public university in Mumbai. (Eds.)
[17] cC, 6 January 1937.

Oxford days. Ever since then he had been haunted by a sense that he had "no natural right to a life of comfort and culture when millions of ... (his) brothers and sisters were dying of hunger". His "whole life" was a "protest" against the kind of life lived by the British in India. In taking this path, he felt "very near to St Francis", so it was fitting that his book on St Francis, the last of his sequence of studies of spirituality, was written at Karanjia.

There is an attractive "Franciscan" note to his Introduction to this work:

> This book has been written in a tiny cell of mud and wattle in the heart of the forest-clad Satpura Mountains, far from libraries, and I am grateful indeed to those who sent books to a beggar so importunate and troublesome. And to Brother Sun who has warmed our hearts, and to Brother Wind for his courtesy in bringing cool refreshment in the heat of the day and to Sister Water who has often encouraged me to persevere, I am also grateful. And you, my little Sisters the Ants, who clambered on my body and across these pages so bravely while they were preparing, you were not so great a distraction as at first I feared. And for that courtesy also I am grateful.[18]

There was nothing romantic, though, about this venture into poverty. He managed to make a joke about the rats which ate his books, wishing that they had been more discriminating in their choice of authors, and about his choosing for himself a few items of clothing donated for the leprosy patients, but he had no illusions about the poverty that he had embraced:

> How easy it is to talk of Holy Poverty when we are comfortable. And then when She comes to us and we find her noisy, dirty, dull and inconvenient (which is what she is), we shrink from the bride we had thought so romantic.

---

[18] Verrier Elwin, *St Francis of Assisi* (Madras, 1935), pp. xv–xvi.

That was towards the end of his first year at Karanjia. Twenty years later, he is still writing book reviews and "pot-boiler" articles for the *Illustrated Weekly*, in the hope of making a little money, and "just managing to live on the edge of the bank balance". It has to be said that Elwin learned to enjoy many aspects of the life that he chose—"we are all children of wildness and freedom", he wrote to his mother with evident satisfaction after a couple of years, and 15 years later he was still saying so, while in an interview in a Bombay newspaper 20 years after coming to Karanjia, he testified that his life with the poor had brought him "great happiness".[19]

There was of course a very important further aspect to his chosen path of poverty. It enabled him to identify with those with whom he lived. He wore a shirt and *dhoti*, he said, "not because it is Indian, but in order to be nearer to the poor". "I cannot help the poor save by becoming one of them", he wrote to the Sisters of the Eremo.[20]

This was also, of course, a deeply religious matter for Elwin, what he called, in a letter to Gandhi, "the real service of Daridra Narayan", and he spoke of the "supreme privilege" to be allowed to be "among His poor", to "follow the Crucified among the crucified". It was a vocation sustained with remarkable gifts of character and grace.[21]

A further aspect of the personality of Elwin that needs to be noted was his capacity for friendship with the tribal people. Of course, his greatest friendship for the whole of the time he lived in Central India was with Shamrao Hivale, who was "everything" to him. In tribal society, Elwin explained, with its pattern of alliances within the single village community, you have many *jawaras* but only one *mahaprasad*, this being "the giver of great grace". *Prasad*, he went on, is "communion,

---

[19] cE, 13 November 1932. He wrote to his mother in 1948: "Truly my lot is set in pleasant places and happy indeed can one be without any of the complications of civilized life. Here I can go barefoot, with a ragged shirt on my back, a roof of leaves over my head, but so long as I have a chair for my bottom and a pen in my hand, I am content." (In a file of newspaper cuttings with cF).

[20] cE, 8 September 1934.

[21] Elwin to Gandhi 12 February 1933, (Gandhi Smarak Nidhi, New Delhi). *The Supremacy of the Spiritual* (Madras, 1933), p. 3.

... the blessed bread", and this was Shamrao's special place. But they both acquired so many *jawaras* that they "did not disturb the general relationship: a whole village was our ... *jawara*". There is a nice passage in his Circular Letter of 29 August 1937, in which he describes his work as a local Honorary Magistrate: to his amusement, his Court-reader, "a perfect Jeeves of a man", calls Elwin "Your Honour". "Nobody else does (he continues) ... the men say Bhai—brother—and an old woman scandalized my Reader one day by calling me *beta* (my son) throughout her evidence." This is a good indication of the easy relationship he was able to establish even when clothed with the borrowed dignity of the Raj. This capacity to relate closely across such a considerable ethnic and cultural divide found its fullest expression in Elwin's marriages, successively to two tribal women, Kosi, a Gond, in 1940, and Lila, a Pardhan, in 1953. He often testified to the enriching and fulfilling nature of the latter relationship in particular.

A further illustration of Elwin's gifts and perceptions in regard to inter-cultural living during these Karanjia years needs to be noted. We have already seen how, in the Christa Seva Sangha in Puna, he was much preoccupied with the nature and parameters of inter-cultural spirituality. At Karanjia, finding his way in a new world yet again, his interest was in the sense of a common humanity underlying seemingly huge cultural divides. He explored and expressed this through the transposition and application of terms from his own English and European culture to the life and character of his tribal neighbours. Thus, he described the social atmosphere of two very different tribal villages in terms of "going from a cocktail party to a conventicle of Plymouth Brethren", while he described the Raj Gond Movement of the later 1930s as "a sort of primitive Nazism", and the first Baigas he met as "not *too* intelligent", remarking that their equivalents at Oxford "would probably get Thirds in History". Many of his analogies and descriptions draw upon Western ecclesiastical nomenclature. Thus, he introduces a notable personality from the Karanjia district:

> Panda Baba is a celebrated Gond magician and he looks it. You would not expect to find anything so ecclesiastical outside Westminster. He does not actually wear gaiters, but there is a sort

of gaiter nimbus about those bare legs of his. He has a significant little stoop and an expression of partly veiled importance, as though he certainly knew more than he cared to tell.

This paragraph then continues startlingly, re-establishing distance, strangeness, unfamiliarity:

> His house is adorned with many symbols of his sacred calling— whips of horse-hair hang beside spiked iron scourges and sharp-pointed rods for thrusting through your cheek or tongue during the ecstatic dance.[22]

He often refers to tribal religious leaders using Christian terminology, as in his description in a letter to his mother about his discovery that the Meheras were practising untouchability:

> I also told the Mehera Archbishop that as a punishment for believing in untouchability, he would be reborn a pig ... they show a little uneasiness now whenever eschatological topics are referred to.[23]

Not surprisingly, with his own great love and knowledge of English literature, many of his analogies are literary. Thus, "the Gonds and the Baigas are more or less absorbed in two things—food and sex, and their conversation is like the prose parts of Shakespeare".[24] This is a striking feature of two books from Elwin's earlier forest years, the years at Karanjia, *Songs from the Forest* (1935), edited jointly with Shamrao Hivale, and *Leaves from the Jungle* (1936). The introduction to the former, in particular, a collection of translations of tribal songs and poems, is a mosaic of analogies and parallels from English literature. The latter is surely the most entertaining and delightful published introduction to

---

[22] Verrier Elwin, *Leaves from the Jungle: Life in a Gond Village.* (London: Oxford University Press, 1936), p. 130.
[23] cF, 21 April 1934.
[24] cC, 8 April 1937.

the enduringly attractive personality of Verrier Elwin. His imaginative cultural parallels, though, are more than mere entertainment. Much of what he was writing at this time, these two books and his circular letters, were for a British readership, for the supporters in Britain of his work, and other friends, and these parallels and contrasts are a brilliant way of communicating the realities of an otherwise unimaginable difference. They also serve an interesting secondary purpose—that of relativizing the British culture of his readers, and at the same time enhancing for them the worth of the tribal world. The only absolutes that Elwin has come to recognize are those associated with a common humanity, as he implies in the text from William Blake which prefaces *Leaves*,

> Man was made for Joy and Woe, ...
> Joy and Woe are woven fine,
> A clothing for the Soul divine.

The final point to make here about Elwin's Karanjia years, is that we are invited to see these as no less concerned with confessing the faith in India than his life and work at Puna. If anything, as a time of "following the Crucified among the crucified", they might be seen as an intensification of what he was and of what he was doing upon others. Accounts of the St Francis Ashram indicate how seriously and committedly Elwin and his companions saw themselves as engaged in a Christian enterprise. The simple mud chapel and altar were established within a fortnight of their first arriving at Karanjia, and, while he was committed to an interreligious community within the ashram, he and his Hindu, Muslim and Christian co-workers (as the place developed) were "bound together in a brotherhood not of syncretism but of service".[25] He was concerned to sustain his own and Hivale's practice of prayer within the Brotherhood of St Francis, as they called it. Sending to his friends in Italy a copy of the set prayers they had devised for regular use in the Ashram, he commented, "Now that our life is so active, I find we need more set times of prayer."[26] He saw this discipline of prayer as supporting an idea

---

[25] *Children of Poverty*, p. 11.
[26] cE, 25 May 1933.

of loving service. While he did not feel called to engage in anything resembling evangelism, the witness of loving service was plainly his ideal. His mother had evidently had misgivings about the venture, but he reassured her:

> Believe me that India for Christ and Christ for India is the only hope and goal of my life, but you must let me go about it in the way that is going to reach that goal.

At about the same time he spelt out what he thought that "way" to be:

> I do pray that among these poorest of the poor, we may be the Hands of Christ to minister to them and His heart for their comfort.

A few years later, after describing their success in curing a case of leprosy, he wrote, "I do not claim to have faith, but we do have love, and love-healing is another form of faith healing."[27]

The impact of this life at Karanjia was significant. While we shall look later at his actual views on the question of conversion in regard to tribals, we do have an impressive contemporary testimony to the impact of his work. On 2 June 1933, he wrote to his friends at the Eremo in Italy:

> They have given me the title of "Din-sevak", which means Servant of the Poor, which I am afraid I hardly deserve.[28]

The context of the remark suggests that those who gave him this title were Gandhi and his companions. This is borne out by an article the following year by A. V. Thakkar in the journal *Harijan*. Thakkar's account in his "Tour Diary" of a visit to Karanjiais is a valuable indication of a contemporary Hindu assessment of Elwin and his co-workers during the Karanjia years:

---

[27] cF, January 1932.
[28] cE, 2 June 1933.

I was anxious for the last two years to visit the place of Father Elwin's unique work ... The uplift of Gonds is very difficult under present circumstances. Four German missionaries came and settled here in the forties of the last century, and all of them were buried in a tomb in the course of a year after arrival. Father Elwin and his assistant Brother Shamrao, or "Bada Bhaiya" and "Chota Bhaiya" as they are popularly addressed by the Gonds, are the only two persons who have stuck to their work out of the six that settled here two years ago. Malaria is rampant, and unless one has a good physique and, more than that, a strong call for service, he cannot stay in this part long.

Father Elwin, though a Christian in the truest sense of the term, is not for proselytization. He does not convert Gonds, but merely serves them. He has no other aim than that of pure unadulterated service from a humanitarian point of view. He does his prayers, with his group of Hindu workers, in Hindu and Christian hymns. For this type of service, novel for Christians, he is thanked neither by Christians nor by Hindus. The former dislike him for his departure from the orthodox way of work, and the latter distrust him as they cannot imagine any Christian tabooing conversion work...

... A highly educated white man divorced himself from all amenities of life, a true follower of St Francis, sacrificing himself in the service of the most neglected section of our countrymen, a habitual wearer of *khadi*, not a mere nationalist, but an internationalist and a true Christian with no desire for conversion is anywhere rare, more so in this country. I wish every social worker will finish his education by a few days stay in the abode of this true servant of humanity.[29]

Here is the heart of Verrier Elwin's confession of the faith in India, in his loving identification with and practical service of the poor, which earned him the title *Din-sevak*.

---

[29] A. V. Thakkar, "My Tour Diary—II. Karanjia", *Harijan*, 23 November 1934.

* * *

Edited and abridged from Daniel O'Connor, Introduction to *Din-Sevak: Verrier Elwin's Life of Service in Tribal India* (Delhi: ISPCK, 1993), pp. 42–53. Dan's system of abbreviation in the footnotes has been retained.

7

Spring Thunder

In 2005, Dan published his account of the O'Connors' years in Delhi under the title *Interesting Times in India: A Short Decade at St Stephen's College*, with a foreword by Narayani Gupta and Afterword by Gopal Gandhi. It was written at the request of his mother who wanted a proper record of the family's decade in India. A more personal story can be found in *Juliet's Letters from India*, edited by Dan after her death in 2016.

Interesting Times in India is a fascinating account of India some 20 years after the independence for which Andrews and Elwin had worked so hard in their different ways, and Dan, with his left-wing political leanings, continues in their spirit in his own time at St Stephen's College as chaplain and teacher. The chapter here printed in a shortened form provides a fascinating glimpse of college life during the late 1960s, when young intellectuals—among them three of Dan's students in particular—were seized with the radical political fervour of the Naxalite movement. It was written at the request of Dan's friends at the Christian Institute for the Study of Religion and Society, Bangalore.

Beginning with the Naxalbari insurgency of 1967 in West Bengal, the Naxalites were a group of left-wing radicals drawn to the communist teachings of Mao Zedong in China, often active in less developed and desperately poor rural areas in Bihar and Andhra Pradesh and drawing upon the idealist enthusiasms of young intellectuals of the time.

Dan's narrative is characteristically modest and at the same time remarkable. As the college chaplain, he was faithful to his students and their idealistic adherence to the claims of the rural poor in Bihar and the north-east of India. In some ways, his ministry was in the tradition of Andrews and Elwin in their love of and devotion to the poor and oppressed in India, and later Dan made at best, with his students, "what accommodations their consciences would permit with the unregenerate world. Many of the others among our college revolutionaries, though not all, very rapidly abandoned their commitment and ideology."[1]

This story of the idealism of youth and Dan's acknowledgment of its worth, makes for absorbing reading.

* * *

Beyond the university and the city during much of 1966, the newspapers carried increasingly grim accounts of a famine in rural Bihar, though the crisis was by no means restricted to that state. Rajasthan, of which I was much more aware on account of my periodic ecclesiastical forays there, was very severely affected as well, its desert districts into their third year of total and seventh year of partial drought, with millions affected, this particular problem reaching into the bordering Punjab districts. West Bengal, Orissa and Madhya Pradesh were also affected, and Eastern Uttar Pradesh was experiencing its worst drought in over a century. Dr B. M. Bhatia, principal of our neighbouring Hindu College, an expert on famine and the Famine Code,[2] noted that governments had always been reluctant to declare famine until starvation deaths began to occur in large numbers. This one, though, received vigorous coverage by the media, and Mrs Gandhi,[3] visiting affected areas in Orissa in blazing hot May and insisting on seeing villages not on the official schedule, declared it to be a national problem.

By the end of the year, Bihar seemed to be the most persistently problematic region, with what had turned out to be the worst famine since Indian independence. The Union education ministry asked vice-chancellors to encourage fund-raising among students for famine relief,

---

[1] Daniel O'Connor. *Interesting Times in India* (Dehli: Penguin, 2005), p. 219.
[2] The Indian Famine Code dates back to 1880 and the drafting of a Famine Code that remained the basis of famine prevention in India for almost a century. The code defined three levels of famine—near-scarcity, scarcity, and famine—and established measures that the government should take to meet the crisis at each level. (Eds.)
[3] Mrs Indira Gandhi became Prime Minister of India in 1966. (Eds.)

and many did so. At St Stephen's, meals were forgone in the dining hall and cash raised. The Delhi papers carried a moving account of a party of eleven young teenagers from Modern School, led by two teachers, going to Bihar on their own modest but courageous mission of mercy, and confronting hunger and absolute poverty such as they had never imagined.

In December 1966, Suman Dubey, a former student of the college, temporarily lecturing in economics but with journalistic ambitions, decided to visit Bihar in the hopes of a story to enhance his journalistic possibilities, taking with him my colleague Brijraj Singh and a student Sanjit (Bunker) Roy. They met and travelled around with Jayaprakash Narayan, the former socialist and by this time Sarvodaya worker,[4] who was responsible for the Bihar Relief Committee. It was, however, their encounter with the outstanding scholar-administrator, Dr Suresh Singh, a deputy commissioner, which led to the involvement of St Stephen's in relief work in Bihar. He asked for a series of small groups of five or six students to come for ten days at a time to act as his eyes and ears in the villages in Palamau district, bringing back to him accurate reports of what was happening.

When Brijraj brought this proposal back to the college, he was pleasantly surprised at Satish Sircar's positive response and willingness to allow this scheme to intervene upon the academic year. The project ran from January to July 1967. However useful it was to Suresh Singh, it was a highly significant time for the students concerned, and for several of them the encounter with the realities of rural poverty and oppression was a life-changing experience. For Bunker Roy, a national sports champion with a very promising career in business already lined up, the Bihar famine experience changed everything. In consequence of what he saw, he set out on a life's journey that led him to set up his highly imaginative and effective development project at Tilonia in Rajasthan

---

[4] Sarvodaya is a Sanskrit term broadly meaning "universal progress". It was taken up by Gandhi and in post-independence India was related to the democratic movement which sought self-determination and equality at all levels of Indian society. (Eds.)

and his internationally admired "Barefoot College".[5] While our student teams were going to Bihar, we[6] left India in April 1967 on the one home leave of our decade, and when we got back in October, the experience was beginning to work in other ways in other minds...

*

... By then, however, another factor had come into the equation, precisely contemporaneous in its origins with the famine. This had its beginnings in the peasant revolt at Naxalbari in West Bengal, which first erupted in May 1967. This was a land struggle on the part of poor and landless tribals equipped with spears and bows and arrows and confronting armed police, with over 200 violent encounters in that particular district over the next three to four months. In a remarkably short time, the Naxalite movement took off in many parts of the country, with violent land seizures and even more violent urban manifestations and a no less violent response on the part of the state. Following on from Bengal, the newspapers reported "the struggle by landless peasants" in Bihar, Assam, Uttar Pradesh, Andhra Pradesh, Kerala, Tamil Nadu, Punjab and Himachal Pradesh. In Andhra, something like a guerrilla war developed, where considerable quantities of mortgaged gold were seized from the landlords and "restored to the real owners". Srikakulam district, comprising some 600 villages, became a virtual alternative state, while Kerala had its "Red Guards" with ambitions to create a "little Albania" in Malabar. Meanwhile, Calcutta seemed to be permanently thudding with homemade bombs. That the original outburst was seen as part of something much bigger, a precursor of an Indian revolution, was evident

---

[5] Barefoot College International was founded by Bunker Roy in 1972, working amongst the rural poor in Rajasthan. It now operates in more than 2,000 villages in 93 countries worldwide. Its mission statement is "to make vocational and educational opportunities accessible to women and girls from the most marginalized communities around the world. We believe providing these opportunities to women is the solution to ensuring long term climate, economic and social resilience for rural communities globally." (Eds)

[6] Daniel and Juliet O'Connor and their two boys. (Eds)

from a broadcast by Radio Peking which welcomed the events in rural Bengal as the arrival of "Spring Thunder". Chinese endorsement was, of course, especially significant, for Mao had launched the communist revolution by organizing, in contradiction to the Soviet line, a peasants' revolt. Organized Left politics took up the cause. Dissident elements of the Communist Party of India (Marxist), the CPI(M), at a "secret" conference, reported in some detail in the broadsheets in October 1968, enunciated the notion of "surrounding the cities" from "revolutionary bases in the villages". In proceeding thus, the Indian people would be "joining hands with the great people of China and other revolutionary masses". The Communist Party of India (CPI) and the CPI(M) manoeuvred to retain credibility, the more so after a third communist party, the Communist Party of India (Marxist–Leninist), the CPI(M–L), entered the area in April 1969.

The liberal English-language press at this time reported that 70 per cent of the population of India were suffering from chronic malnutrition, and was therefore not surprised at what was happening. The oppressed sharecroppers of Bihar and Bengal had been "brazenly exploited" by a feudalism condoned by the entire rural establishment. "No wonder", the *Hindustan Times* reported in June 1969, that the landless labourer "should in desperation finally seek a violent Naxalite solution". By 1971, the CPI(M–L) chairman Charu Mazumdar was talking of an army with rifles snatched from the police marching across "a vast area" of West Bengal and "a revolutionary tempest" raging over much of India. No wonder also, as one of my English honours students was to write, recollecting these events later in tranquillity at Oxford, "there was a time when the word Naxalite was ... loaded with nameless fears and aspiration, stirring hopes or despair".

*

This same student, Rabindra Ray, observed that the students and urban "petty-bourgeois intelligentsia" who eventually became the main component of the Naxalite party and movement "fought in the cause of a class not their own". It was this phenomenon that explains in a general way the involvement of individuals and groups from Delhi University and, not least, St Stephen's in the "Spring Thunder" that rumbled throughout India in the later years of our decade.[7] In remarkable ways, significant elements in what had been a demoralized and direction-less student community, a community who, as the vice-chancellor had observed, did not know what they wanted, were transformed.

That St Stephen's had a significantly disproportionate part in this is evident from the way the name of the college keeps cropping up in my newspaper cuttings for 1970 and 1971. "The so-called Naxalites of Delhi University belong to the two premier institutions on the campus, St Stephen's College and the Delhi School of Economics", said one *Hindustan Times* article in January 1971, though students in several other colleges and institutions, including Miranda House, Indraprastha College and the School of Social Work were also mentioned. Two months later, a "special report" in the *Times Weekly* gave an even higher profile to the college: "Outside of St Stephen's, no other institution seems to be the focal point of unrest." Interestingly, this report recalled the early twentieth-century precedent of the extreme nationalists around the St Stephen's student Har Dayal, influenced as he was, as my C. F. Andrews researches at this time were disclosing, by both Marxist and nihilist ideas.

St Stephen's, of course, presented a wide spectrum of responses and involvements. This was never easy to compute. There was an element who were quite indifferent to what was going on, part of a new and singularly unedifying social development in Delhi, a "fast-growing world of pop groups, long hair and drugs" as one more concerned student put it in the *Enquirer*. He was alarmed at "the *pride* Stephanians take in being absolutely good-for-nothing". However many of these there were, it was clear that the majority of students remained marginal to the process of radicalization, though not always to its excitements. An emergency meeting of the students' representative body in December 1970 declared itself actively opposed to "Naxalite activity" within the college. About that time, their president, Deepak Vohra, was set upon by some of the activists. I visited him in hospital on the morning after: no bones were

---

[7] O'Connor means by this the decade that he and Juliet were in Delhi, 1963–72. (Eds.)

broken, and I got the impression, though I could of course have been mistaken, that it was in some respects a symbolic hospitalization.

It has to be said of this rejectionist majority that they were not all by any means indifferent to the lot of their disadvantaged urban neighbours. Through the college's Social Service League, a fair number busied themselves in trying to help them, though they remained, typically, unengaged politically. Some of the more dogmatic of our revolutionaries despised this sort of thing, though in conversation one or two of the more mature among them, when I pressed them on the subject, acknowledged the social service activists as allies. A few of those keen on doing something practical in the way of social service got into rural good works, too. One group was led by Romesh Bhattacharji, recently graduated and a trekking enthusiast, by this time in customs, and his wife, Shobhana. They developed from 1970 what was to be a long running project to assist a remote, hungry and neglected Himalayan village called Namik. Over a number of years, small groups of students helped in this, with our house, as long as we were there, the godown for sacks of grain and clothing.

In addition to the politically unengaged, there was a broad penumbra of Left-inclined students, in varying degrees either opposed or sympathetic to the movement. Some of this group of students provoked a Naxalite leaflet, which actually named one of them; they were "comical elements" who "talk[ed] Marxism to oppose the people". Others were more sympathetic, often from a moral or a romantic perspective or a mixture of the two, among them a Christian student from Kerala whose general sympathy was cruelly shaken when news came of the killing of his father, a tea estate owner, by local revolutionaries.

Possibly it was within these latter parameters that a drama production in September 1970 stood. This was Mario Fratti's *Che*, a play about the revolutionary Che Guevara.[8] The play, as Sunil Chand observed in his review, dealt with "immediately relevant social issues" and dealt with them "fiercely". It was presented in college, designed and directed by Kapil Sibal, with most of our usual college and Miranda House drama

---

[8] Mario Fratti (1927–2023) was a playwright and writer, born in Italy and becoming a naturalized American in 1974. His drama *Che Guevara* has been performed in New York, Toronto and the Venice Festival. (Eds.)

enthusiasts taking part. Juliet did the costumes, and we had a whole platoon's worth of guerrilla camouflage uniforms hanging on our veranda for all to see. The college's army cadet unit provided the rifles, courtesy of "Major" Arya, our next-door neighbour. Box offices were a huge success, and the play ran for four nights, a new record for the college. We were astonished and slightly alarmed, though, when we discovered that the police had asked for a copy of the programme and had shown an interest in all the names included on it, most of them, if not all, highly "respectable", the police interest being a small indication of the climate of "nameless fears" that pervaded the university at that time.

An interesting case of detached and critical sympathy among the students was the position taken by one of my English honours students, Dawa Norbu, a refugee from Tibet. While still a student with us, he wrote up his childhood experience of the coming of the Chinese communists to his provincial hometown of Sakya. This was published as the fascinating *Red Star Over Tibet* in 1973 but was written in the thick of the college's Naxalism, and written quite specifically, as he said, in response to the Maoist students he met, an attempt to establish what communism really meant for the peasants, "to try and avoid propaganda from both sides". (In 1972, we had carried the photographs to be used in the book to the publisher in the UK when our decade had come to an end.) An equally complex case was that of a Muslim student from Kashmir, very close to the activists and perhaps one of them, who at the same time asked me to get him an Urdu version of the Bible, which I was able to do.

Among members of staff, some, though by no means all, were concerned and interested in what was going on. Our two CPI(M) members, Suhash Chakravarty and S. Ganguli, were in the thick of the debate, while one or two younger members of staff had police searches on their homes. Our somewhat authoritarian dean, Willie Rajpal, was inclined to be ruthless, but Satish Sircar was, I thought, wise and prudent in his handling of the whole affair. At a seminar organized by the Delhi University Teachers' Association to discuss whether or not the police had a role on a university campus in countering Naxalite activity, he expressed the conviction that in all but immediate emergencies the police should keep out. Only the teaching staff could solve long-term problems. With a predictable St Stephen's approach, he suggested they could do this by the establishment of "continuous rapport" with the students and "providing them necessary physical amenities". In the less public forum of our Christian Staff Fellowship, the principal admitted that he was "secretly rather proud" of our revolutionaries.

*

The real thing, though, was something other than all this, with no question of "both sides". Those who were most intensely caught up in it increasingly closed their minds to alternatives—this was, in a sense, one of the most critical features of the movement. Some, in fact, who had been perfectly civil participants in the college community, began to confine their relationships ever more exclusively to co-revolutionaries, growing secretive and in some cases arrogant and intolerantly dismissive of those who were not with them. In their evermore closed world, I had the impression of their being drawn into a narrowing vortex, with, at least in some cases, sense, proportion and good judgment abandoned. Perhaps only that sort of intensification of conviction and determination provided the means to walk away from their familiar world. I never ceased to admire and respect the passionate sense of justice and the self-sacrificial concern for the poor in those I knew best among them, but this respect and admiration was accompanied by a troubling impression of ideology taking over.

How many true believers there were in college is rather difficult to be sure about—we are talking, after all, of very young adults, some only too quick to adopt the ideological certitudes involved, others feeling their way uncertainly and experimentally. In the university at large, a *Hindustan Times* journalist in January 1971 estimated that there was a "hard core" of about 50 students and a dozen teaching staff, but with "a large number of known, and secret supporters and admirers". In St Stephen's, perhaps 30 to 35 came into the "true believer" category. Of these, 15 "disappeared" in 1970, some in May, others in October, to join the struggle.

Of these true believers, I knew and talked with several, but there were three in particular whom I have come to count as lifelong friends and who have subsequently been so open about their involvement that I prefer to tell the story through them rather than name others, some of whom no doubt have wanted to put the entire episode behind them. One or two were senior in college to my three friends and, in one case at least, an important influence upon them, though he defected to the Indian Administrative Service subsequently.

The three were Arvind Narayan Das, who came up to St Stephen's in 1965 as a history honours student; Dilip Simeon and Rabindra Ray, both of whom came up the following year, Dilip reading history and Rabindra reading English. Rabindra was an exceptionally intelligent, sensitive and articulate member of one of my honours classes. Before they went underground, Arvind had completed and the other two had started their master's degree courses. All three subsequently earned doctorates. In fact, virtually all of the true believers were able, often gifted honours and postgraduate students, in science as well as arts subjects. They came mostly from educated middle class households, from almost all of the communities represented in college—Hindus, Muslims, Christians and Parsis.

Arvind, Dilip and Rabindra had all gone to Bihar during the college's famine project, and Arvind has provided in his book *Changel* (1996), his "biography" of his ancestral village, an account of how that experience affected him. During his early childhood and holiday visits to his "feudal, familial" village in north Bihar, he was quite unaware of the endemic, abiding exploitation throughout the countryside, which was concealed by "an enduring system of patronage–clientelism". He had heard lively political discussions on his mother's side of the family. He had also, perhaps, picked something up from a reputed revolutionary among the five Bengali spinster sisters who ran the little prep school that he attended in Patna.[9] He had heard about Marx, albeit in decidedly negative terms, from the Jesuit teachers, mostly Irish–American, in the school that he and Rabindra attended in Patna, though he later spoke to me appreciatively about these teachers. His upbringing had, nevertheless, been "generally apolitical", his father, a government servant, being deliberately unattached. This had kept Arvind "apathetic to the plight of others". It was only when our college project took him to Palamau in

---

[9] Historically known as Pataliputra, Patna is the capital and largest city of Bihar. (Eds.)

1967, "where hunger stalked the parched land", that he began to discern the realities of rural life and to see the truth of the post-independence communist slogan: "This independence is false since the people are still hungry." The brief from the deputy commissioner, Suresh Singh, to monitor the relief works and try to prevent leakages and corruption in the cluster of villages to which he, Dilip and another student were assigned, ensured that "the ugly visage of property became clearly apparent". He watched the moneylenders collaborating with duplicitous contractors to profit from the public works programmes prescribed by the Famine Code, and there was corruption and exploitation in the light manual labour schemes for the elderly, with extortion even in connection with the food doles for the totally indigent. He noted how the local rich were perverting the entire relief process to consolidate their own property and power. Witnessing the death of a hungry tribal, he realized that "the political economy of death is part of the political economy of exploitation". On his return to Delhi with the other volunteers from the college, the outworking and reverberations of this experience gradually began to manifest themselves.

*

It was some three years from the time of the Bihar famine experience to the time when Arvind and the 14 others left college and went underground in 1970. These were three strikingly eventful years. One aspect was the formation and development of ideology. A number of organizations and linkages provided the locus for this. There was already in the university a Marx club. It had been founded back in 1950, with such distinguished members in its earlier years as Professor V. K. R. V. Rao, the creator of the Delhi School of Economics, and Dr D. S. Kothari.[10] When it was thrown open to students in the 1960s, it became very popular. Arvind described it as run by 'some of the finest people in the university', though he was also drawn to the "galaxy of intellectuals" in the Delhi School of Economics.

---

[10] D. S. Kothari (1906–93) was a distinguished scientist and educationalist. He was president of the Indian Science Congress and the Indian National Science Academy. (Eds.)

These two centres included Bipan Chandra, whose excellent book on the rise of economic nationalism appeared in 1966, a psychology lecturer, Ajit Pal, and our own Dr Ganguli. Temporarily there was also Ranajit Guha,[11] during his attachment to the Delhi School of Economics in 1970–1, when he met some of our students and decided to give up his projected study of Gandhi in favour of an analysis of peasant insurgency. The Marx Club's deliberations in the later 1960s were increasingly dominated by the far Left, who effected a split among its younger adherents, driving the more moderate into an organization called Sankalp, while the more radical reconstructed themselves as Yugantak. This might best be described as a politico-cultural group. The more activist political focus of the students concerned from around 1969 was the Student Youth federation, an association with international connections. This last may well have been the point where university students and young industrial workers met. They certainly did meet, and Arvind introduced me in his room one night to a young Delhi Cloth Mills worker whom he described as his guru.

Ideological development was greatly stimulated by events in China following the launch of the Great Cultural Revolution in 1966, and Mao's Little Red Book began to be in evidence. Arvind urged me to read Edgar Snow's *Red Star Over China* (1937) in order to understand what was going on. It was, I concluded in a letter to my family "something like the Acts of the Apostles in the extreme Left's New Testament". We also had the benefit at one stage of a first-hand if somewhat starry-eyed account of what was going on in China. This was from Professor Joan Robinson, the Cambridge economist, sister-in-law of Bishop Christopher Robinson of the Delhi Brotherhood. Fresh from a visit to China and unmissable in her Mao cap, she was much lionized during the few days she spent about the university.

Another site for ideological exploration was a series of cyclostyled publications, the first being the *Enquirer*, produced in St Stephen's by the Debates Committee, the opening issue appearing in November 1968. This aimed to be "a forum for serious discussion". The assistant

---

[11] Ranajit Guha (1923–2023) was a distinguished historian. He emigrated from India to the UK in 1959 to work at the University of Sussex. (Eds.)

editor, after the first three issues, was concerned that vital issues such as language, integration and economic policy should be considered, for, as he put it, "the fact is that Stephanians *are* eventually going to play a major part in administering this country". There was, he seemed to be saying, too much emphasis on secessionism and revolutionary movements. It was undoubtedly in dealing with these latter topics that the *Enquirer* proved to be such a lively intervention, attracting contributions chiefly from the gradually coalescing hard core of student revolutionaries, including pieces by Arvind, Dilip and Rabindra, though also from wider circles of what one of them, characteristically gloomy about the college, called "the dying breed from the age of rationality and reason". Poetry and fiction were strictly banned. Topics included Marxism, the Vietnam War, student unrest (not only in India; current agitations in universities in Belgium, Brazil, France, Italy, Japan, Lebanon, Poland, Spain and West Germany were also referred to), the "free world" and communist aggression, the ethics of revolution, the Indian state, planning in India, the USA in UNCTAD,[12] and specific consideration of particular regional issues in Nagaland, Kashmir and Czechoslovakia. Dilip was in fine form as he concluded a piece on the state with, "The ruling classes and their flunkeys—the belching Marwaris, the pompous bureaucrats, the cocktail-swilling socialites, the perquisite-seeking sophisticates, the club-going wasters and the parliamentary cretins—all of whom today remain impervious to the miseries of the exploited classes, will realize, only too late, that they are being flushed down the drain of history." Arvind, in an article "On the State of our Republic", contrasted a similarly depicted ruling class with "the real friends of the people, those who love their fellow human beings and want to work for their welfare".

Following on, the *Enquirer*, and starting in October 1969, the Discussion and Debating Society of the Law Faculty Students' Union (Day Shift) took up the cause with a similar cyclostyled production, the *Questioner*, to which a number of our students contributed. Alongside these relatively readable publications, the political wing of the Student-Youth Federation prepared a worthy but dense tract, the *Foundations of Scientific Socialism*. This was "For Workers Only", but the workers would

---

[12] United Nations Conference on Trade and Development.

have had to be endowed with unusually robust intellectual skills to make anything of it. I got something of an overview of the developing ideology in August 1969 when a visiting American university chaplain, fresh from the excitements of Students for a Democratic Society and other campus ebullitions in the United States, asked me to arrange a meeting with Arvind at our house for him and some twenty of his charges. The terms semi-colonial, semi-feudal, comprador, bureaucrat, imperialist and capitalist flew about our sitting room as the Indian situation was explicated.

Alongside and succeeding these exercises, a more evangelizing or conscientizing cluster of endeavours broke upon the college and the university. There was, first, at least a couple of series of public seminar-type events. One of these was a series hung upon the Gandhi centenary commemorations of 1969. Its content is perhaps reflected in our special issue of the *Stephanian* in October 1969, with some particularly interesting pieces and photographs on Gandhi's association with the college, but also with Arvind's "Blasphemous Analysis". This presents Gandhi as first stimulating and then arresting "a great historical upsurge" by representing the interests of "the rural petit bourgeoisie" and failing to recognize the rural landless labourers and the very small farmers as "the real peasantry in India".

The other seminar series was a "Week of Revolutionary Heroes" held in the university Arts Faculty. This was organized by the Delhi State Student–Youth Federation. It included, on successive days, a seminar commemorating Engels, under the heading "revolutionary consciousness", then one commemorating Lenin, headed "revolutionary practice", a third one commemorating Che Guevara and "revolutionary struggle", rounded off with a rally outside the Arts Faculty on the theme of "revolutionary victory and continued struggle", commemorating Ho Chi Minh and the Indian martyrs. I was invited and attended one session.

The college theatrical talents were also harnessed to the cause. In one case, this involved street theatre at the factory gates of Delhi Cloth Mills, using workers' songs from an earlier generation of campaigning and struggle. This was reputedly reported on Peking Radio. One small irony of this aspect of things was that the chairman of Delhi Cloth Mills, Dr Bharat Ram, who was also chair of Indian Airlines and the first non-westerner to become president of the International Chamber of Commerce, was also a St Stephen's graduate. In another theatrical endeavour, in early January 1970, a review with the title *India '69* was staged at Miranda House and Tagore Hall, with a cast dominated by our college. Vietnam was part of the background, but two images linger—one of three world statespersons, Mrs Gandhi, Nixon and Brezhnev, depicted in common reactionary cause, and the other, with unashamedly lurid lighting effects, India's Green revolution turning irresistibly into a red one.

The former image cropped up again in the Student–Youth Federation leaflet referred to, which describes India as "this Yankee–Russian controlled comprador–bureaucrat landlord state". The leaflet is addressed to "the pseudo-Marxist Indian Administrative Service renegade clique", students who pretend to be Marxists but, quoting Comrade Charu Mazumdar, "sit for the IAS examination and become administrators, that is, go over to the enemy camp". It warns them that "the masses punish the traitors more ruthlessly than they punish all other class enemies". Another leaflet was from the executive committee of a group calling itself Janashiksha and was addressed to the wretched vice-chancellor. It took up two relatively straightforward issues—the preference for a revision of the semester system in the English department and for "a more relevant method of teaching" in history and social science—but makes the most of the opportunity to attack the entire education system as catering solely to the interest of "the outdated comprador–feudalist polity". Also, that government by the "foul ruling class" was "irrational, inefficient, outdated, treasonous, corrupt, barbaric, cruel, brutal and totally useless" and the entire foul class was "doomed". The format is similar to that of many revolutionary statements appearing around the world at that time with its concluding message "Remember your Humanity and Rebel!" And the appended "Immortal Fire".

I am inclined to think that these leaflets were a less effective form of conscientizing propaganda than the overnight appearance of slogans on the walls of the university and its institutions. This was a practice learnt from the Red Guards of the Chinese Cultural Revolution and was known among its Indian practitioners as "walling". Some of the slogans that appeared were straight quotations from Mao, or the rather standard ones such as those that appeared immediately below the stone cross on our college main tower: "China's path is our path, China's chairman is our chairman". Some were more original, however, and on one occasion I dropped in at Arvind's room to find a creative slogan-concocting session in progress. These were designed to match the institution where they appeared, like the one for a women's college which read "Arranged Marriages to Businessmen is Abduction by *Dacoits*",[13] or one for the college of commerce, "The Private Sector is Legalized Thuggery". The university *chowkidars*[14] were of course under orders to prevent walling, but one night at least, when the purpose of the exercise was explained, the chowkidars joined in and assisted in the slogan painting.

The practice was extended beyond the university campus, and one of our second year students was arrested while painting a slogan on the boundary wall of the supreme court in December 1970 in defiance of a prohibitory order promulgated by the district magistrate. Other slogans appeared in January 1971 at Gandhi's samadhi[15] at Rajgat. At this time also, we had a rash of nocturnal sloganizing on our lecture room blackboards, one announcing "Reactionary Teachers, We will have Your Skin for Shoes for the Poor." One of these blackboard messages was a warning the principal would have to "pay" for calling the police to the college, though I do not think he did call them during this period, despite life being very difficult for him.

Certainly around December 1970, there was a feeling that we were under siege, and I wrote in a letter that there was "tension in the air" with selected "reactionary" students being threatened. According to the *Times of India*, there was "a plot ... to set fire to the college library and to plant a bomb in the chapel", and we had temporary floodlighting in the college grounds at night, with a detachment of sturdy hill men recruited as extra *chowkidars* for a few weeks. By this time, though, our

---

[13] *Dacoit* is a Hindi word meaning a bandit. (Eds.)

[14] Watchmen or janitors. (Eds.)

[15] Rajgat, or Raj Ghat, in Delhi is the final resting place of Mahatma Gandhi. Samadhi is a term in Hinduism related to the state of total concentration when the mind, the process and the object of concentration become one. (Eds.)

15 most serious revolutionaries had been away for some months. These alarms, nevertheless, and the later walling and blackboarding, some carrying the signature CPI(M-L), which occurred after the May and October 1970 disappearances, indicate that 15 did not exhaust our tally of revolutionaries.

*

The call from Charu Mazumdar[16] was to "go to the villages and integrate", though the *Hindustan Times* report in January 1971 of a rumour that Mazumdar had visited Delhi to put this to the students was incorrect. He had certainly visited Delhi, staying in a worker's *basti*[17] with a friend of Dilip's, but this had been for a meeting of north Indian organizers of the CPI(M-L). Without benefit of such an encounter, a first small wave of about a dozen Stephanian Naxalites, including Arvind and Rabindra, left college in May 1970. Dilip and four others left in October. Their leaving was all rather elusory from a college perspective, as it was meant to be—they would disappear and reappear and disappear again, and it was only after a time that one was reasonably certain that they had actually gone. Rabindra, as he later put it in his book, left Delhi with some other members of the Student-Youth Federation in 1970 "to preach revolution in the north Bihar countryside", and "remained there for a couple of years under the direction of the North-Bengal North-Bihar Border Region Committee of the CPI(M-L)".

All the ramifications of the movement with which our college revolutionaries identified, and not least the paradox of a party arising out of an agrarian mass uprising that went on to immerse itself in urban riot and lawlessness and then in urban terrorism and brutality on an appalling scale in Calcutta, are for others to dissect and try to explain. Rabindra has himself made a bold attempt at this in his book *The Naxalites and Their Ideology* (1988). For us in the college, there

---

[16] Charu Mazumdar (1918-72), was popularly known as CM. A militant Naxalite, he was founder and general secretary of the Communist Party of India (Marxist-Leninist). (Eds.)

[17] A *basti* is a very poor neighbourhood in a town or city. (Eds.)

were only snatches in Arvind's *Changel*. He and Rabindra went on to work in Purnea, the latter's ancestral district, and "encountered immense generosity among the poorest, those who were themselves on the verge of starvation" and "they also met greed and cupidity". Most of all, he writes, "they discovered their own naivety and came to terms with their ignorance which more than a decade and a half of expensive education had cultivated". The entire experience was "enough to blow their minds, together and individually". Both of them found that "the dividing line between reality and rationality is extremely thin and it is possible to cross and recross that line with felicity". There are more snippets about some of the people whom they befriended and were befriended by—a poor peasant, a landlord's armed retainer, the father of a bonded labourer, a Santhal bird-catcher and others—and there is a description of the food on which the landless labourers survived. There is a reference to the "bitter class conflict that always simmered under the surface of idyllic village life", the "barely dormant" rural volcano, but nothing about their work for the party.

At one point during their two years underground, there was a knock on our front door late one night, and there stood Arvind and Dilip, in Delhi on some party assignment. We kept our back door unlocked in case they needed to make an unobserved exit, but they were able to stay for a leisurely session over coffee and tell us something about their experiences. They explained that the party required those sent to the countryside to simply—to use Rabindra's word—preach. Anything in the way of "actions" was to be entirely in the hands of the villagers. Many landlords and moneylenders were of course killed at this time, but whether the preaching of our activists prompted anything of the sort they did not say. Arvind told us about some of the nocturnal sessions they had with the villagers and how he used his knowledge of the Sanskrit scriptures to reassure them that they were on the right track. This was a gift which he was to employ again, much later when he was research editor of the *Times of India* at the time of the Babri Masjid outrage,[18] refuting Hindutva claims quite brilliantly. He also told us how they were

---

[18] The Babri Masjid was an ancient mosque in Ayodhya, India. It was attacked and destroyed by Hindu nationalists in 1992. (Eds.)

learning something about subsisting off the land at the most basic and desperate level, from people who were obliged to live like this more or less habitually.

Following our nocturnal conversation, I mentioned after chapel next morning to a student whom I thought I could trust, that we had had this visit. I had misjudged the strength of this student's sense of civic duty. By the time I set off for lectures that morning, a plainclothes sleuth had arrived and positioned himself across the drive from our garden gate, and remained there for the day trying to impersonate a tree, though our two friends had been gone many hours before he turned up. Our watcher was picked up on the motorcycle of a uniformed colleague at knocking-off time in the evening, and that was that. Though slightly farcical, it had been a useful indication to us of the seriousness of the situation.

Dilip had a very different sort of experience from that of Arvind and Rabindra. His cultural and ethnic origins—a distinguished Roman Catholic family in Goa on the one side, and a north India Christian family on the other—determined that he would not be able to merge into the rural background as Arvind and Rabindra did, more or less, in their native Bihar. In consequence, the task conjured up for him was to establish an underground communication network across the Indo-Gangetic plain along the line of the Grand Trunk Road under cover of his role as a trucker's mate.

Dilip's highly entertaining account of this in his short story "O.K. TATA, Mobil Oil (and World Revolution)" suggests that his cover held reasonably if not unfailingly. Truckers' mates were—

> human appendages to the trucks, odd-job hands who leapt out at brief stoppages with tyre-levers with which they knocked the tyres to hear them ring, to confirm they were not punctured, rushed out at octroi barriers to pay the clerks, leaned out of the cabin windows slapping the door in city traffic and yelling at rickshaws, two-wheelers, cyclists and pedestrians, stood behind the vehicle when it was being reversed shouting affirmatives, wiped the smudges of shattered insects off the windshield regularly at night, washed the truck at long halts, supervised loading and unloading, spread the on-board tarpaulin on to

consignments tying it down with the on-board rope, performed hard labour with jacks and rods during tyre changes, checked engine oil and radiator water levels, stayed awake for twenty four hours unless instructed to sleep, and were honoured occasionally by being asked to take the wheel.

Like Arvind's and Rabindra's experiences, it must all have been a rather rude contrast with life at St Stephen's. As party work, though, the assignment seems to have been highly unsatisfactory, with only the most tenuous party contacts at some places and, in many, none at all, while very early on he discovered that the proletarians to whom his oily avocation introduced him "were not all straining to overthrow the semi-feudal semi-colonial status quo with armed revolutionary violence". That was less true, from what Arvind wrote, of the people that he and Rabindra and others met in rural Bihar.

(Eds Note. All three of the radical students whom Dan calls his "Naxal heroes" came and spent time with him later in the United Kingdom, and all three flourished in later life, though St Stephen's College did not welcome them back. Dilip Simeon, who has affirmed the accuracy of Dan's account, became a distinguished labour historian and public intellectual. He was professor of history at Ramjas College, University of Delhi, and has frequently stayed with the O'Connors over the years. He has created a public body for conflict-resolution and still teaches at the new Ashoka University. Arvind Narayan Das became a journalist and social scientist as well as a documentary film maker. He visited Dan O'Connor in Edinburgh in the later 1970s. Rabindra Ray went on to study at the University of Oxford, his D.Phil a stinging attack on Naxalism, and he later taught at the Delhi School of Economics.)

* * *

Edited and abridged from, Daniel O'Connor, *Interesting Times in India* (New Delhi: Penguin Books, 2005, pp. 186–207, 219–20.).

8

"Perpetual Succession": USPG and the Changing Face of Mission

In September 1997, Dan was invited by the United Society Partners in the Gospel (USPG),[1] which was approaching its tercentenary in 2001, to write a new history of the Society to replace an earlier volume, *Into All Lands* (1951) by H. P. Thompson. As Dan had recently suffered a heart attack and undergone major surgery, his wife Juliet remarked, "Well, it may kill you, but you'll die happy!" The history was published in 2000 as *Three Centuries of Mission*, written largely by Dan together with contributions from 14 other scholars from around the globe. Happily it did not kill him, but he went on to add to the story in his inaugural lecture of USPG "LINKS", the friends' organization of Anglican mission agency USPG. It was delivered under the title "Perpetual Succession" in the chapel of King's College, London on 18 October 2001, and is reprinted in an edited form here

The lecture begins with a portrait of Joshua Watson (1771–1855), once known as "the best layman in England" and a member of the High Church group of Anglicans known as the Hackney Phalanx. The Phalanx was eager for the renewal of the Church of England; this included the training, at the new King's College, London, of SPG overseas missionaries, bringing about a major renewal of the Society and ushering it into the nineteenth century. The excerpt from the lecture here reprinted takes up the story with an account of the life of the Revd John Ebenezer Marks (1832–1915) and his work as a teacher and missionary in Burma

---

[1] USPG was founded in 1701 as The Society for the Propagation of the Gospel in Foreign Parts (SPG).

(now Myanmar). Marks stands in stark contrast to the two later Anglican missionary priests in India who have featured so largely in this book, C. F. Andrews and Verrier Elwin. Openly proselytizing in the schools that he founded, Marks firmly linked imperialism, indeed militarism, with God's purpose. Dan's purpose here is to illustrate that the heroes of an earlier age of mission and empire, men like Marks, stand now in contrast to later heroes in the mission field who were, and are, committed anti-colonialists and critics of former British imperialism.

Dan remarks that this lecture marked the end of a great deal of publicity surrounding the publication of his new history of USPG. He used the lecture "to enable the Society's supporters to see how the Society had reinvented itself in creative ways over three centuries—and was still doing so".[2] The "unedifying story" of Edward Marks illustrates the close nineteenth-century ties between the Society and Empire. Dan further notes that "Karl Rahner's notion of 'non-simultaneity in the Church' was nicely illustrated in the presence among our students at the College of the Ascension in Selly Oak in the 1980s of a very fine young Burmese layman who had been baptized 'Edward Marks' in honour of the unscrupulous imperialist of a century earlier".[3]

The lecture ends with an affectionate note on Dan's old friend from Selly Oak days, the scholar R. S. Sugirtharajah, whose *Dictionary of Third World Theologies* was also published in 2000.

* * *

... I start with this glimpse of Watson and his circle to make the point that one feature of the Society's history has been its capacity for originality, its capacity to renew, sometimes almost to reinvent itself, for changing circumstances and challenges. Of course, the eighteenth-century story of the Society's immensely creative role in the First British Empire, colonial North America and the Caribbean, was a thoroughly original venture and

---

[2] In unpublished correspondence with DJ.
[3] Correspondence with DJ.

achievement. We have told it in the book[4] in some detail, because it has almost invariably been ignored by evangelical historians, for whom the world began with William Carey.[5] It certainly began again, though, for SPG, with the vision and labours of Watson and the Hackney Phalanx.

Their work was at the beginning of what Latourette[6] called "The Great Century", and inaugurated the Society's part in "the age of the most extensive geographic spread of Christianity".[7] That story, however, as we look back on it now, suggests that that word "Great" needs to be qualified in some way. Since completing the new history of USPG, I was asked by the publisher of a new dictionary for an entry on the nineteenth-century SPG missionary, John Ebenezer Marks. I had mentioned Marks briefly in *Three Centuries of Mission*, but now had to look at his record in greater detail. His story is told in his autobiographical *Forty Years in Burma* (1917), with much further detail provided in his regular reports to the Society.[8] These give us a remarkably vivid illustration of colonial mission.

Oddly, the story starts in Hackney, where John Ebenezer Marks, born in the East End, was pursuing what looked likely to be a modest career as a schoolteacher at the Hackney Free and Parochial Schools. His pupils included a gang known as the Hackney Bulldogs, not quite the world of the Hackney Phalanx. His call to educational mission with SPG took him to Myanmar (Burma) in 1860. It took him also to what the Society at the time of his death in 1915 called "a place among the great educational missionaries of this age", recognized with a Lambeth DD in 1879. He founded nine schools in all, modelled on the school in

---

[4] Daniel O'Connor and Others, *Three Centuries of Mission: The United Society for the Propagation of the Gospel, 1701-2000* (London: Continuum, 2000).

[5] William Carey (1761-1834), Baptist minister, who went to Calcutta in 1793, and founded Serampore College. He is sometimes known as "the father of modern missions". (Eds.)

[6] Kenneth Scott Latourette (1884-1986), American historian of missions. (Eds.)

[7] K. S. Latourette, *History of the Expansion of Christianity* (London: Eyre & Spottiswoode, 1941), Vol. IV, p. 1.

[8] John Ebenezer Marks, *Forty Years in Burma*, ed. W. C. B. Purser (London: Hutchinson & Co, 1917). Marks' reports are taken from the SPG monthly publication, *Mission Field* (MF hereafter).

the recently published *Tom Brown's Schooldays* (1857). During the course of his 40 years in Burma, he saw some 15,000 pupils pass through them under his undoubtedly charismatic influence.

I could happily spend the rest of this lecture on the quite extraordinary story of John Marks and his "Royal SPG School" in Mandalay. He had already founded a school in Rangoon (now Yangon), in Lower Burma which was already under British imperial rule. Upper Burma was still independent, Mandalay the capital. At the invitation of the Buddhist King, Mindon (1814-78), the last but one king of Burma, the school was built at royal expense in the precincts of the Palace, to accommodate one thousand pupils, including several royal princes from among the king's numerous sons, with this Buddhist king paying also for the construction of the adjacent church—Marks was by now ordained after brief studies at Bishop's College, Calcutta. The font was provided by Queen Victoria. King Mindon also built Marks a house nearby, with a triple-tiered roof to mark his royal privilege, and Marks' own meals were provided by the Palace, the king insisting it was his duty, as the Buddhist equivalent of a churchwarden, to feed his priest. The princes came to school under gold umbrellas, two gold umbrellas each, each with some 40 attendants. Marks had a good deal of difficulty in running it as a school because the other pupils insisted on continuously prostrating themselves in the royal presences in the classrooms, and it took him a while to get that sorted out. "But the princes are thoroughly good little fellows without the least pride", Marks reported. "I could not have better pupils—more obedient, affectionate and diligent."[9] At least two novels have touched upon this colourful place and period, though they are no more colourful than the reality.[10]

There are some memorable details to the story, as when Marks brought Bishop Milman of Calcutta for an audience in the Palace. The king inspected the bishop down the length of the audience hall through

---

[9] *MF*, October 1869.

[10] F. T. Jesse, *The Lacquer Lady* [1929] (London: Virago, 1979), and A. Ghosh, *The Glass Palace* (London: HarperCollins, 2000). (Amitav Ghosh (1956-) was educated at St Stephen's College, Delhi, where O'Connor himself taught. He later earned a D.Phil from the University of Oxford. (Eds.)

a pair of binoculars. (That must have been rather galling for the bishop, himself the cousin of Lord Salisbury.) There are other memorable aspects, including those told by Marks' later SPG colleague, George Colbeck, as when two ladies-in-waiting came in disguise by night for baptism. The whole project, however, was extremely precarious from a political point of view. An American Baptist friend compared Marks' grace-and-favour house to an attractive little villa built on the slope of a volcano. This was because of King Mindon's quite explicit intention to use Marks. He wanted him as a go-between with the British. For example, he expected Marks to go to London to negotiate terms with Queen Victoria for Upper Burma's continued independence. Marks refused, pleading political neutrality. In conflict with Mindon Min's plans, the British intended to seize Upper Burma by force, partly to thwart French ambitions in the region. A contemporary imperial commentator, referring to Mindon's successor, King Thibaw, wrote in a contemporary imperial way that "the British Empire was tired of the vanities and pretensions of the Burmese Court".[11]

The British at the time described it as a sort of "military picnic".[12] Colbeck gives a very moving picture of the overthrow of the last king of Burma, not least the moment when King Thibaw, surrounded by a column of British soldiers with fixed bayonets, was led from the Palace, coming down the steps holding hands with two of his queens, and was marched through the bewildered, silent crowd of his subjects to the steamer that would carry him away to permanent exile in India. Marks himself also described a slightly later experience, when the palace had been commandeered by the British. In the grand hall of the palace, converted to a garrison chapel, Marks celebrated holy communion and preached to a church parade of British soldiers. "Here in this golden apartment", he wrote, "in which I had so often walked, barefoot and anxious, waiting for hours for the appearance of one of my prince-pupils with the joyful words, '*Kaw daw mu thi*' ('the King calls you'), I now stood with my back to the throne preaching to a large and attentive congregation."[13] The

---

[11] Scott O'Connor, quoted in Marks, *Forty Years in Burma*, p. 221.
[12] Marks, *Forty Years in Burma*, p. 227.
[13] Marks, *Forty Years in Burma*, p. 230.

throne, incidentally, was soon dispatched to a museum in Calcutta. The SPG School in Mandalay, though no longer "royal", continued for many years. More of this particular story later.

In Lower Burma, along the Irrawaddy, Marks founded a number of other schools, describing how "the people came and begged me to establish" schools for their sons.[14] He used pupil-teachers recruited from his school in Rangoon, on the pattern of his own progression in the East End of London from pupil to pupil-teacher. Most of these pupil-teachers Marks had himself baptized, and he hoped that some would eventually move on to ordination, which indeed some did. Among these was John Tsan Baw, the first Burmese Anglican priest. We should here mention other aspects of his extraordinarily devoted and energetic work, including his encouragement of women missionaries to open girls' schools. He saw these as more important than the boys' school "in the evangelization and civilization of this country".[15] There was also his evangelistic work in Rangoon, among the Chinese community, and also among the Tamil "coolies"—indentured labourers—"poor and despised" as he noted, brought in by the shipload from South India.[16] From among these latter, Marks built a strong congregation with its own Tamil catechist, Abishakanathan, later ordained and on SPG's list. Around 1879, the Tamils created a branch of the YMCA as a means of evangelism. Marks chaired their meetings. There is a sequel to this which I shall refer to in a moment. He also translated parts of the New Testament and completed and published the first Burmese edition of the Book of Common Prayer. But these things were all on the side from his point of view. His teaching and running of schools were his passion and the principal feature of his work.

The other school to mention in particular was St John's College, Rangoon. "In our school we had two meals a day", he wrote, "rice and curry in the morning, and curry and rice in the evening".[17] St John's was, from its foundation in 1864, the leading boys' school in Burma. Its

---

[14] *MF*, April 1868.
[15] *MF*, October 1867.
[16] *MF*, November 1869.
[17] Marks, *Forty Years in Burma*, p. 126.

impact on the emerging colonial élite was very significant as it produced generations of recruits for the developing institutions of the country, administrative, educational, legal and commercial. It also produced impressive numbers of Christians. Marks regularly reported baptisms in the school chapel—his 1877 report referring to 67 baptisms in the previous six months, including 50 Burmans and Karens. Among the Burmese baptized was the son of the leading Buddhist in the city, a judge who was the custodian of the Great Pagoda.

There are a number of features of this "Great Century" story which are strikingly characteristic. First, regarding educational mission. Marks ran his schools in an openly proselytizing way, and required parents to accept this as a condition for admitting their sons. No one, not even the devout Buddhist King Mindon, ever seems to have objected. The king, of course, had his own specific political agenda, of which Marks was well aware. Marks' explanation of the general enthusiasm for his proselytizing schools was that people saw the educational package that was offered to them as a passage to the modern world. There were no doubt two aspects to this. Thus, Mindon Min wanted modernity for his kingdom while determining to remain outside the Empire. And he wanted it badly. He asked Marks to bring 50 of his St John's College boys to Mandalay to translate the *Encyclopaedia Britannica* into Burmese. This was a request too far, even for this incredibly energetic missionary. On the other hand, many parents no doubt felt the need to make friends with the new imperial culture. As Marks explained, parents wished their sons "to learn the *bah thah*, a term that comprehends the language, literature, customs and religion—in a word, English".[18] The education he provided, which was for him pre-eminently a missionary project, clearly had also both colonialist and modernizing functions.

Secondly, there was a question about imperialism and God's purpose. Looking back after 35 years in Burma, Marks asked what God's purpose had been in adding Burma to the British Empire. His answer was clear: "That the banner of the Cross might be raised."[19] Presumably this helps to explain why he was such a highly political missionary. He was on

---

[18] *MF*, February 1881.
[19] *MF*, January 1896.

terms of intimacy with the successive British rulers of the province. The "Chief Commissioner and the General" would be invited to events in the school chapel in Rangoon. On a visit to Calcutta, he was invited to visit the Viceroy, and on leave in England in 1875, he had "long and pleasant interviews" with the Secretary of State for India, Lord Salisbury.[20] Most telling, though, was his dabbling in politics in connection with the downfall of Mindon's successor, King Thibaw, a former pupil of his. As news of Thibaw's misrule in Mandalay reached Rangoon, Marks wrote a letter to the city press calling for vigorous protest against the king. He then spoke at what an enthusiast called "a magnificent mass meeting".[21] After this, the military takeover of Upper Burma took place. That there was some connection, at least in some peoples' minds, is suggested by the actions of Sir Charles Bernard, about to become the first British ruler of Upper Burma. On receiving the official communiqués as they came in from the field force, Sir Charles copied them all and sent them to our SPG missionary at St John's College. All this, however, was because Marks believed that imperial rule facilitated the raising of the banner of the Cross.

Thirdly, there is the question of mission and other faiths. Marks' encounters with Burmese Buddhism were revealing. He saw Buddhism as useful from a missionary point of view. It "frees men from caste, and gives them an open mind to receive the Gospel".[22] He saw the religion, nevertheless, as a bundle of "perversions", "heathenism", on which "aggressions" were to be made, not least through his schools, where absolutely no concessions were ever made. Certainly, he often wrote with warmth, affection and respect of Mindon Min, "a pious and learned Buddhist", but in his well-documented discussions with the king, it is clear that he never wavered from his starting point, the stereotypical view of Buddhism as "a false system . . . a religion of despair . . . practical atheism . . . [with] no vivifying power whatever".[23] There was considerable curiosity about Buddhism in Victorian England, but to Marks this was

---

[20] Marks, *Forty Years in Burma*, p. 212.

[21] Marks, *Forty Years in Burma*, p. 34.

[22] *MF*, January 1896.

[23] Marks, *Forty Years in Burma*, p. 145. *MF*, January 1896.

ill-informed "nonsense". Much more serious and much more significant than his opinions, though, were some of his practical actions. Thus, he describes how a group of townsfolk at Zalum on the Irrawaddy, "very anxious to have a ... school, ... turned the Buddhist .. [monks] ... out of a large monastery, ... had it thoroughly cleaned and altered to my plans, and then gave it to me for an SPG school".[24] On a much larger scale of significance, however, was his acquiescence or more in the destruction of the Burmese Buddhist monarchy. If Marks himself did not know, and he must at least have been dimly aware, the British "knew that this would mean the collapse of a whole cosmological and moral order anchored in the royal capital". As a senior monk expressed it:

> No more the Royal Umbrella
> No more the Royal Palace
> And the Royal City ...
> This is indeed an Age of Nothingness
> It were better we were dead.[25]

Another of Marks' actions had consequences, significant but unforeseen. We need to recall here his part in the formation of an evangelizing YMCA in Rangoon. There was a Buddhist response, an explicit response, in the formation of a Young Men's Buddhist Association in 1906. This YMBA was initially religious and cultural in its orientation, but within a decade it was becoming increasingly "political", and is widely seen among historians of modern Burma as the first stage in the modernizing anti-colonial and nationalist movement.

Fourthly, SPG and imperialism. Soon after opening his school in Rangoon, Marks had formed there what we might call an army cadet corps. The Bishop, John Strachan, a former SPG missionary, had opposed this, but that had not deterred John Marks. Its ethnic make-up was engineered to correspond with that in the army proper. During the

---

[24] Marks, *Forty Years in Burma*, p. 118.
[25] R. Ileto, "Religious and Anti-Colonial Movements", in N. Tarling (ed.), *The Cambridge History of South East Asia* (Cambridge: Cambridge University Press, 1992), Vol. II, p. 218.

Third Burmese War, the St John's College Rifle Corps was a designated part of the garrison of Rangoon—a contribution, in other words, to the imperial army. Marks was awarded the Volunteer Decoration and always thereafter wore it, pinned to his clerical scarf. Shortly after the war, colours were acquired from England for the school's Corps—that is, a flag. It was a Union Jack. In the centre were the letters SPG. In a speech on the occasion, a Captain Becket made reference to "the great and good Queen Empress, upon whose dominions the sun never sets, and we trust never will set". He said of the College Corp's new flag, "It will remind you that the power of this Empire surrounds such beneficent agencies as the SPG, protects them in their good works, and is itself nourished and supported by such efforts in all countries that own the British name."[26]

I have told this interesting story of John Mark's 40 years in Burma not simply to share a bit of new research since the publication of *Three Centuries of Mission*, and certainly not to mock the good intentions and good achievements of the nineteenth-century mission, but to underline the context and look fairly closely at a characteristic understanding of mission in that context. John Marks was a characteristic rather than an original figure, creative and innovative within the context and parameters of colonialism ... There were other types of creativity and innovation also in that period, and there was far more to SPG and UMCA and CMD[27] than this, including some of the most committed and effective anti-colonialists that the modern missionary movement has known.[28] They are our heroes today, but we need somehow to hold them alongside those who were heroes at that time, and John Marks was certainly one of them.

---

[26] *MF*, January 1887. Of course, though it is not always acknowledged, the entire missionary movement from Britain, of all denominations, was part of this phenomenon. See especially, A. Porter, "Religion, Missionary Enthusiasm and Empire", in A. Porter (ed.), *The Oxford History of the British Empire, Vol. III, The Nineteenth Century* (Oxford: Oxford University Press, 1999), pp. 222–46.

[27] UMCA—Universities' Mission to Central Africa. CMD –Cambridge Mission to Delhi. (Eds.)

[28] For example, the slightly later C. F. Andrews in India.

✯

[Finally] I draw your attention to a book. It was published, like *Three Centuries of Mission*, in the year 2000. We just managed to get a reference to it into our history at the proof stage. Its title is *A Dictionary of Third World Theologies*.[29] It claimed a place in USPG's new history because its principal editor, Sugirtharajah, had been a tutor at the College of the Ascension in the 1980s.[30] He has always said that it was his appointment by USPG to the College and to Selly Oak that marked the beginning of his distinctive work. His other writing and research have been quite as remarkable as the *Dictionary*. From his initial book, *Voices from the Margin* (1991), published just ten years ago, he has written and edited a stream of ever-more challenging books on the interpretation of the Bible in the post-colonial and neo-colonial world. One feature has been his editing of collections of studies by other Third-World scholars, women and men, giving them an international platform for their work. This finds a sort of summation in this *Dictionary of Third World Theologies*. Its editors rightly call it 'unique' because it is the first time that a dictionary has been devoted to issues specifically related to the Third World and its theological concerns (some 150 topics), and also for the first time written solely by men and women (over 100 of them) normally relegated to the periphery. Unique also, because, as their Introduction says, these "former recipients" of other people's knowledge "turn into dispensers of their own knowledge". It is also, of course, widely ecumenical. I include it in our epilogue to celebrate the truth that, if the "mother churches" in Europe at present are much diminished, their offspring, originating among the ambiguities of the "Great Century", are now making their own diverse and glorious appropriations of the gospel. Of course, the vast majority of these are not in books, but in the lives and sufferings of individuals and communities, but this *Dictionary*, in its representative character, points towards all that.

---

[29] Edited by Virginia Fabella and R. S. Sugirtharajah (Maryknoll, NY, Orbis Books, 2000).

[30] At the same time as O'Connor was the College's Principal. (Eds.)

If the works of LINKS, and of USPG as a whole, can continue to serve such appropriations of the gospel, and help the churches here to learn from them, the "perpetual Succession... by the same Name" might well be worth sustaining for a bit longer.

* * *

Edited and abridged from the Inaugural Lecture of USPG "Links" (the friends' organization of Anglican mission agency USPG (2001).

9

The Geography of Anglicanism

The last essay by Dan O'Connor in this book is one of his most recent pieces, commissioned for inclusion in the *Oxford Handbook of Anglican Studies* (2016), edited by Mark Chapman, Sathianathan Clarke and Martyn Percy. There are glimpses of much of his earlier work in this remarkable essay. It is a brief and illuminating history of Christian mission and British Empire and its aftermath in the wider global Anglican Communion. Dan has remarked that, though not a geographer, he always had an affection for maps, here drawing the atlas of Anglicanism in various shades and colours. In his slightly earlier book, *The Chaplains of the East India Company, 1601–1858* (2012), Dan portrayed the history of the East India Company as initially surprisingly pious but later "a violent and corrupt player on the world stage, its chaplains for the most part deeply compromised".[1] He has expressed his gratitude that he was able to celebrate in his writings the lives of some of the later anti-colonial missionaries, men like Andrews and Elwin, who played their part at the end of the British Empire.

In examining the "geography" of Anglicanism, Dan begins with the English domination over the peoples of Scotland, Wales and Ireland and the "internal colonialism" that was to lead to the worldwide British Empire and that carried with it the spread of the Anglican Church, for good and for ill. But the picture is by no means without hope. If the Lambeth Conference remains split in so many ways, Archbishop Rowan Williams was still able to speak of "a global claim on our services", while his successor, Archbishop Justin Welby, comes with "a proven record of good work on issues of reconciliation".

---

[1] Unpublished correspondence with DJ.

As always, Dan writes clearly and with a sense of justice and suspicion of power, whether it is of the state or of the church. He speaks with a wisdom that is granted by a lifetime of service and teaching in the church in India, in Scotland and in England.

* * *

Historical pointers

An essential but not exclusive determinant of the geography of Anglicanism has been colonialism and imperialism. Within the writer's memory, English coinage carried the formula "Fid.Def.Ind.Imp", the faith of the Church of England being defended by a sovereign who ruled India.

The Empire of Great Britain

An early question for the post-Reformation Church of England was the matter of the "Atlantic isles", and the internal colonialism that turned them into "the Empire of Great Britain". At this stage several elements in the template for the geography of Anglicanism were laid down. Thus, in 1536, an Act of Union legalized the relationship of England and Wales, with the Welsh dioceses part of the Province of Canterbury, followed by an act to authorize Welsh translations of the Bible and the Book of Common Prayer. Other parts of this Empire were less easily secured. An Episcopal Church, reformed in part by its own bishops, emerged in sixteenth-century independent Scotland. In its subsequent history, it was largely—aside from the occasional "bullying" by its larger southern sister—independent of the Church of England and always "Episcopalian" as distinct from "Anglican". This complicated the template and contributed to an enrichingly distinct element to what was to be known as the "Anglican Communion"—a phrase first coined by the Scottish bishops. Colonizing impulses nevertheless ran even through this part of the "Isles". The Protestant Reformation had made little progress in the outer parts of Scotland and beyond the Pale in Ireland. The Gaelic-speakers of the Scottish Highlands and Islands were seen at the beginning of the seventeenth century as "a barbarous, irreligious ... people", and Ireland, still predominantly Catholic, as "that barbarous land where the people know not God" and live "like beasts". Note the animal metaphor, characteristic of racist formulations. James VI and I aimed to bring these populations from "rude barbarity" into "perfycte obedience and civilitie".[2] Andrew Knox, Bishop of the Isles, contributed his Statutes of Iona (1609), which earned him translation to a further "civilizing" ministry in Donegal as Bishop of Raphoe, and Bishop James Law used his close friendship with James to bring Orkney into line. Similarly, John Bramhall as Bishop of Derry vigorously enforced canonical norms in an effort to "Anglicize" the Church in Ireland. A further means of "civilizing" Ireland and Scotland entailed "planting", with English and Inland Scottish settlers of sound Protestant stock sent to people and cultivate "plantations" in Ireland; a similar scheme was successful in Orkney and Shetland, but unsuccessful in the Outer Hebrides. Already, then, legitimacy mattered, and bishops, liturgy, and scriptures, in an Anglicanism sharing interests with the state. Already, too, the settling of Protestants is established as a political tool and an aspect of the contestation with Roman Catholicism. What was to be an enduring rhetoric of barbarism and civility, with the added component of racism, was part of the rationale.

The Atlantic Empire

As this empire-building project was being pursued, knowledge of the Spanish, Portuguese, and Dutch "discoveries" of the non-European world was being disseminated in England by Richard Hakluyt. As chaplain to one of Elizabeth's leading statesmen, and England master-geographer, he was a significant figure in the developing geography of

---

[2] J. H. Ohlmeyer, "'Civilizing of those rude partes': Colonization within Britain and Ireland, 1580s–1640s", in N. Canny (ed.), *The Origins of Empire*, Oxford History of the British Empire, Part I. (Oxford: Oxford University Press, 2001), pp. 130ff.

Anglicanism. To promote an English Protestant colonization of North America, he produced a *Discourse on Western Planting* for Elizabeth in 1584. This confirms some of the leading conditions for the geography of Anglicanism: first, legality, in this case resting on an earlier Welsh "discovery" of North America; secondly, "planting", as a means to "the advancement of the kingdom of Christ", by establishing groups of British Protestants in a viable social and economic community. Importantly, this would enhance the social and economic life of England by reducing the "swarminge of beggars". Painting the eastern woodlands of North America as a cornucopia of fertility and abundance, Hakluyt details the trades and professions required to create a "lucrative market". The Church's part will include "devines" to promote a godly society, preachers with Bibles to deter the mutinous, and the building of churches to provide employment. Strengthened with episcopal structures, Protestant England will create a bulwark against Catholic Spain in Florida and the Caribbean. The native American will present no problem, being convertible to the gospel if approached by the colonists with discretion and mildness. Reality modified Hakluyt's vision of a "Western planting" in various ways: first, discretion and mildness were largely lacking in the approach to native Americans, who would have to endure a holocaust at the hands of the settlers, with only a small minority ever attached to the Anglican Church. Secondly, the arrival of the *Mayflower* just 36 years after Hakluyt's *Discourse* signalled a very diverse settler population, with every imaginable Protestant group flourishing and free, alongside which Anglicanism had to find its place.

Despite Hakluyt's propaganda, the Church of England was slow to assume responsibility in North America. Only late in the seventeenth century, Henry Compton, Bishop of London and one of the powerful Lords of Trade and Plantations, took up the matter. To get Anglican clergy to America, he appointed as his commissary in Maryland the remarkable priest, Thomas Bray.[3] After a brief visit, Bray addressed both the needs of America and the problem of an excess of ill-paid clergy in England

---

[3] Thomas Bray (1658–1730) was born in Shropshire and educated at Oxford. He went to Maryland in 1699, returning to England in 1701. He was a key figure in the establishment of the SPG. (Eds.)

by personally recruiting over a hundred for North America, and then, with vision and skill, creating a means of perpetuating and expanding Anglicanism both there and subsequently wherever British sovereignty prevailed. The means included both the Society for Promoting Christian Knowledge (SPCK) in 1699 and, in 1701, the Society for the Propagation of the Gospel in Foreign Parts (SPG). These two societies, almost exclusively until the nineteenth century, ensured Britain's colonial geography was Anglican. The SPG provided most of the 600 Anglican clergy who served in North America up to Independence, and the SPCK significantly effected there, through its extensive provision of libraries and education, an Anglican cultural plantation. Its commitment to supplying Bibles, invariably bound together with the Book of Common Prayer, became over the next two centuries a leading contribution to the liturgical thrust and identity of Anglicanism worldwide. An exceptional number of Scots was a significant element among these clergy, including several distinguished commissaries, while the persistent failure of the Church of England to provide a bishop throughout the colonial period had important consequences. The eventual, post-independence acquisition from Scotland of a "free, valid and purely Ecclesiastical Episcopacy",[4] along with a Scottish-style synodical polity which accorded well with republican sentiment, helped create what American (following Scotland) called an Episcopal rather than an Anglican Church. Part of its completeness was a missionary movement free from the constraints of British imperial geography and largely functioning within American spheres of influence. Thus, in the nineteenth century, women's and men's missions from that church, and the efforts of missionary bishops, extended the church across North and into Central America and the Caribbean, and beyond into China, Japan, Taiwan, and the Philippines.

---

[4] Preamble to the Concordat signed by the Scottish Bishops and Samuel Seabury in October 1784 (MS register of the College of Bishops).

An Eastern "Footing"

Almost simultaneous with western developments, a variant type of Anglican presence was evolving in the East, with another priest-geographer, Samuel Purchas, Hakluyt's disciple, in support. In this case, following the papal bulls of donation which divided the world between Spanish and Portuguese imperialisms, Anglicanism found itself in contestation with the latter, though also with Dutch Protestants in the Indonesian archipelago. The four volumes of *Hakluytus Posthumus* or *Purchas his Pilgrimes* of 1625 builds upon Hakluyt's work and was a guide for the first decades of the East India Company's activities. Despite the evaluation today of the Company as the precursor of such unattractive modern transnational corporations as Enron, it started as an intensely pious Anglican project, and gained what the SPG missionary Patrick Gordon, in his *Geography Anatomiz'd* (1693), with its overview of the "terraqueous globe", called a "footing" for the gospel in South India and Bengal and elsewhere. Its credentials as a Christian venture were taken for granted. Purchas was chaplain to the long-serving Archbishop of Canterbury, George Abbot, whose brother chaired the Company for many years. The archbishop took an active interest in Company affairs, publishing his own *Briefe Description Of The whole Worlde* (1599). As a theological geographer, Purchas saw the English merchants adventuring their capital as true "pilgrims" distinct not only from the surrounding heathen but also from the Roman Catholics with their "Pilgrimage of Vanitie". This fed into the geography of Anglicanism deeply ambiguous, mystificatory suggestions about "Gods Providence...which...effected ...extraordinary Wonders", which were to become a central tenet of the imperial project in the nineteenth century.

The Second British Empire

Simultaneous with American independence and the emergence of an equally independent American Episcopal Church were the beginnings of a vast British imperial and colonial expansion, soon outstripping all its European rivals and global in its reach. Anglicanism accompanied this through both its existing semi-confessional SPG and new voluntarist agencies.

Particularly significant in this latter category, fruit of the Evangelical Revival, was the Church Missionary Society (CMS), initially a Society for Missions to Africa and the East, and growing to be the largest Anglican agency in the nineteenth century. Starting with work among apprenticed ex-slaves in Sierra Leone in 1804—which also, echoing earlier policy, had cleared London's streets of thousands of those called at the time "negro beggars"[5]—later decades saw pioneering work with indigenous populations, in some cases, as in Nigeria and Uganda, ahead of formal colonial establishment, and also in Kenya, Tanzania, Uganda, Congo, Rwanda, and Sudan. Other CMS work, some with settlers, spread to India, Australia, Canada, New Zealand, China, and Japan. In the Middle East, CMS missionaries worked in Palestine, Jordan, Iran, and Egypt. Other new Anglican agencies, related to the Oxford Movement, also approached indigenous peoples, chief among them the Universities' Mission to Central Africa, inspired by a lecture at Cambridge by David Livingstone in 1857, and giving an Anglo-Catholic orientation to Anglicanism in what is now Zambia, Malawi, Mozambique, Botswana, and parts of Tanzania. Caught between these two tendencies, SPG entered reluctantly into the new competition for support, extending the Anglican geography, nevertheless, into many parts of and beyond the Empire's formal structures.

The work of the underrated Thomas Middleton, first Bishop of Calcutta from 1814, brought pre-Tractarian high-church principles to bear in drawing together the Company chaplains, missionaries, and Indian Christians in an emerging South Asian Anglicanism. Middleton greatly admired the Indian Christian community already established in South India through a century of work by Lutheran missionaries, many financed by SPCK and the East India Company. His incorporation of some of their congregations into the Anglican Church was, from his perspective, the best thing he could do for them, though Lutheranism harbours a continuing grudge. They made for a strong and dynamic element in Indian Anglicanism, as they have continued to do in the united

---

[5] R. Coupland, *Wilberforce: A Narrative* (London: Collins, 1945), p. 225.

Church of South India. Elsewhere in the subcontinent, Anglicanism was to remain little more than a faithful "footing" in the ocean of Asian religiosity.

Having originally turned to Richard Hakluyt for geographical information, and acquired traders' maps of eastern North America, the SPG from 1842 produced its own interpretation of Christian progress with its *Colonial Church Atlas, Arranged in Dioceses*, thereafter frequently revised. Similarly, throughout the period, from 1857, the *Church Missionary Atlas* was constantly reprinted in successively enlarged editions, as was the *Atlas of the UMCA* (Universities' Mission to Central Africa). These were accompanied by a mass of popular literature: the SPG published in alternate years the journals of bishops in *Missions to the Heathen* and in *The Church in the Colonies*, marking Anglicanism's dual existence. SPCK's celebration of Queen Victoria's Jubilee in 1887 with *The Jubilee Atlas of the British Empire* is a useful reminder of what was seen from the imperial metropolis as the seamless weave of Anglicanism and the second British Empire.

Geographical features of an imperial Church

Anglican space
The connections between the spatial and the Anglican in the imperial process fall into four categories.

Settlement, controlled and encouraged by the British Government
This was a major element over some four centuries in the making of Anglican geography, though of course not all settlers were Anglicans. Emigration from Britain was highest in the period 1815–1914, including 13.7 million to the USA, 4.2 million to Canada, 2.4 million to Australia and New Zealand, and 0.8 million to South Africa, a total of over 22 million. There are many fascinating byways in this story, such as that reflected in an SPG report of 1857 noting the large numbers of "downright avowed infidels ... mechanics ... chiefly from Manchester, Rochdale and London" emigrating to Australia, while the "character of those who proceed to Canada ... [was] exceedingly promising ... small farmers,

farm labourers ... almost exclusively members of our Church, and therefore most enthusiastically loyal to our gracious Queen". Others, in 1863, were "first-class people, not as formerly the refuse of the country". Chaplaincy and gifts of Prayer Books, Bibles, etc., were provided at the port of London and at Liverpool to serve these emigrants, with a system of commendation to the developing colonial church. Migration was still high after the World War II, not least into Southern Africa, and to Australia with assisted passages. The settler churches gained some of their distinctive character from the mission agencies involved—particularly SPG and CMS, who provided many hundreds of clergy—but also from such factors as politics and class in their colonial societies.

Settlement could be involuntary, as in slavery
Anglicanism was associated with this chiefly in West Africa, the Caribbean, and North America. Caribbean slavery included the contested story of the Barbadian sugar plantations and their Anglican slaves. Not everyone would call this an altruistic experiment, but it led to a Caribbean Anglicanism and to slave-descended clergy serving in the West Indian Mission to West Africa. In North America, Anglican clergy ignored the law to provide education for the slaves, and, despite the barbarity of the entire institution, a later black historian could write of black dedication to the Episcopal Church because it was seen as a divine institution established before racial inequality.[6] After abolition, colonial agriculture depended on indentured labour, with several millions, known as coolies, shipped about the Empire, mostly from South India, some of them Christians, and with Indian Anglicans attempting to minister to them. Enforced settlement was frequently practised to remove dangerous elements from Britain, as after Monmouth's Rebellion and the Jacobite risings, or as steps were taken to reduce the numbers in English prisons by transportation to Australia. Until the influx of free immigrants during the Australian gold rushes of the 1850s, the settler population was composed largely of convicts and their descendants. Economic pressure carried

---

[6] H. T. Lewis, *Yet with a Steady Beat: The African American Struggle for Recognition in the Episcopal Church* (Valley Forge, PA: Trinity Press International, 1996), pp. 4–5.

white indentured labour to America and the Caribbean, while enforced clearance of the Scottish Highlands and famine in Ireland created new populations in Canada, Australia, and New Zealand. In all these cases, the Church of England and its colonial associates were committed to providing a ministry and education to these new populations.

A third feature relates to the indigenous people where occupation or settlement took place
Here, there were two developments. The first was displacement. Variant versions, none benign, feature across the entire Anglican geography. The first issue of SPG's monthly, *The Mission Field*, described the original Boeothic people of Newfoundland driven into extinction by the 1820s, and followed by a virtual holocaust across North America. Only 3 per cent of the Aboriginal inhabitants of Australia survived the eras of colonization, 13 per cent in New Zealand, and none in Tasmania, while, further into the Pacific, missionaries reported the slaughter of islanders and a growing slave trade in Melanesia. Anglican attitudes varied. In Canada and Australia, industrial schools, a collaboration of church and colonial government, though later heavily criticized and often a path to degradation and death, were seen by the church as a passage for indigenous people to both Christianity and the modern world. Some missionaries campaigned against the displacement and mistreatment of native peoples, but the Bishop of Grahamstown in the 1860s described how in British Kaffraria, previously "filled with savages", English farmhouses were now replacing "Kafir kraals, ... the countryside. ... being filled with life". A second development was co-option by marriage. In the Indian subcontinent, Britain's soldiers, the world's largest standing army, fathered a large Eurasian community. With many brought up and educated as Anglicans, and permanent outsiders to India's older ethnic society, migration to Australia, New Zealand, and Canada was common.

A fourth feature was segregation, the pale around Dublin providing an early example
In North America, the English started in forts, although it was the local people who finished in reservations. In Canada, the Anglican clergy received generous grants of land known as the Clergy reserves, with

comparable arrangements in Australia. In India, starting with Fort George, Fort William, and Bombay Castle, each with its Anglican church, the seeds were planted of India's three most vast conurbations. All three soon had a White Town (in Madras originally known as Christian Town) and a Black Town, the former spacious and orderly and with grand buildings around the church, the latter crowded, growing exponentially, and severely policed, with churches and ministry following eventually. In India from around the 1750s, Anglican churches for Europeans and Eurasians became a feature of the advancing distribution of military cantonments, Indian converts subsequently getting separate churches. Segregation there applied also to cemeteries. Colonial town planning throughout British territories in many parts of Africa and elsewhere observed this pattern of segregation, with Anglican and other church presences only appearing in African areas by lay, missionary, and indigenous initiative. South Africa was a prime twentieth-century case, with the Anglican Church developing in the Black and Coloured areas a large church-building programme to counter the oppression of apartheid.

An Anglican fault line

The civility/barbarity dichotomy which marked the Church's mission in the "Empire of Great Britain" was a persisting fault line in Anglican geography. The terminology of barbarian, savage, heathen, pagan—over against civilized—had a much older and wider European history, but gained a commanding currency throughout the British Empire and the Anglican Church. Thomas Bray was clear about it, disapproving of the Native Americans who "roam about in the Woods, Hunting after Prey as the Wild Beasts do" and who need to be delivered "from a Savage to a Civil and Human Life". The civilizing function of mission was always present in Anglicanism but gained renewed emphasis from the Enlightenment and among Evangelicals in early nineteenth-century India. Thus, in 1805, the evangelical East India Company chaplain, Claudius Buchanan, published his influential *Memoir of the Expediency of an Ecclesiastical Establishment for British India* which would provide *a Foundation for the Ultimate Civilization of the Natives.*

The means of civilizing most emphasized in Anglicanism was education, seen as moral training and a preparation for evangelization. The Church's massive role here usually preceded and often outstripped in scale that of the colonial and imperial authorities, though often funded by official grants-in-aid. An entire system of primary to tertiary institutions—in some respects an advance of what was happening in Britain—was a feature of Anglican mission. Anglican women missionaries found, along with their contribution in medicine, a highly significant educational vocation. The medium of instruction was a lively debate, not least in nineteenth-century India. There the debate between the "orientalists" and the "anglicists" was resolved in favour of English education, the law-member, Macaulay's famous minute of 2 February 1835, being often cited as the determinative moment. However much they might have been at the time a "mask of conquest", missionary education and the medium of English were transformative factors in global human geography. The term "improvement" regularly accompanied talk of civilizing, and was further amplified by movements, particularly in the nineteenth century for social reform, including several in India led by chaplains and missionaries, and in Africa against the slave-trade, under the auspices from 1839 of a Society for the Civilization of Africa. One little-explored aspect of "improvement" was the eighteenth-century notion characterized in England by rural development and the work of people like "Turnip" Townshend. In 1816, Bishop Middleton, on tour in India, complained that the country through which they passed, largely uncultivated, displayed "no features whatever of public spirit or improvement". His Baptist contemporary, William Carey, was more practical, founding the Agricultural and Horticultural Society of India. In the post-imperial world, under the name "development", the phenomenon had a continued and contested existence.

The "civility" Anglicanism promoted through education was often, and with no doubt complex motivation, eagerly sought after. An early and enduring image is of the four Mohawk leaders on bended knee at the court of Queen Anne receiving copies of the Book of Common Prayer in 1710. They also asked for teachers and got them. Likewise, both in South India, where the upper castes campaigned for English Education, and in Bengal where, following Macaulay's Minute promoting education in

English and denigrating Indian culture, the support of Indian reformers encouraged an "English fever", the long-term consequences were massive. The missionary J. E. Marks in Burma in the later nineteenth century explained that parents wanted their children "to learn the *bah thah*, a term that comprehends the language, literature, customs and religion— in a word, 'English'". The numerous "bush schools" throughout Africa and Asia, feeding a series of élite institutions of secondary and tertiary education, were characteristic of Anglicanism to which people flocked. Kolumba Msigala in East Africa, who opened many schools, was told by Chief Undi in 1937 that he wanted a school because "Your religion builds up a town ... (and) brings civilization."[7] Commenting on the Universities' Mission to Central Africa's élite St Andrew's College at Kiungani, Zanzibar, a historian observed that the school "produced, and was meant to produce, young men who often thought like Europeans, but at least produced young men who had the knowledge and confidence to criticize Europeans".[8]

"Civilization" understood in this way almost invariably involved defamation of indigenous religion. The evangelical missionary Henry Martyn, arriving in Calcutta in 1805, found his delight in the elegance of the White Town ruined by the thought of the "diabolical heathenism" beyond. Behind this was a century-long denigration of Indian culture and religion, pioneered by some of the leading SPCK Lutheran missionaries and raised to a new pitch of contempt in the campaign led by William Wilberforce in the 1790s for the admission of missionaries to India. It was to characterize the nineteenth-century Anglican and other missionaries in India, with only rare exceptions, chiefly in the small university missions.

Another aspect of the dichotomizing was the racism which developed so strongly throughout British possessions in the nineteenth century, and this explains the absence of indigenous leadership in the churches. An impressive attempt to overcome this was in the case of the CMS secretary, Henry Venn, with his vision of a separate "Native Church" with indigenous leadership. The consecration of the Yoruba, Samuel Crowther

---

[7] J. Iliffe (ed.), *Modern Tanzanians: A Volume of Biographies* (Nairobi: Historical Association of Tanzania, 1973), p. 6.

[8] *Modern Tanzanians*, p. 6.

as Bishop of the Niger in 1864 initiated the fulfilment of Venn's vision, but the missionaries undermined Crowther's position, their adherence to the intolerant imperialism of "Keswick" theology unmistakably racist. A later advocate of ideas similar to Venn's was the SPG missionary Roland Allen, impressed with Confucian culture and deeply hostile to imperialism, whose writing influenced the formation of the Three-Self Patriotic Movement in communist China, which aided the survival under Mao of Protestant Christianity.[9]

The dichotomy had a curious outworking in the matter of colonial clergy. The nineteenth century saw a considerable increase in the numbers recruited throughout the colonies for the colonial church. Accompanying this was legislation in England in the way of Colonial Clergy Acts, intended—in the words of one of their champions—to "prevent the country being visited with an *inundation* of *foreign* and *half-educated* Clergymen".[10] St Augustine's College, Canterbury, was opened in 1848 to provide an entry point to ministry in the colonies for the many who could not afford a university education, even if the stigma of "colonial" became attached to them. We see it in a light-hearted form in W. S. Gilbert's ballad, "The Bishop of Rum-Ti-Foo", while it was endured by irritated clergy originating outside Britain in the form of "colonial cringe" well into the postcolonial era, which proved an aspect of an enduring fault-line in the mental geography of Anglicanism.

---

[9] The credibility of the Three-Self Patriotic Movement in China is held very much in question by the unregistered House Churches. It was founded in 1954 on the principles of removing foreign influences from the church in China, and assuring the government of its patriotism. The three principles of self-governance, self-support (freedom from foreign money) and self-propagation were first articulated by Henry Venn in the middle of the nineteenth century. (Eds.)

[10] S. S. Wood, *An Apology for the Colonial Clergy of Great Britain.* (London, 1828), p. 10. Italics in original.

Postcolonial harbingers

There was always dissent from an imperialistic Anglicanism, and a measure of freedom achieved. Thus nineteenth-century Tamil Anglicans such as Vedanayaga Sastriar and Krishnapillai wonderfully expressed their faith in Tamil poetry, and others developed their own effective agency in mission. Bishop Robert Caldwell encouraged them in the latter, though he dismissed proposals to have a Tamil bishop. In Africa also, phenomenal church growth in Nigeria towards the end of the century had seen the rise of a popular "folk" church among both the peasantry and the urban working class, local agency showing minimal dependence on outside support, while in South Africa (though Anglican "Ethiopianism" was severely controlled), the struggle against racial oppression was taken up by women and men, black and white together, under such courageous leaders as Archbishop Desmond Tutu. A small group of mostly high-church Anglican missionaries such as J. W. Colenso and A. S. Cripps in Southern Africa, R. Allen in China, and C. F. Andrews in India, defied imperial Anglicanism and were given new names by the people amongst whom they worked. The broad picture of this sort of vitality and integrity has only come to be widely acknowledged, researched, and celebrated more recently. None of it has a specific geographical locus, but it represented a Christianity standing free of the culture of colony and empire.

Anglicans and the terraqueous globe

"A Epitome of the Church's Work"

This phrase in the SPG Report of 1870 described missionary work among aboriginals in Guyana and the 16 other groups in this British colony in South America, people from Africa, Asia (including both India and China), North America, assorted Atlantic islands, and Europe. This was seen as a missionary challenge, but it also disclosed something of the globalizing impact already being experienced in places that were far from the colonial metropolis but distinctly cosmopolitan. Part of Anglicanism's response to this emerging reality, in addition to a vigorous missionary movement, was the sort of networking represented initially among the episcopal friends of Joshua Watson and the Hackney Phalanx and then by the Lambeth Conference, the first meeting of which had been in 1867. That it included bishops of the American Episcopal Church clarified its formal independence of colony and empire.

A global context

What the reporter observed in 1870 British Guyana pointed forward towards the extraordinary changes that took place throughout the world in the twentieth century. These indicated that increasingly human life was experienced and understood within a global context. The very naming of two of its most problematic periods as "world" wars makes the point. The creation, in the immediate aftermath of the second of these, of the United Nations Organization and its diverse agencies was a source of hope, never as yet fully realized. Economic change accompanying the dismantling of the British and others European empires saw a prolonged struggle between systems representing capital and labour and entailing a "cold war" of some 40 years, much of it fought by proxy in over a hundred local wars in what was termed a "Third World" where the world's poorest people lived and bore the brunt. The capitalist option was challenged by Pope John Paul II. If the United States emerged as the world's only superpower, launching new resource wars and speaking of a "Project for the New American Century", its dominance seemed far from guaranteed in the light of the BRIC phenomenon, the economic rise of Brazil, Russia, India, and China, suggesting an emerging multipolar world order. Accompanying this period of vast economic and political change was rapid social change, the position of women in society probably having the most far-reaching consequences, but significant also was the speed of urbanization, locating ever larger numbers in vast "megacities". Constant conflict and economic imbalances made migrancy and the consequent increasing pluralism of societies a feature. Alongside economic change, the other great accelerator in the globalizing process was the expansion of knowledge and of scientific and technological achievement, including the globalizing of communication through the internet. The great challenge confronting the globe's human occupants in their ever vaster numbers was crystallized in the observation of a devout Christian woman that

> the two worlds of man—the biosphere of his inheritance, the technosphere of his creation—are out of balance, indeed potentially, in deep conflict. And man is in the middle. This is the hinge of history at which we stand, the door of the future opening on to a crisis more sudden, more global, more inescapable and more bewildering than any ever encountered by the human species and one which will take decisive shape in the life span of children who are already born.[11]

Anglicans in a globalizing world

In 1947, 90 years after the first Lambeth Conference, the process of decolonization began with the independence of India and a partition that also produced Pakistan (and Bangladesh subsequently), with Burma and Ceylon/Sri Lanka becoming independent at the same time. This was the beginning of the end of British imperialism. In the year following, Geoffrey Fisher became the first Archbishop of Canterbury to visit Australia. It was a first step in his highly effective promotion of a pan-Anglicanism that was to take him subsequently—where he made the most of the ease of air travel—to many of the African countries approaching independence, urging them to take up the matter of indigenous leadership in a transformed Anglican Communion. Decolonization in West and then East and Central Africa came in a torrent in the 1960s, 23 independent nations emerging between 1961 and 1963, though powerful and wealthy White racist communities in Southern Africa hung on to power for another 30 years. Fisher's project was prophetic, as some statistics regarding the Lambeth Conferences at this period make clear. Thus, in 1948, 6 per cent of bishops attending the Conference from Africa were black, while by 1978 the figure was 80 per cent. The same period

---

[11] B. Ward and R. Dubos, *Only One Earth* (Harmondsworth: Penguin 1972), p. 47.

saw a growth in the number of bishops attending from Africa from 37 to 102, while these as a percentage of all attending bishops rose from 11 per cent to 25 per cent. Talk of a change in Christianity's centre of gravity began in the 1960s, though it was only a rather crude characterization of what was happening. South Asian developments also changed the geography of Anglicanism, with a united Church of South India formed in the year of Indian independence and Anglicanism losing itself in the wider body, its bishops only admitted to a "wider episcopal fellowship" within the Lambeth family after some decades. The union that followed in North India in 1970 met Anglican requirements from its inception. There were also some losses in the period. In addition to the severe testing of Anglican churches in South-East Asia and of the Nippon Sei Ko Kai during World War II, Anglicanism in China following the Maoist revolution was transposed into the Three-Self Patriotic Movement, while the Anglican Church in North Korea after the communist takeover disappeared without trace.

Anglicanism's global networks

New measures were taken enabling Anglicans to adjust to a post-imperial world and to realize new relationships in a globalizing context. The term "partnership"—first formally adopted at an ecumenical meeting of the International Missionary Council in Canada in 1947—was widely adopted, for example in the business of the leading mission agencies of the Church of England. An Anglican Congress in Minneapolis in 1954 further worked out the principles and practice of inter-provincial partnership in a strategy known as "Mutual Responsibility and Interdependence in the Body of Christ", a strategy implemented with some success for a number of years. Measures to consolidate the work of the Lambeth Conference itself included the appointment in 1960 of an Executive Officer of the Anglican Communion and the formation of an Anglican Consultative Council (ACC), with equal numbers of bishops, priests, and lay people, its first meeting being in Limru, Kenya, in 1971. The ACC initiated a consultative process, Partnerships-in-Mission, to give mutual support to the member churches of the Communion in their mission, though the

Church of England, with a lingering colonial mindset, was a reluctant host to a consultation. Another globalizing use of modern technology, like Archbishop Fisher's use of improved air services, was when the wealthy parish of Holy Trinity, Wall Street, New York in the 1980s funded the provision of fax machines to every Third World provincial office, the forerunner of internet and website links across the Communion. The constructive use of these means is seen in the Anglican Communion's ten global networks set up for environmental, peace and justice, women's, interfaith, and other concerns. At a regional level also, new groupings were created, such as, for example, the Caribbean Anglican Consultation maintaining from 1991 a dialogue with North American Anglicanism, or the Council of Anglican Provinces of Africa, with its "HIV AIDS, TB and Malaria Network" confronting the problem of global epidemics. Beyond its own circles, Anglicanism participated in other globalizing processes, such as the work of the World Council of Churches, an Anglican Centre founded in Rome in 1966 at the time of the Second Vatican Council as a base for Anglican representation to the Vatican, and an Observer at the United Nations in New York.

The network damaged

Problems affecting the global relationships of Anglicanism developed from the 1970s in the interface of hermeneutics and culture, initially with regard to the ordination of women, and then with regard to sexual ethics. In the former case, Anglo-Catholics in England and Anglo-Catholic missionaries sought to influence church policy in Central Africa and elsewhere. In the latter, fundamentalism featured, a response echoed in other world religions faced with rapid cultural change. Phrases such as "Global Anglican" and "Global South" were appropriated, and some 200 bishops were persuaded to absent themselves from the Lambeth Conference. A geographical dimension was identifiable here also. Dioceses and provinces originating in English conservative-evangelical missions in South America, and in Africa, including some affected by then East African Revival, were strongly represented among the absentees, as were dioceses in South-East Asia that had been influenced by English charismatic missionaries in the 1980s. On the other hand, out of the struggle for racial justice in Southern Africa emerged a further commitment, to advocate "gender-justice". Funding for the dissenters came from the political right-wing elements in the Episcopal Church in the USA, with a managerial role by ex-missionaries and ex-missionary bishops from England. Hardly surprisingly, the terms "colonialism" and "neocolonialism", and cultural theory's terminology of "imperial prudery" and "colonial masculinity", came into play. Theory also seemed applicable when fieldwork research in South-East Asia disclosed the gap between the younger clergy and laity, who were untroubled about gender issues, and their episcopal leaders who claimed that such concepts had no place in their local culture, a case of the culture of Anglicanism repeating the colonial silencing of the subaltern.

The vocation of global Anglicanism

The large majority of bishops who attended Lambeth 2008 testified to the value of "indaba", a Southern African method for groups seeking a common mind, that was adopted for the event. They said it freed them from the tensions that assailed the Communion and for opportunities to appreciate its wider life, "broader and richer"—in Archbishop Rowan Williams' words—than those matters alone. His third address directed attention powerfully to the vocation and practice of Anglicanism:

> A global church and a global faith ... (that was) not just about managing internal controversy. Our global, Catholic faith affirms that the image of God is the same everywhere—in the Zimbabwean woman beaten by police in her own church, in the manual scavenger in India denied the rights guaranteed by law; in the orphan of natural disaster in Burma, in the abducted child forced into soldiering in Northern Uganda, in the hundreds of thousands daily at risk in Darfur and Southern Sudan, in the woman raising a family in a squatters' settlement in Lima or Buenos Aires. *This* is the Catholic faith: that what is owed to them is no different from, no less than what is owed to any of the rest

of us... This is the Catholic Church; this is the Catholic faith—a global vision for a global wound, a global claim on our service.

Justin Welby became Archbishop of Canterbury and assumed the leadership of the Anglican Communion in February 2013. He brought to this testing role a spirituality both evangelical and catholic, a long experience of working internationally—not least in Africa—both in the churches and in the secular sphere, and a proven record of good work on issues of reconciliation, all modestly held but carrying their own promise for the promotion of Anglicanism's global inheritance.

From, Mark D. Chapman, Sathianathan Clarke and Martyn Percy (eds), *The Oxford Handbook of Anglican Studies* (Oxford: Oxford University Press, 2016), pp. 271–84. Reprinted with minor editorial changes by permission of the Oxford University Press.

Appendix

From Juliet O'Connor, *Juliet's Letters from India* (Amazon, 2018), and Beth Collier, *Beyond Words* (London: SPCK, 1987)

After Juliet's death in 2016, Dan collected, edited and published two volumes of her writings: *A Stockton Childhood* (2018), of which the second part is by Dan himself, and *Juliet's Letters from India* (2018). Each has its own special flavour. *A Stockton Childhood* begins with a fragment of Juliet's writing that seems to be an introduction to a history of her family. The history itself has not been found, but the fragment introduces us to her ancestor Admiral Sir Francis Augustus Collier (and before that his father Admiral Sir George Collier [1738–95]). These naval forebears were to figure again later in her life.

Juliet's Letters from India—a short excerpt from which appears below—are letters written to her parents during the O'Connors' decade living in Delhi. They are full of vivid and minute descriptions of everyday life and vignettes of the early days of the marriage. For example: 11 July 1964—"I slept like a log on the train coming here, but D was awake prac all night fighting to keep the bugs off me—in swarms, vile creatures."[1] 21 July 1964—"Some lovely birds in the garden—green bee-eaters, v. elegant, and two golden orioles in the neem tree, brilliant yellow & a piercing cry."[2] In the Interlude "Mushaira", reprinted here, it should be born in mind that this Muslim celebration was taking place at the end of a war with Pakistan that was essentially a conflict between Hindus and Muslims—the latter in Pakistan, and Muslims, perhaps some of these poets, in Delhi were compelled to fight against their religious brethren in Pakistan.

---

[1] Juliet O'Connor, *Juliet's Letters from India* (Amazon, 2018), p. 66.
[2] *Letters from India*, p. 67.

The final excerpt is from "Beth Collier's" *Beyond Words: Prayer as a Way of Life* (1987). Juliet wrote this book under the pseudonym "Beth Collier" in admiration of her ancestor who is mentioned in her childhood recollections, Admiral Sir Francis Augustus Collier (1785–1849), between 1826 and 1830 the commodore of the West African Station, during which time he fought slavers and freed some 3,500 slaves. She remembers her father telling her, looking back to their distinguished forebears, that "If it was not for a silly family quarrel, you would have been a Lady." But we see in Juliet's words reprinted here that it would have taken far more than a family quarrel to make her anything less than a lady. They are an appropriate way to end this book.

Juliet's Letters from India, pp. 231–4

INTERLUDE "Mushaira"

[The reference on 15 December to the end of the Indo-Pak War which saw East Pakistan become Bangladesh introduces a piece Juliet wrote about a "celebratory" event at the Lal Qila (the Red Fort) that we were taken to by our friend, Professor Khwaja Afmad Faruqi. Dan.]

One of the most moving events I have ever witnessed in India was an open-air poetry reading. Called a "mushaira", it is a traditional Muslim form of entertainment which can be enjoyed by all castes and classes. The mushaira we attended was set against the backcloth of the Lal Qila, the Red Fort of Delhi, the old Mughal palace of a long line of proud rulers.

The white marble glittered in the moonlight, and further off, domes and minarets made a romantic silhouette against the deep blue sky. Through the sculptured archways and delicately carved stone screens, it was easy to imagine the drifting muslin of courtesans glimpsed for a moment as they slipped quickly back to the harem. It did not require much imagination to be back in the high days of magnificence in the Mughal court, and feel the heartbeat of its beautiful and bloody history.

In such circumstances, it is hard to concentrate even at such a bewitching assembly as a mushaira.

The festival of verse is always held at night, and may last until the waking crows and jackdaws disturb the muse as the sky changes through grey pearl to turquoise and then to pale azure with the rising sun.

The audience were seated partly on luxurious oriental carpets, partly on rough cotton durries, and partly on western chairs. The extras, for there are always extras in India, found spaces on the grass or steps or parapets of the formal courts and now dry pools of the old water gardens.

On such an occasion, a university professor may be seated next to the humblest of labourers. We saw just such a juxtapositioning, and it would be hard to say which appreciated the evening more. The labourer was not alone as there were many who had spent the day barefoot, pushing barrows through the streets, and had only the clothes they wore and would sleep under the stars. Others had spent the day in air-conditioned offices, perhaps telephoning the capitals of the world, had wardrobes full of western suits, and would sleep in silken luxury. For the literate and the illiterate, the evening held equal delight because they all loved the language with its wit and flexibility. Delhi has a large Muslim population and many others also speak Urdu.

In front of the former royal apartments, a high platform had been built, backed by a truly regal shamiana screen. It was surrounded by potted plants and covered with white sheeting.

As the poets, all wearing traditional dress, took their places, they removed their shoes and made themselves comfortable on the cushions and bolsters provided. Most of the poets were recognized by the audience and were applauded when they appeared on the platform. Some acknowledged the crowd and others remained aloof. There was a good deal of changing places and shuffling before the programme began, and those familiar with the poets enjoyed watching this positioning and enjoyed the animosities and friendships it indicated.

When the master of ceremonies took the centre of the stage and welcomed the audience, he was applauded, and we all settled down for a long night of verbal dexterity, delicacy and fireworks.

As the hours went by, each poet came forward in turn and recited his work, usually from memory. One or two of the older ones needed help from their notes, but this was viewed sympathetically. The hushed audience were totally involved in the event. During the recitals, a particularly clever couplet, a neat turn of phrase, or a witty juxtaposing of ideas would be applauded, sometimes with the Urdu equivalent of "bravo", sometimes with a roar of appreciation and even clapping. The poets' eyes twinkled, their chests swelled with pride, or they regarded the audience with a sly expression whilst they produced an even more apt line.

Occasionally, one of the poets waiting in the background would be seen hastily scribbling, perhaps changing a line for a better effect or to secure more praise from the audience than another poet.

The whole event tingled with life and there was plenty of audience participation. Sometimes, an older, well-known poet would be asked to recite a particular popular poem, and those in the audience would hold their breath and glance at each other, waiting for their favourite lines to be spoken. A long sigh and nodding of heads would greet the expected ingenuity, delicacy or pathos.

Eventually, when all the poets had exhausted their store of new poems, and the familiar ones had been recited too, they would be led from the platform by the Master of Ceremonies, heads held high and glancing to neither left nor right, in the knowledge that they had again ensured their places in the hearts of their public, and that their gift, although appreciated by many, was not a commonplace skill.

The audience dispersed, the magic was spirited away, and the raucous vitality of India, like a hot blanket, engulfed us again. Food-sellers cried their wares, beggars accosted us, carts clattered past and stray dogs rummaged through stinking heaps at the roadside.

For one night, the poets had carried us beyond the uncomfortable and the mundane. Those of high estate and those of none, academic and labourer, sharing a delight in the language and imagery of dreams, had met across the gulf which normally separated them. After such an experience, the reality of everyday India becomes once more bearable.

*

"Beth Collier", *Beyond Words,* **p. 109**

For the future
Wherever and whoever you are, you have a special place to fulfil and enjoy. Enjoyment is probably not the first word that comes to mind if you are finding life a struggle, but there are so many small blessings we have to be thankful for. Even those who are imprisoned by physical or mental circumstances can usually think of a situation worse than their own.

If you are called to a life of prayer, heartily rejoice that God has seen fit to draw from you qualities that have lain dormant during their maturing and now enable you to be ready for his service, and for a fuller life in the beautiful or difficult circumstances you are given.

Look forward to the future and never give up; God is for ever.

"Bless the Lord, O my soul; and all that is within me, bless his holy name. (Psalm 103)

Afterword

Harish Trivedi

I first met Daniel O'Connor in September 1969, on being appointed a lecturer in English in St Stephen's College, Delhi, where he was already serving in that capacity. We were colleagues for a period of just two years, for in September 1971, I left for Britain, and when I returned in 1975, I found that Dan and his family had already returned to England for good in 1972. Then *kismet* (as Kipling and other Anglo-Indians called it) brought us together again in 1985 in Birmingham, for a longer stay together until 1988 when I finally returned to India.

In St Stephen's, Dan had been for me—and for many others of our colleagues too perhaps—primarily a figure in a white cassock, whose role as a lecturer was apparently secondary to his missionary role as the Chaplain of the college. He seldom spent much time in the Senior Combination Room—as our basic staffroom was called in imitation of Oxbridge colleges—where we sat chatting and drinking cups of tea between lectures. But Dan was always busy elsewhere, gliding in and out silently, smilingly and a little mysteriously. In Birmingham, paradoxically, where we were not colleagues but lived within an easy walking distance of each other, we constantly met *en famille* in each other's homes and spent much "quality time" together.

It was then that we really got to know each other and became friends, which we have continued to be over all these decades, through his two subsequent visits to Delhi, and my more numerous visits to Britain and to his successive homes in Ely, Wakefield (where he took me on a literary pilgrimage to Haworth), and Edinburgh. Even when we could not meet, we regularly read each other's work and kept in touch through letters or email. On the occasion of the centenary of St Stephen's College, I invited Dan to contribute his memoirs to a special issue of the college magazine that I was editing, entitled *St Stephen's in Our Times* (1981), and 42 years on, I am delighted that I have the privilege of contributing this afterword to a selection of his publications written over a lifetime.

In what follows, I shall first recount a couple of personal episodes from our long friendship, for Dan cherishes and attaches value to his friendships with a host of people almost as a part of his faith, and seems to believe as John Keats did in "the holiness of the heart's affections". I shall then proceed to discuss briefly a few of his works among those reprinted in this volume, now and then seeking to complement his views from my own parallel experiences, so that there may be a sense of an international, interfaith and intercultural dialogue.

The little terrorist and the credit card

When Dan I got together again in Birmingham in 1985, he and Juliet and their two sons and I and my wife Poonam and our two sons constituted quite a symmetrical familial ensemble. Back in Delhi in 1971, Poonam and I had just got married in August that year before we set off three weeks later for Britain—just as Dan and Juliet had just got married in England and then set off for India in 1963. My wife and I recall that the O'Connors were among the more sociable colleagues of mine. They promptly had us over to dinner at their home in the College in that narrow window of three weeks.

When we met again after 14 years, it was through the good offices of the late David Baker, who taught history in St Stephen's, assiduously kept his countless friendships in good repair, and knew exactly where Dan was. Immediately on our arrival in Birmingham, Dan and Juliet made us feel as if we had last met only yesterday. It was through their recommendation that we had booked a flat near them in Selly Oak in a grand old establishment then called the Methodist Overseas Guest House, which often had vacancies as the number of Methodist missionaries coming back on home leave had drastically declined.

Neither Dan nor Juliet could be called effusive (isn't that bad form!), but Juliet came across as rather more outgoing and genial and was in this respect too an asset to Dan. In Birmingham, Juliet helped Poonam shop for various household things in an inexpensive market at the bottom of the Rotunda in the city centre, and when Poonam's wallet was stolen on one of their visits there, she told me she would have been rather more distraught had it not been for Juliet's soothing presence at her side. Many were the "little nameless ... acts/ Of kindness and of love" (in Wordsworth's fine phrase) that we could depend on the O'Connors for.

The conversations between Dan and myself tended to be of a more academic nature. While Poonam kept busy working on her doctorate at the Shakespeare Institute in the University of Birmingham, I too had a project of my own which was to work on Edward John Thompson (1886–1946) who wrote eight novels, four plays and about a hundred poems all located in India and was in his day compared not unfavourably with E. M. Forster. He had served as a missionary in India, as his father too had before him, and a trilogy of his novels, of which the middle one is pointedly entitled *A Farewell to India* (1931), has two British missionaries serving in Bengal as the central characters. It helped my cause tremendously that this novelist's son, E. P. Thompson the historian, allowed me unrestricted access to his father's papers, now in the Bodleian Library, which were still with him in his huge house near Worcester which I visited once a week for the better part of three years.

Dan naturally warmed to my chosen theme, but when he read the novels I was working on, his enthusiasm was not exactly enhanced. The two missionary protagonists in Thompson's novel, in their frequent soul-searching elegiac introspections feel that the great age of missionary endeavour had already passed by the 1920s and that they had been "left stranded by history". Dan and I often talked about the larger ebb and tide of missionary movements, and he surprised me one day by suggesting that Christianity was growing in the world at a faster pace than it had ever before. Such was my regard for his expertise in the matter and for him generally as an unimpeachable source on whatever he talked about that it never struck me for a moment to check this. Yet it was true. In fact, Christianity is still growing globally at this present time.

Dan often came to see me at my flat in the afternoons when Poonam was away at the university and our elder son at school though our younger fellow, all of two years old, would be at home with me, after I had collected him from his stint of two hours at a playgroup run by the neighbourhood church. While Dan and I chatted away animatedly about various matters, little Mudit would feel left out and neglected, and he would sometimes climb on to my lap and put both his little hands across my mouth to stop me from talking to Dan. Dan would laugh and call him "the Little Terrorist". And indeed, Dan still remembers him fondly by his old sobriquet.

It was a pleasure for me to name "Dr Daniel and Mrs Juliet O'Connor" in the very first paragraph of Acknowledgements in my book *Colonial Transactions: English Literature and India*.[1]

Dan and India

All the nine selections from the impressively vast corpus of Dan's writing that are put together in this volume form a cogent progression. They also reveal that although Dan and Juliet spent only "a short decade" in India, in Dan's own phrase, his engagement with that country has dominated his life's work and looms large in it. As David Jasper and Ann Loades say in the Introduction in this volume, Dan's unpremeditated and premature departure from India was something he "never got over", and "India has always remained at the heart of his life".[2]

As it happens, I, too, have spent altogether a short decade in Britain: four years studying for my own doctorate, three years while Poonam was doing hers and I was minding both the Little Terrorist and the novelist Thompson, and then two stints of one year and six months respectively in London as a visiting professor. But in my case, there was an opposite movement, so to say. I had come utterly bewitched by British literature as a worshipper at its shrine, and then found that it was not, and never could be, my literature in the easy inherited sense that it is the literature of those born and bred in one's own country. Accordingly I moved away to Comparative Literature involving both British and Indian literatures, then more and more to Indian literature and Translation Studies, while taking a critical postcolonial view of this whole spectrum.

---

[1] Calcutta, 1993; Manchester University Press, 1995.
[2] See above, p. 11.

Looking back, I feel that the key difference between Dan's progress and mine was that while British literature was my profession, India became Dan's vocation in that profound sense of self-discovery and epiphany which only persons of faith can experience. Dan discovered in India, and identified to a large extent with, two major predecessors of his, C. F Andrews and Verrier Elwin, who like him had started out as British missionaries but then let their experience of India define their mission. They did not seek to convert India but laid themselves open to being converted or at least transformed by it, in not a theological but an experiential sense. Though Dan did not spend his whole life working in India as both Andrews and Elwin had, he carried his India back to Britain for he had opened himself to that country just as they had and submitted to it. Dan's two books each on Andrews and Elwin may well be read as his own autobiography by other means; he is the hidden but fully engaged presence in each of those books as an alter ego of the protagonists.

Faith and muti-faith

When I spent those three years as Dan's neighbour in the 1980s, I soon discovered that that neck of the creek in Selly Oak was more thickly covered in Christian history and theology per square yard than perhaps any locale I had ever known. I lived in a huge missionary building while Dan was the Principal of the USPG College of the Ascension and lived on the premises surrounded by Christian students from many countries. There was a cluster of four or five other theological colleges close by, and there was a new Central Hall for the common use of all the colleges. Dan would invite me to some of the events there, and as I got to know some of the regulars at such events and they got to know me, I was occasionally invited to lecture by different universities on various subjects with a religious or spiritual dimension.

In his book of memoirs, *Interesting Times in India: A Short Decade at St Stephen's College* (2005), Dan writes at one point that his pastoral duties in the College included organizing meetings of small groups of Christian students and teachers, and that these were regarded by "non-members" (i.e., the non-Christians who constituted the vast majority of the teaching staff), with a degree of suspicion.[3] He says it perhaps half-jokingly, but I as one of the "non-members" can testify that there was no reason for this attitude at all. For one thing, the number of Christians in the College was very small, perhaps no more than five or ten per cent, in broad consonance with the proportion of Christians in the total population of the country which has remained steady over the decades at about three per cent. And for another, the Christians in our College came across as being exceptionally gentle and even meek. Even in that nominally Christian College, Christians thus were thin on the ground and may have felt, justifiably, somewhat secretive and isolated.

So, when I met Dan again in Selly Oak, I saw a different Dan, a Dan entirely in his element. As part of his efforts to help me settle down and feel at home, he introduced me, as indicated above, to friends and institutions I may not have come across at all had I kept myself to my primary circle of the English Department staff at the University of Birmingham. Through such introductions to a different sphere, not only were my horizons considerably widened, but I also found that I had begun to look in a new way on missionaries and other people living a life of practising their faith. Further, I also became involved in reading about religion and deepening my understanding of religion, especially my own religion Hinduism, in a way I had not while living in India. And probably none of this would have happened had I not met Dan again in his post-Delhi days.

Let me limit myself here to only two instances of a new window that Dan thus opened for me. He introduced me to Roger Hooker, a missionary who had been out in India at about the same time as Dan, but had spent his time in largely non-Anglophone institutions in Allahabad, Bareilly and Banaras, learning Hindi and Sanskrit for about ten years as few missionaries of his generation did. When I met him, he, too, was living in Birmingham, tending to a distinctly multi-religious parish in Moseley where he spoke to several neighbours in Hindi or Panjabi. As Hindi is my mother-tongue and I too had read Sanskrit at the University of Allahabad, we got along like a house on fire. He propagated a multi-faith approach which did not stop him from telling some nicely

---

[3] O'Connor, *Interesting Times in India*, p. 132.

modulated multi-faith jokes. An English bishop, he once narrated, was addressing a multi-faith assembly and at the end said, "Let us now pray together." Sensing a little difficulty, he added, "Of course, you may pray to your gods in your own different ways, and I'll pray to God in His." We sometimes punned and joked together in Sanskrit. When Roger completed his highly scholarly study, *The Quest of Ajneya: A Christian Theological Appraisal of the Search for Meaning in his Three Hindi Novels* (1998), he did me the honour of asking me to contribute a Foreword to it. This book may be the only study of a major Indian writer of the modern period attempted from this specific perspective. This book made me see how inter-faith dialogue can be conducted not only in pragmatic daily interaction but also at a level of high literary complexity.

Another door that Dan flung open for me led to an even wider, richer and more productive experience in terms of my understanding of religions. It was as if in his modest, unobtrusive manner, he was conducting me on a tour of forms of multifaith awareness. He introduced me to Dr Mary Hall, a red-haired Irish nun who was as tall and towering as Dan himself is short and mild. She had founded in Selly Oak a Multi-Faith Centre where a team of resource persons she had recruited ran six-week courses on the major religions of the world for anyone who cared to enrol for them for a small fee.

Now it just so happened that when Dan took me to her, the holy, saffron-clad *guru* who used to conduct the Hinduism classes had cried off at the last moment. After an affable five-minute conversation Mary asked me if I would help her out by stepping in, not omitting to mention the not insignificant honorarium I would be paid per two-hour session, and for distinctly mixed motives, I said that I would. When I wrote to my family about this new development in my life, my father a believer, was quite horrified and sent me a list of ten books I must absolutely read as a crash-course before I went lecturing. I had already read a couple of them anyhow, I had read extracts from the Vedas and the Upanishads in my university classes in Sanskrit, and I derived strength from the knowledge that of the six systems of belief in Hinduism, one is so catholic and permissive that it allows you to hold and declare that you do *not* believe in God.

As I soon learnt to say in my lectures, Hinduism has no one God, no one Prophet, no one Book, no fixed sabbath, no creed, and no prescribed protocol for converting anyone to Hinduism, for it allows that there are many valid ways to God not only within Hinduism but also outside it. Of course, complementing this "High Hinduism" of philosophy and theology, as the early missionaries called it, there was also a "Popular Hinduism" comprising thousands of gods and a myriad personal modes of worshipping them, but the High and the Popular coexisted without the one cancelling the other. Anyhow, my Hinduism For Beginners seemed to work well enough, indeed it proved Highly Popular, and Mary was soon sending me out on special missions, once to give a lecture to the inmates of a prison not far away, and on another occasion to engage in a dialogue with a Hindu priest in a temple within Birmingham, for the benefit of the students in our course whom we had taken there to get a feel of what they studied. Disconcertingly for me, the temple was housed in a large church building which had been desacralized but not otherwise modified—as if offering a physical demonstration of the new multi-faith configurations in Britain.

Dan thus served to introduce me to my own religion as perceived and practised in a broadly non-Hindu context—*in partibus infidelium* with a difference, as it were. I could witness and experience models of multi-faith dialogue in a liberal society which was newly learning to live as a multi-faith society while trying to keep its old liberalism intact, especially in those early decades of coloured immigration and often heated local responses to it. All this added up to a new kind of cross-cultural and multi-religious education for me, with Dan not only facilitating the process but also watching it from the sidelines quietly, indulgently and with that little smile of his and that twinkle in his eye.

A postcolonial missionary

In his book of memoirs of his decade in India, Dan describes the clerical dimension of his life in India in a chapter titled "Learning to Be a Post-colonial Missionary". This is clearly a self-description in retrospect, or *post facto*, for in 1972 when Dan left India, the term "post-colonial" (now routinely spelt "postcolonial" without a hyphen and with a disambiguation of meaning between the two spellings), had not been invented. What many regard as the foundational text of postcolonialism, Edward Said's *Orientalism*, was not published until 1979, though the word "postcolonial" does not occur in it and became current in theoretical circles only about ten years later. It was after some more years had passed that the distinction was established that "post-colonialism" with a hyphen was a simple chronological marker signifying that something had happened after a country became independent, while "postcolonialism" without a hyphen signified a theoretical–political way of reading texts including those published long ago, such as *The Tempest* or *Mansfield Park*. In Dan's case, the first meaning applied while he was still in India, and the second came into play in some books and papers that he wrote later.

Looking back now on my Birmingham years spent with Dan, it seems to me that just as he was my guide or facilitator to the phenomenon of British multi-faith exchanges and practices in those times, I might in turn have happened to introduce him to a post(-)colonial discourse which was then at its nascent stage. I had read and re-read Edward Said while still in India, I had already turned my back on canonical British literature after completing my dissertation on Virginia Woolf in 1975, and the work I was then engaged in, on the novelist Edward Thompson, was solidly postcolonial in the political-theoretical sense.

At the University of Birmingham, my colleague David Lodge, already famous as both a novelist and a critic, convened a semester-long faculty discussion group in which we struggled with texts such as the erudite, innovative but stylistically obscure essay by Homi Bhabha entitled "Signs Taken for Wonders: Questions of ambivalence and authority under a tree outside Delhi, May 1807" (1985). It described an early meeting of some hopeful missionaries with a group of somewhat amused and sceptical Hindu pilgrims, and it explored terms such as "hybridity" and "mimicry" which were to became key-terms in postcolonial discourse, while it also highlighted the "sly civility" with which learned brahmins deflected missionary endeavours to convert the Hindus. I immediately took a photocopy of this text to Dan, who took a quick look, gently laughed at its less than lucid prose, and promptly made another copy to pass on to his young theological colleague R. S. Sugirtharajah who, incidentally, later became a pioneering scholar of the spread of the Bible from a distinctly postcolonial point of view. Dan has always known which seed may fructify where.

Of Dan's own writings, the most clearly postcolonial include his book, *The Chaplains of the East India Company, 1601–1858* (2012), in which he forthrightly characterized the Company which founded the British Empire in India as "a violent and corrupt player on the world stage". The essay in the present volume which represents this radical strand of Dan's work the best is the last one, "The Geography of Anglicanism", in which the idea of "Geography" also embraces History. Dan himself makes plain his stance in the very first sentence of his essay: "An essential but not exclusive determinant of the geography of Anglicanism has been colonialism and imperialism."[4]

The long journey of ever broadening and indeed ever deepening self-discovery on the part of Dan O'Connor that is mapped by the selections in this volume represents the work of a lifetime, not quite a pilgrim's progress perhaps but certainly a faithful seeker's progress through widely varying inter-cultural and inter-religious contexts at home and abroad. It extends from the Masters thesis that Dan wrote in 1973 at Durham on Bishop John Cosin's *Devotions* (1627), which forms the subject of the first essay in this volume, to his last piece here which is a look at the spread of Christianity in the world in circumstances that were understood in one kind of way in the era of imperialism and are interpreted quite differently now in our age of the postcolonial and beyond. Dan has not only kept pace with this evolving process but also helped disseminate it through his teaching, publications and, no less through the friendships and fellowships that he has forged with a whole variety of people in many different locales throughout his richly productive life. I count it as a fortunate circumstance indeed that I too have been among the innumerable personal friends and intellectual fellows of Dan's since 1969, through over half a century in history which has spanned in geography more than half a dozen of his homes and mine across two continents. And it is a further bonus that I was given an opportunity to trace this

---

[4] See further above, pp. 161–81.

progress (and in an indirect and partially intertwined way, my own) in this Afterword and thus to relive our long connection. All readers of this volume who accompany Dan on this journey, including those who have never met him, will experience equally the excitement and illumination of Dan's own explorations and discoveries, in an aptly distilled selection.

Harish Trivedi taught English in St Stephen's College, Delhi, from 1969 to 1984, and in the University of Delhi from 1984 to 2012. He is the author of *Colonial Transactions: English Literature and India* (1993) and has co-edited *Kipling in India: India in Kipling* (2021); *Literature and Nation: Britain and India 1800–1990* (2001); and *Post-colonial Translation: Theory and Practice* (1999). He has edited Kipling's *Kim* for Penguin Classics and E. M. Forster's *A Passage to India* for Penguin India (2022). He has authored a History of South Asian Literature for *Literature: A World History*, eds David Damrosch et al (2022, 4 vols).

The writings of Dr Daniel O'Connor: A select bibliography

1967: (with P. G. Stanwood), *John Cosin: A Collection of Private Devotions*, Oxford: Clarendon Press.

1969: *T. S. Eliot. Four Quartets: A Commentary*, New Delhi: Aarti.

1971: "Study of Religion and Social reality", in Harbans Singh (ed.), *Approaches to the Study of Religion*. Patiala: Punjabi University, pp. 103–7.

1973: "Dialogue as Communion: C. F. Andrews and Munshi Ram", in G. Gispert-Sauch SJ (ed.), *God's Word Among Men: Papers in Honour of Fr. Joseph Putz, S. J*, Delhi: Vidyajyoti, pp. 73–83.

1974: Introduction to *The Testimony of C. F. Andrews*, Confessing the Faith in India Series, No. 10, Bangalore: The Christian institute for the Study of Religion and Society, pp. 3–64.

1990: *Gospel, Raj and Swaraj: The Missionary Years of C. F. Andrews, 1904–14*, Frankfurt: Verlag Peter Lang.

1991: "Holiness of Life as a Way of Christian Witness", *International Review of Mission* 80:317 (January 1991), pp. 17–26.

1993: *Din-Sevak: Verrier Elwin's Life of Service in Tribal India*, Confessing the Faith in India Series, No. 17, Bangalore: Christian institute for the Study of Religion and Society.

1994: *Relations in Religion*, The Westcott (Teape) Lectures, 1992, New Delhi: Allied Publishers Ltd.

1996: *A Liberating Force and a Friend: The Life and Work of Din Sevak Verrier Elwin*, The Eighth Verrier Elwin Memorial Lectures, Shillong: North-Eastern Hill University Publications.

1997: "John Cosin: A Collection of Private Devotions 1627", in Margot Johnson (ed.), *John Cosin: From Priest to Prince Bishop: Essays in Commemoration of the 400th Anniversary of His Birth*, Durham: Turnstone Ventures, pp. 194–205.

2000: (with others), *Three Centuries of Mission: The United Society for the Propagation of the Gospel, 1701-2000*, London: Continuum.

2001: Entries on William Hodge Mill (pp. 386-7); K. M. Banerjea (pp. 436-8); N. N. Goreh SSJE (pp. 455-6); H. A. Krishan Pillai (pp. 460-2); S. C. Appasamy Pillai (pp. 510-13); Pandita Ramabai Sarasvati (pp. 530-1); C. F. Andrews (pp. 553-60); Sundar Singh (pp. 626-9); A. J. Appasamy (pp. 629-30); Emani Sambayya (pp. 696-7); Lakshman Wickremesinghe (pp. 737-41); Roger H. Hooker (pp. 749-51), in Geoffrey Rowell, Kenneth Stevenson and Rowan Williams (eds), *Love's Redeeming Work: The Anglican Quest for Holiness*, Oxford: Oxford University Press.

2001: "'Perpetuall Succession': USPG and the Changing Face of Mission", The Inaugural Lecture of USPG "LINKS" (the friends' organization of Anglican mission agency USPG.) Delivered in King's College Chapel, London, 18 October 2001, London, USPG.

2005: *Interesting Times in India: A Short Decade at St Stephen's College*, New Delhi: Penguin Books.

2005: *A Clear Star: C. F. Andrews and India, 1904-1914*, New Delhi: Chronicle Books. (This is a later edition of *Gospel, Raj and Swaraj* [1990]).

2011: "Gandhi, *Dinabandhu* and *Din-Sevak*: Critical Solidarity from Two Anglican Missionaries", *Studies in History* 27:1 (2011), pp. 111-29.

2012: *The Chaplains of the East India Company, 1601-1858*, London: Continuum.

2016: "The Geography of Anglicanism", in Mark D. Chapman, Sathianathan Clarke, and Martyn Percy (eds), *The Oxford Handbook of Anglican Studies*, Oxford: Oxford University Press, 2016.

2018: Juliet O'Connor (editor, Daniel O'Connor) *Juliet's Letters from India*, Amazon.

2018: Juliet O'Connor (editor, Daniel O'Connor), *A Stockton Childhood*, Amazon.

2019: "India", in Jeremy Gregory (ed.), *The Oxford History of Anglicanism. Vol. II: Establishment and Empire, 1662-1829*, Oxford: Oxford University Press.

In addition:

1987: "Beth Collier" (Juliet O'Connor), *Beyond Words: Prayer as a Way of Life*, London: SPCK.

Index

A Passage to India (Forster)　vi
Abbot, Archbishop George　166
Abbott, Claud C.　2
Abishiktananda, Swami　13
Acland, Bishop Richard　114
Adivasi　74, 77
Agricultural and Horticultural Society of India　172
Ahimsa　66, 69
All India Trade Union Congress　104
Allen, Roland　174
Alternative Service Book (1980)　37
American Episcopal Church　176, 180
Amritsar Massacre　59
Andrewes, Bishop Lancelot　34
Andrews, Charles Freer　vi, vii, 12, 13, 14, 18, 21, 47–60, 64–69, 81, 83–112, 134
Anglican Communion　162
Anglican Consultative Council (ACC)　178
Archer, W. G.　75
Arya Samaj　50, 51, 97
Ascension, College of (Selly Oak)　19–21, 150
Asian Drama (Myrdal)　43–4

Baigas　116, 124
Baker, Bishop John Austin　4
Barefoot College　132
Baw, John Tsan　154
Bernard, Sir Charles　156
Beyond Words ("Beth Collier")　vii, 20, 183, 186
Bhagavad Gita　56
Bhatia, B. M.　130–2
Bhattacharji, Romesh　135
Bihar Famine (1966)　130, 139

Blake, William　125
Book of Common Prayer　28, 33, 35, 37, 154, 165, 172
Bray, Thomas　164, 171
Brayne, F. L.　119
Brown, Gordon　18
Buchanan, Claudius　172
Burton, Henry　35

Caldwell, Bishop Robert　175
Camara, Bishop Helder　69
Cambridge Brotherhood (Cambridge Mission to Delhi)　13, 49, 61
Carey, William　151, 172
Caribbean Anglican Consultation　179
Chadwick, Owen　6, 7, 25
Chaplains of the East India Company, The (O'Connor)　161
Chatterji, Margaret　39
Chaturvedi, Shri. Benarsidas　53
Chaudhuri, Nirad Chandra　7
Che Guevara　142
Che Guevara (Fratti)　10–11, 135–6
Chillingworth, Bishop David　25
Christa Seva Sangha (Pune)　70, 113, 120, 123
Christian Institute for the Study of Religion and Society (Bangalore)　9, 14, 16, 20, 48, 82, 84, 129
Christianand, Pancras　40
Christianity in World History (van Leeuwen)　8
Church Missionary Society (CMS)　19, 167, 173
Clear Star, A (O'Connor)　49
Colbeck, George　153
Colenso, Bishop J. W.　175

Collection of Private Devotions (Cosin) 4, 10, 27–37
Collier, Admiral Sir Francis Augustus 183
Colonial Church Atlas (SPG: 1842) 168
Colonial Clergy Acts 174
Compton, Bishop Henry 164
Communist Party of India 17, 133
Cosin, Bishop John vi, vii, 3, 6, 27–37
Council of Anglican Provinces of Africa 179
Cow Protection Society of Calcutta 93
Cox, Harvey 49
Cripps, A. S. 175
Crowther, Bishop Samuel 173–4
Cuddesdon Theological College (Oxford) 3, 4, 27

Dalits 62, 80–1
Das, Arvind Narayan 17, 138–48
Dayal, Har 134
Defty, Gordon 6
Delhi 49, 183–5
Delhi University 8, 133–4
Devanandan, P. D. 9, 83
Dictionary of Third World Theologies (Ed. Sugirtharajah) 159
Din-Sevak (Ed. O'Connor) 21, 113
Divine Mother 55–6, 60
Dubey, Suman 131
Durham Book, The 37
Durham University 2–3, 27

East India Company 166, 167, 171
Elwin, Verrier vi, vii, 21, 23, 62, 70–7, 113–28
Eremo, Sisters of the 122
Evelyn, John 28

Famine Code 130
Farquhar, J. N. 91
Fiji 103
Fisher, Archbishop Geoffrey 177, 179
Forrester, Duncan 18
Four Quartets, The (Eliot) 10
Francis, St (Franciscan) 121, 125

Gandhi (Attenborough) 65
Gandhi, Indira 15–16, 130, 143
Gandhi, Mahatma vi, 12, 14, 16, 42, 57, 58–9, 61, 64–9, 71, 73, 77, 83, 96, 98–9, 106, 111, 113, 115, 122, 142
Gandhi's samadhi (Rajgat) 144
Geography Anatomiz'd (Gordon) 166
Gilbert, W. S. 174
Gispert-Sauch, G. 40, 47
God's Word Among Men (Ed. Gispert-Sauch) 13
Gond Seva Mandal 73, 115, 118
Gonds 117, 123, 124
Good Shepherd, Murrayfield 18
Gordon, Patrick 166
Gosling, David 2
Gospel, Raj and Swaraj (O'Connor) 14, 48
Graham, Sir Lancelot 120
Gulliver's Travels (Swift) 41–2

Habgood, Archbishop John 1–2
Hackney Phalanx 149, 151, 176
Haggart, Bishop Alastair 18
Hakluyt, Richard 163–4, 168
Hakluytus Posthumus (*Purchas his Pilgrimes*) 166
Hardie, Keir 104
Hardinge, Lord Charles (Viceroy) 51, 58
Harland, Bishop Maurice 5
Herbert, George 33
Heylyn, Peter 36
Hinduism 91–4, 99
Hivale, Shamrao 72, 73, 74, 77, 78, 113–28
Holland, W. E. S. 50, 51
Hooker, Richard 33
Hooker, Roger 13
Hoyland, J. S. 53–4

Indentured labour 104
Interesting Times in India (O'Connor) 24, 129
International Missionary Council (Canada) 178

INDEX 203

International Missionary Council (Jerusalem) 94
Into All Lands (Thompson) 149

John, Bishop Ernest 15
John Paul II, Pope 16, 62, 176
Johnson, Margot 27, 37
Juliet's Letters from India (Ed. O'Connor) 24, 129, 182, 183-85

Kabir (poet) 110
Karanjia 113-28
King, Martin Luther 69
Kirill, Patriarch of Moscow 19-20
Knapp-Fisher, Bishop Edward 3
Knox, Bishop Andrew 163
Kothari, D. S. 139

Lambeth Conferences 177-8, 180
Lewis, H. D. 39-40
Lightfoot, Bishop J. B. 49
Little Gidding 34, 36

Macnicol, Nicol 92
Mahabharata 76
Mao Zedong 129, 133, 140, 143, 174
Marks, John Ebeneezer 149-50, 151-8, 173
Martyn, Bishop Henry 173
Marx Club (Delhi) 139-40
Maurice, F. D. 90
Mayflower 164
Mazumdar, Charu 133, 143, 145
McCullough, Bishop Nigel 23
McGill, Canon James 5
MECCA (Ministry and Ecumenical Council of the Church Assembly) 4, 6
Michael, Bernado 48
Middleton, Bishop Thomas 167
Milman, Bishop Robert 152, 153
Milton, John 34
Mindon (King of Burma) 152-8
Mission Field, The 170, 172
Mountague, Richard 33, 34
Mozoomdar, P. C. 108

Msigala, Kolumba 173
Mugabe, Robert 6, 69
Myanmar (Burma) 151-8
Myrdal, Gunnar 40, 43-4, 46

Narayan, Jayaprakesh 131
Naxalites 16-17, 129-48
Nehru, Jawaharlal 15, 16, 62, 73, 75, 85, 114
New College, University of Edinburgh 22
Norbu, Dawa 136
North East Frontier Agency 114
North Eastern Hill University (Shillong) 23
North India, Church of 178

O'Connor, Daniel George (Father) 1
O'Connor, Gladys (Mother) 1
O'Connor, Juliet (née Wood) vii, 4, 5-6, 8, 10-11, 15, 18, 19, 23, 25, 29, 182-6
O'Connor, Kath (Sister) 4, 11
O'Dwyer, Sir Michael 58
Osmond, Percy Herbert 28
Oxford Handbook of Anglican Studies, The (Eds. Chapman, Clark, Percy) 24, 161
Oxford Movement 167

Pannikar, Raimundo 13
Paul VI, Pope 8
Populorum progressio (Paul VI) 8
Pound, Ezra 100
Primer 32
Prynne, William 34, 35
Punjabi University (Patiala) 9, 39
Purchas, Samuel 166

Rahner, Karl 150
Ram, Bharat 142-3
Ram, Munshi 13, 47-60, 61, 83, 91, 92
Ramayana 75-6, 102
Ramsey, Archbishop Michael 3
Rao, V. K. R. V. 139
Raven, Charles 1, 4, 9, 86

Ray, Rabindra   10, 17, 133, 138–48
Red Star Over China (Snow)   17, 140
Red Star Over Tibet (Norbu)   136
Robinson, Joan   140
Roy, Sanjit ("Bunker")   131
Rudra, S. K.   12, 53, 58, 95
Runcie, Archbishop Robert   7

Sahi, Jyoti   14, 21
St Andrew's College, Kiungani, Zanzibar   173
St Andrews, University   18
St Augustine's College, Canterbury   174
St John's College, Rangoon   154–5, 158
St Stephen's College (Delhi)   v, 6, 7–11, 12, 15, 17, 28, 39, 47, 50, 53, 61, 129–48
Salisbury, Lord Robert Gascoyne-Cecil   156
Samartha, Stanley   82, 83
Sarasvati, Swami Dayananda   47, 50
Sastriar, Vedanayaga   175
Schweitzer, Albert   70
Scottish Churches House (Dunblane)   21–2
Sealy, Irwin Allan   10
Selly Oak   vii, 19–21
Shakespeare, William   10, 99, 124
Sharp, C. H. C.   50, 51
Sikhs   78–9
Simeon, Dilip   17, 138–48
Singh, Brij Raj   8, 131
Singh, Harbans   39, 40–1, 46
Singh, Suresh   131, 139
Sircar, Satish   6, 7, 131, 139
slavery   169–70
Smart, Peter   35
Smith, Wilfred Cantwell   13, 45
Sollicitudo Rei Socialis   63–4
Songs from the Forest (Elwin and Hivale)   74
South India, Church of   178
Stanwood, P. G.   27
Stockton Childhood, A (J. O'Connor)   5, 24, 182
Strachan, Bishop John   157

Student Christian Movement (SCM)   7
Sugirtharajah, R. S.   150, 159
Surtees Society   27, 30
Sykes, Marjorie   53

Tagore, Rabindranath   vi, 12, 14, 51, 58, 67, 83, 87, 91, 100, 109
Tambaram Conference   96, 103
Teape Lectures   9, 13, 22, (seminars) 25, 61–82
Teesside Industrial Mission   5
Temple, Archbishop William   120
Testimony of C. F. Andrews, The (Ed. O'Connor)   14
Thakkar, A. V.   115, 126
Thibaw (King of Burma)   153, 156
Thomas, M. M.   9, 14, 82, 83, 96
Thompson, Edward   vi
Thomson, James (poet)   3
Three Centuries of Mission (O'Connor et al)   24, 149, 158
Three-Self Patriotic Movement (China)   174, 178
Times of India   144, 146
Tolstoy, Count Lev Nikolaevich   66
Tom Brown's Schooldays (Hughes)   152
Towards the Understanding of Jesus (Simkovitch)   106
Trivedi, Harish   8
Tutu, Archbishop Desmond   175

Underhill, Evelyn   120
Union, Act of (1536)   162
United Nations Organization   176
United Partners in the Gospel (USPG)   viii, 19, 23–4, 149–60, 168, 175
Upanishads   103–4

Vatican II, Council   16, 179
Venn, Henry   173
Vidyadyoti College of Theology, Delhi   13, 49
Vivekananda, Swami   67, 81
Vohra, Deepak   134–5
Vrindaban   93

Wakefield Cathedral 22-3
Walls, Andrew 22
Watson, Joshua 149, 150-1, 176
Welby, Archbishop Justin 161, 181
Westcott, Bishop Brooke Foss vii, 9, 12, 14, 61, 104
Wilberforce, William 173
Williams, Archbishop Rowan 161, 180-1
women in India 101-2
Wood, Bishop Alexander 62, 113
Wordsworth, William 3
World Council of Churches 16, 21, 179